TALKING SHOP

PETER BETJEMANN

TALKING SHOP

THE LANGUAGE OF CRAFT IN AN AGE OF CONSUMPTION

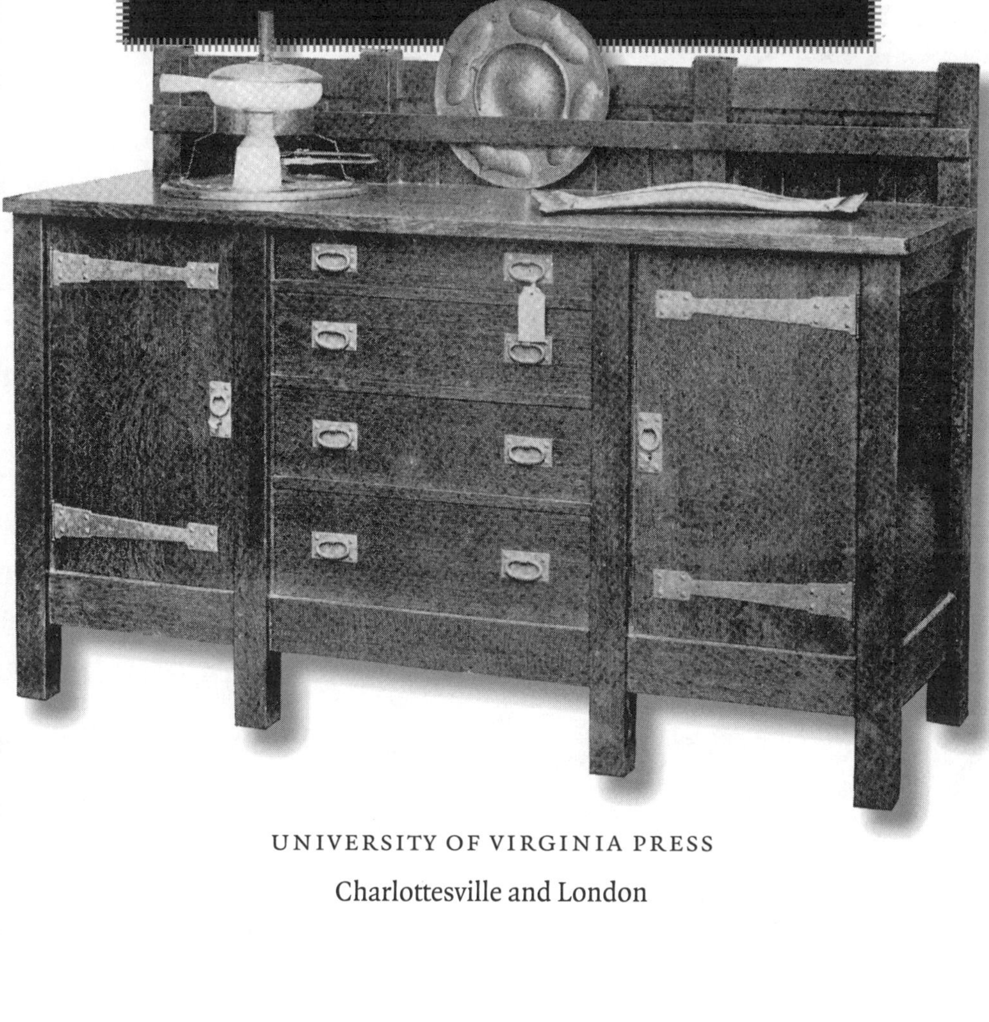

UNIVERSITY OF VIRGINIA PRESS

Charlottesville and London

University of Virginia Press

Printed in the United States of America on acid-free paper

First published 2011

1 3 5 7 9 8 6 4 2

Library of Congress Cataloging-in-Publication Data
Betjemann, Peter, 1973–
Talking shop : the language of craft in an age of consumption /
Peter Betjemann.
p. cm.
Includes bibliographical references and index.
ISBN 978-0-8139-3121-0 (cloth : alk. paper) —
ISBN 978-0-8139-3169-2 (e-book)
1. American literature—19th century—History and criticism.
2. American literature—20th century—History and criticism.
3. Material culture in literature. 4. Authenticity (Philosophy) in literature.
5. Artisans in literature. I. Title.
PS374.M39B48 2011
813′.409355—dc22
2011000694

CONTENTS

ILLUSTRATIONS

ACKNOWLEDGMENTS

This book is about craft as a public discourse, and in that sense its completion constitutes its own argument—for I have depended above all on the insights, inspiration, and support of others as I have made and remade, constructed and dismantled, its pages.

The idea for *Talking Shop* was born when, in my own amateur pursuit of a craft, I had the good luck to learn from John Zachary, formerly owner of Catamount Woodworks and now a partner in Water Street Furniture Studios, Leeds, Massachusetts. John's steady, unpretentious application of his skills revealed to me the daily rhythms of the best artisanship and prompted my thinking about how nineteenth-century authors and artisans essayed to translate those rhythms to the page. The vast, polyvocal discourse of craft I ended up researching was not immediately apparent during the days I spent in John's one-man shop, but that discourse, I came to see, took its own inspiration from the example of craftspeople like John. I have been fortunate to know other artisans whose choice of life has, more than anything, sustained my interest in this project. In practices ranging from stonemasonry to winemaking, carpentry to gardening, it is an honor to name Dori Betjemann, Peter Betjemann, Chris Churilla, Dai Crisp, Jay Gray, PK McCoy, Scotty Kelley, Trevor Norland, Amanda Sever, and Nathan Warren.

Among literary critics, I owe a great debt to Myra Jehlen, whose consummate scholarly craft and readings of the early manuscript set a plumb line toward which I could only hope to hew. William Howarth, Bill Gleason, Peter Antelyes, and H. Daniel Peck shaped the ideas in this book in ways both direct and indirect; my readers at the University of Virginia Press did much for the manuscript in its final stages, and no scholar could ask for a more satisfying and useful editorial process than the one shepherded at Virginia by Cathie Brettschneider. Coincidentally, I happened to read Miles Orvell's *The Real Thing*, which introduced me to the writings of Gustav Stickley, at the same time as I was trying to learn how to make the furniture joint—the so-called through mortise and tenon—with which Stickley is most associated; that happenstance propelled my research for the next decade, and I would particularly like to acknowledge the Winterthur Museum and Library in Delaware for a fellowship that allowed me to study Stickley's original papers and trade catalogs. The remarkable Center for the Humanities at Oregon State University provided time and space for my research on Benvenuto Cellini—and as I wrote my way toward an actual chapter on the fiery goldsmith, Christopher Leoni unpacked Cellini's equally fiery Italian for me.

In his autobiography, the famously immodest Cellini makes much of his sharp eyes—but the sharp eyes actually more central to *Talking Shop* are those of my copyeditor, Beth Ina. For help with the bibliography, I also thank Kristi Shelton, and for material support of my research, the Department of English at Oregon State University. In the course of everyday life in Corvallis, my colleagues at OSU anchor a wonderful community of writers, scholars, and, most important, friends. For special help on the project, or for their comradeship while I was away from it, I am grateful to Kerry Ahearn, Betty Campbell, Norman Carlson, Tracy Daugherty, Neil Davison, Colin Day, DeSales Harrison, Anita Helle, Karen Holmberg, Patricia Lacy, John Larison, Ted Leeson, Jon Lewis, Aria Minu-Sepehr, Rebecca Olson, Michael Oriard, David Robinson, Marjorie Sandor—and, especially, Erik Gray and Tara Williams.

Portions of chapter 1 appeared in "Craft, Telos, and the Representation of Labor: Nineteenth-Century Readings of Benvenuto Cellini," *Nineteenth-Century Prose* 36:2 (Fall 2009): 1–30; portions of chapter 3 appeared in "Craft and the Limits of Skill: Handicrafts Revivalism and the Problem of Technique," *Journal of Design History* 21:2 (2008): 183–93; and portions of chapter 5 appeared in "Henry James's Shop Talk: *The Spoils of Poynton* and the Language of Artisanship," *American Literary Realism* 40:3 (2008): 204–24. I thank the journals' editors, Oxford University Press, and the University of Illinois Press for their generosity in making it possible to reprint that material. For the images, I have depended on the holdings and the courtesy of the John Hay Library of Brown University; the Victoria and Albert Museum; the Winterthur Museum and Library; Dalton's American Decorative Arts, Syracuse, New York; and the Stickley Museum at Craftsman Farms, Parsippany, New Jersey.

No craft demands greater communicative energy than the work of building and sustaining human relations. For modeling a beautifully crafted language of family, I can name no better artisans than Keith Scribner, Jen Richter, Luke Scribner, and Chloe Scribner. My parents, one a woodworker and the other a knitting teacher, are the deepest inspiration for this book because their best work is their endlessly patient craft of communication; when it comes to love—

to say nothing of housed dovetail joints or slipping stitches purl-wise—they are always and ever talking shop. Without my realizing it until near the end of the project, my brother Erik Betjemann, who cannot hear, may have launched everything to the degree that his craft of self-expression—both manual and verbal—has had me thinking for decades about what the relations between the hand and the voice might look like.

Hachikō, a dog represented in a statue in Tokyo, stands for fidelity, devotion, patience, and indomitable trust—and also, at least for the two days I spent there with Julianna Gray in 2006, for the willingness to give oneself to the unsequenced, the unknown, and the unplanned. This entire spectrum of virtues, from reliably delivering what you say to improvising around what you find, shapes the meaning of craft developed in the following pages. More important, it defines what I most love in Julianna, and the craft of partnership and family life at which she is so expert. Under the sign of Hachikō, for what has been and for what is to come, this is for her.

TALKING SHOP

INTRODUCTION

THE YANKEE STONECUTTER

In June of 1842, the American sculptor Horatio Greenough laid down his chisel in his Florence studio. Embarking for the United States to oversee the installation of his massive statue *Washington* in the rotunda of the Capitol, he also embarked on a new kind of labor: the writer's. At the end of his yearlong visit to his home country, Greenough's first two essays appeared alongside stories by Nathaniel Hawthorne and poems by John Greenleaf Whittier in *The United States Magazine and Democratic Review*. Expressing his dismay at the imitativeness of the built environment he saw in the United States, Greenough's essays assert the relation of form to function and, tapping the Jacksonian mythos of practicality promoted by the *United States Magazine*, celebrate the structural integrity he associated with handicraft. What makes Greenough's literary career my starting point in this book, which studies the adaptability of craft to textual media, is that Greenough's writing on practical workmanship is saturated with language about language itself.

Daring, as he describes it, "to utter a few words of discontent," Greenough wonders whether a new aesthetic "language can be born" as an alternative to the "conflicting dialects and jargons" of derivative styles—particularly the Greek, Gothic, and Egyptian—that appear to have blocked the original development of American art and architecture.[1] The new language Greenough proposes constitutes not a lexicon of ornament but a willingness to engage in frank and vigorous communication, a habit Greenough identifies with the craftsman's discourse: in the studios of the Old World, he writes, apprentices did not sit "passively listening" but "discussed with their fellow students the merits of different works, the advantages of rival methods."[2] In the nine years between the pieces in the *United States Magazine* and the publication (in the final year of Greenough's life) of his collection *The Travels, Experiences, and Observations of a Yankee Stonecutter*, he went on to argue a series of points about labor and authenticity that he described as derived from the "traditional lore of handicraft."[3]

These points of recovered "lore" became, in turn, core assertions of the formal crafts movements of the later nineteenth and early twentieth centuries. Aesthetics, Greenough claimed, should be properly related not to history or to certain visual qualities (a position he identified with Enlightenment taxonomies of beauty and sublimity) but to purpose, use, and "principles of construction"

(137); understood in that way, the presumed gap between high art and the "so-called lower trades" closed.[4] Anticipating the emphasis of the Arts and Crafts Movement on vocational training, Greenough urged his country to establish "working Normal schools of structure and ornament" for "mechanics who need aesthetical guidance in their operations" (20–21). A craft-centered ethos of function would connect modern production to vernacular examples: the South Sea islander's purposeful shaping of his "war club" mirrored, for instance, the nineteenth-century engineer's fabrication of a "compact, effective, and beautiful" machine by eliminating nonessential weight.[5] Yoking primitivist ideologies and emerging technologies, art and construction, form and purpose, Greenough's essays of the 1840s anticipate the strenuous efforts of such figures as William Morris, Gustav Stickley, Charles Rennie Mackintosh, and Frank Lloyd Wright to make craft and craft principles relevant to modern life. For Ralph Waldo Emerson, who read the *Yankee Stonecutter* volume in manuscript, Greenough's essays announced "in advance the leading thoughts of Mr. Ruskin" and contained "more useful truth than any thing in America." "I should think," Emerson went on in a letter to the sculptor, "the entire population well employed if they would suspend [all] other work for one day & read it."[6]

Emerson's suggestion of a national day off to read Greenough is of course figurative, a way of complimenting the author on the cogency of his revolutionary ideas about design and labor. But in imagining work suspended by a book about work, Emerson unwittingly addresses a profound anxiety about the relation of text and practice that courses through Greenough's formulation of craft-centered design as, in particular, a vigorous discourse and a revivified lore. After his trip to the United States, Greenough found less time for sculpture; more travels, professorial and diplomatic appointments, and growing family responsibilities (his three children were born between 1845 and 1850) dramatically altered his schedule and directed some of his energies from the studio and the chisel to the desk and the page. The decrease in Greenough's sculptural output may explain why authorship appears in his texts as a weaker echo of actual building as often as it appears the agent of craft's revivification. Although reprinting texts that had enjoyed a fine reception, *The Travels, Observations, and Experience of a Yankee Stonecutter* opens by disparaging the "amateur job" the sculptor will make of literary composition; if the author takes "this feather in my hand," it is only "to beguile time and keep out of worse mischief" (v). Greenough describes a "book-maker" questioning stoneworkers about their toil, using an artisanal language of "making" for both authorial and manual labor but firmly identifying himself with the latter class of laborers: when queried by book-makers, he writes, "we hang the lip and look silly," for "we who cut stone temper our tools and choose our blocks by rules that be not in the Encyclopedia or Conversations Lexicon."[7] The objects produced by these mute artisans, he says elsewhere, should themselves observe a proper "silence."[8] Functionalism mandates that objects should be appreciated neither for the "quotations" of foreign styles that they make nor for the explanatory narrative of the maker, but for their relation to their site, the practical requirements of their construction, and their use (99).

The functionalist logic by which Greenough defended the crafts, in this example, mitigated against the translation of crafted things: he worried, in effect, that builders would talk over their buildings and that style would drown out structure. And yet the linguistic metaphor for imitative design that Greenough adopted—in describing "conflicting dialects," stylistic quotation, and the "inverted commas" that historical styles seemed to place around architecture and objects—also led him, time and time again across his oeuvre, to frame his writing as a way to reassert rhetorical control over the vocabularies of imitation.[9] "Nature spake" truer "laws of building" than Greenough found in the conventional lexicons of ornament; such laws became interpretable through the study of the "storied relief" and "eloquent statue" of ancient times.[10] Complaining that the true "name and functions of architecture" had been "usurped" (136), Greenough half-apologetically asserts "a truly American right—the right of talking" as the necessary agent of his ideas about structure and function. Greenough's reminder that "each man is free to present his notions on any subject" defends the stonecutter's decision to pronounce his "words of discontent" (146) on the same grounds as his idealization of the Old World apprentice's freedom to opine on the master's work. And as he talks through his ambivalence about talking, Greenough ends up finding a functionalist defense of authorship. "There are threads of relation which lead me from my specialty to the specialties of other men," Greenough writes of his inspiration to compose. To "seek another form [than words], another dress than that with which my thought was born," would be for Greenough to "disjoin" origins and expression, violating the integrity of the medium to which he pinned the authenticity of handicrafts labor in the first place.[11]

Greenough's authorial identity thus defends the functionalist correlation of beauty and a particular medium (the "form . . . of my utterance," in and as text, transcribes the original nature of his thought "as it came" [197]) at the same time as his writing threatens to drive him away from physical practice, compromising the autonomous silence that he felt should belong to useful things. That *The Travels, Observations, and Experience of a Yankee Stonecutter* appeared under a pseudonym, "Horace Bender," epitomizes the complicated and equivocal relation, for Greenough, of craft production to literary production. The text offers on the one hand an antischolastic "stonecutter's creed," a Thoreauvian manifesto that turns on an extended analogy between artisanal labor and nature's processes—and through which the author claims to "find my way back to practice" from the abstract "labyrinth" of having read aesthetic philosophy.[12] On the other hand, the book splits Horatio Greenough's *actual* sculptural practice, always performed under his own name, from the literary persona, Horace Bender, through which he channels the putatively practice-centered creed; the preface to the book in fact asks readers not to guess at the true identity of the author. The curiously ductile name "Bender," for a figure who breaks and cuts stone, further widens the gap between the authorial persona of the "bender" and the artisanal practice he celebrates. Whatever physical matter the stonecutter works will, he says, "stay put"; "if I strike off a bit with my chisel, it stays off for all time."[13] But words appear malleable, subject to being stated "over again in another shape" (x). "Bender," in fact, was the maiden name of Greenough's mother. But knowing that source does not render the contrast between "bending" and "stonecutting" any less striking—except to the degree that it further confuses the connections between author and artisan by making "Horatio Greenough" and "Horace Bender" at once relatives and, at the same time, the names that Greenough used to obscure and divide the relation between his labors of writing and sculpting.

THE GRAMMAR OF ORNAMENT: CRAFT'S TEXTUALITY

The unstable relation of Greenough's creative personae—the craftsman and the critic, the stonecutter and the bender, the artisan and the author—exemplifies the subject of *Talking Shop*. Tracing the complex interweavings of craft and language that emerged in the nineteenth and early twentieth centuries, it posits that a rapidly proliferating vocabulary, literary ethos, and print culture of workmanship (in which Greenough's texts were important documents) complicated distinctions between manual and literary labors, between objects and texts, and between bodies and their representation. For thinkers ranging from Plato to craft's most visible recent advocates—the pragmatist philosopher Richard Sennett and the philosopher-mechanic Matthew Crawford—skilled workmanship has instead appeared a repository of a practical, firsthand, and experiential relation to real things and concrete problems. While I am deeply sympathetic to these perspectives about craft as an individual practice and, as Sennett and Crawford propose, a model for reframing our ideas about productive work today, this book places craft in nearly the reverse position in cultural history. The era between 1840 and 1920, I argue, constructed lines, connections, and correspondences between skilled handiwork and text, and thus paved the way for craft's mobilization as a highly portable discourse—one viably articulated in print and apotheosized in the twenty-first century by the ubiquity of the "artisanal" as a tag for everything from local products and breads to coffee beverages, cocktails, and furnishings styles. I open this study with Greenough's specifically literary "search after the great principles of construction" not because his texts were singular or even very early instances of advocacy for design's predication on usefulness.[14] The publications of the eighteenth-century Italian architect Francesco Milizia, for instance, almost certainly shaped Greenough's precepts—and the interest of writers in artisanal processes appears clearly enough, as Sennett notes, in the contents of Diderot's *Encyclopedia* and in the Enlightenment's appetite for texts explicating housekeeping, parenting, and education as kinds of craft.[15] Rather, I open with Greenough because the pace of industrial mechanization in the nineteenth century moved a class he defended—the "so-called lesser trades"—into the spotlight of the reformist credo and, most important, because Greenough's unstable rhetorical authority epitomizes the evaluative intricacies attending craft's emergence as a textual and a narrative subject. As the vehicle of his reformist energies as well as an apparent threat to his artisanal identity, Greenough's literary career, reinventing his labor, begins to unfold some of the complexities of exporting and translating workmanship across boundaries of genre, medium, and practice.

Tracing the larger cultural rhythms of this process, *Talking Shop* describes the naturalization of handicrafts as a cultural and aesthetic ideal (an ideal represented familiarly, but by no means only, by the popularity of the Arts and Crafts Movement in the United States and the United Kingdom) by focusing on the negotiations of physical practice and representation that translated artisanship from the workshop to the public sphere. Print media forms the obvious archive for this study, but print in fact represents only one of the vectors along which workmanship developed as discourse. In the middle chapters in particular, I analyze crafts artifacts themselves as bearers of translatable meanings; written descriptions, accounts, and vocabularies of craft were matched by the reverse enthusiasm, for crafts artifacts that invited transliteration. Gustav Stickley's primacy in the American Arts and Crafts Movement, for instance, had a great deal to do with his deliberate effort to produce a material effect that could be cogently described in catalog and magazine copy. But Stickley's proclivity for imagining physical things in textual terms was not just a shrewd marketing strategy. Rather, as I will be suggesting, it derived from the philosophical underpinnings of crafts revivalism: theories of work and workmanship in the generation before Stickley's stressed the ways in which handicrafts objects addressed viewers as readers, communicating their intentions to people in intelligible and translatable idioms.

Even so, craft does appear most often in the following pages as a literary subject oriented to a broad reading public. Alongside his furnishings, to stay with the current example, Stickley offered the American public a vigorous literary forum, his magazine *The Craftsman* (1901–16). Practical articles on woodworking and gardening appeared next to works by a range of now canonical figures (Bliss Carman, Hamlin Garland, Henry Wadsworth Longfellow, Amy Lowell), obscure fiction writers (Annie Hamilton Donnell, Paul Harboe, Helen Fitzgerald Sanders), and architects and designers (Ernest Batchelder, Louis Sullivan, Candace Wheeler). Authors in forums like *The Craftsman* were sometimes tradespeople themselves, and in the most interesting cases they tied their practical experiences to the literary traditions on which the crafts revival depended. The New Orleans ceramist Harriet Joor, for instance, interrogated the purposes of artisanship by tapping an example that she presumed her readers might know: Joor's morally ambiguous story "A Lover of the Beautiful" (1905), discussed in my fourth chapter, clearly derived from Hawthorne's ruminations about craft in "The Artist of the Beautiful" (1844), discussed in the second chapter. Despite the centrality of such intertextual dialogue to the emergence of craft as a cultural value, however, *Talking Shop* does not try to comprehensively reconstruct a history of artisanship from forgotten literary texts by crafts workers or their advocates. Instead, my chapters closely analyze examples in which craft slides between different manifestations—as material artifact, stylistic tag, fictional subject, moral principle, authorial practice, technical lexicon—so as to trace the patterns by which authors, artisans, readers, and consumers negotiated and naturalized the emergence of artisanship as a textual phenomenon. That process is legible in elite as well as popular literature, canonical as well as unknown sources, essays as well as fiction, and objects as well as print. The canonization of the Italian Renaissance goldsmith Benvenuto Cellini as the era's paradigm of the artisan, one of my major examples, offers a ready instance of how different kinds of cultural activity interlocked to popularize craft. Translators, critics, and readers seized on Cellini's bombastic autobiography, unpublished in its own era but a nineteenth-century blockbuster. Metalworkers embraced Cellini as a model of their trade. Connoisseurs created a vigorous market for Cellini's works and for Cellini-like pieces, lauding the technical interest the pieces provoked even as many found his florid style distinctly inferior to the examples of the generation—da Vinci's—that preceded him. Composers and musicians, including Hector Berlioz and Franz Liszt, made several attempts at staging an operatic version of Cellini's life. Writers introduced Cellini to every possible reading constituency, retelling his story in novels, nonfiction, children's books, and technical works for the trades.

Vaulted into prominence by the sensation (and the sensationalism) of his autobiography, Cellini thus appeared at the center of a public discourse about workmanship energized nearly three centuries after he composed his text. As craft came to be tightly correlated with its translatability and its narrative appeal, furthermore, the author and the artisan appeared interlocked in another, more private scene—that of the writer's compositional effort to represent crafted artifacts, an effort obviously predicated on naming and describing. Such ekphrastic exertions were put under heavy pressure by the prominence of cultural questions about the actual compatibilities of words and things, the writer's textual medium and the artisan's physical one. In his 1921 classic *The Craft of Fiction*, Percy Lubbock declared that the correlation advanced in his title is beset by the fundamental problem that narrative is physically "shapeless"; unlike physical artifacts produced by artisans in workshops, fiction "melts and shifts in the memory."[16] Anticipating Lubbock's anxieties, texts that interrogated connections between craft and language could also be strikingly self-conscious about the obvious paradox they presented: that such texts were themselves implicated in the emerging print culture of craft. In *The Spoils of Poynton* (1897), for instance, Henry James—Lubbock's favorite example of a literary master builder—appears to satirize a woman's habit of classifying exquisite furnishings of the "more laboring ages" according to a conventional lexicon of historical workmanship. For the woman, Mrs. Brigstock, everything appears " 'in the style' of something else."[17] But Mrs. Brigstock's vulgarity, presented as her penchant for translating the work of master artisans into stylistic tags, also affords James an occasion for ironically commenting, in his preface to the novel, on the potential vulgarity of his own authorial practice; James himself looks not unlike Mrs. Brigstock when he characterizes "the sweetest Louis Seize, all assorted and combined" or "an exquisite old house, early Jacobean" (53, 7).

James's correlation between the novel's most buffoonish character and the novelist himself looks ahead to a later theme. What is important to say now, however, is that the historical development on which James's anxiety turns—the incorporation of the details of workmanship into a vocabulary of style, including the "Louis Seize" and "Jacobean"—appears throughout this book as an important vector of craft's print culture. Thomas Sheraton's *Cabinet Dictionary* (1803), one of the famous guidebooks produced by eighteenth-century English cabinetmakers to "assist [gentlemen] in the choice" of furnishings (the others were by George Hepplewhite and Thomas Chippendale), offered "an explanation of all the terms used in the cabinet, chair, and upholstery branches" and set the pattern by which later producers and consumers were taught a language of traditional details.[18] Sheraton describes his work as a "dictionary," and a spate of publications in the mid-nineteenth and early twentieth century encoded ornament in similarly lexical or linguistic terms. Texts like Henry Shaw's *Encyclopedia of Ornament* (1842), Owen Jones's *Grammar of Ornament* (1856), and Alexander Speltz's *Der Ornamentstil* (1900; English edition *The Styles of Ornament*, 1906) tagged dozens of styles from many periods and cultures. In so doing, they drew attention to traditional crafts practices—Speltz addressed his volume to "architects, designs, painters, sculptors, wood-carvers, chasers, modelers, cabinet-makers, and artistic locksmiths"—even as they provided the mass market with a potent resource, as a vocabulary of the "Chippendale" or the "Colonial," for turning out period furnishings and selling imitation goods.[19] Understood as documents in craft history, grammars of ornament relate consumer objects, print culture, and manual labor; they name, taxonomize, and make legible both antiques and machine-made goods by representing their details as the historical practices of woodcarvers, engravers, and "artistic locksmiths."[20]

In describing craft as textual and narrative, then, I mean to highlight a host of relations cutting across several modes and genres of production. Craft appears in the following pages as a technical lexicon, a literary topos, an authorial labor, a theoretical discourse about how true workmanship could be recognized, a grammar of consumer styles, and a nameable aspect of material objects. The definitions of the artisanal used in this book vary because such variability is exactly my point about the period between 1840 and 1920; the stakes of James's ruminations on craft's semiotics or Gustav Stickley's anxiety about introducing fiction into *The Craftsman* (which he did in 1905) only become clear in the context of an energetic, multimodal discourse that both invigorated workmanship and pulled it away from the singular site of the workshop. To the degree that *Talking Shop* is about a general (that is, a varied and pervasive) adaptation of craft's medium, it can be best understood as depending on a series of prior histories tracing the nineteenth-century popularization of the handmade—but while addressing, as a critical subject in its own right and with a correspondingly singular set of implications, the problematic condition of using text to represent craft. What have been studied heretofore are certain public discourses to which craft was relevant, rather than the fact of its textuality itself. Political writing about labor is the most familiar example: the emergence of working-class newspapers, literature, and other early instruments of trade consciousness carried the voice of the workshop to the eighteenth and early nineteenth centuries. Consider, as instances of the historical backdrop for *Talking Shop*, Laura Rigal's *The American Manufactory: Art, Labor, and the World of Things in the Early Republic* (1998) and William Sewell's *Work and Revolution in France: The Language of Labor from the Old Regime to 1848* (1980).

These monographs, studying two different countries in the decades before the ones treated in the present book, reveal that revolutionary-era republican discourse depended on links between nation building and physical building. As crafts practice entered the general vocabulary through eighteenth-century guidebooks, encyclopedias, and technical manuals, workmanship became a usable political trope, typified for Rigal by Francis Hopkinson's poem "The Raising" (1788). Staging the "performance of production" by drawing on the vocabulary of the trades, Hopkinson describes "king-posts" and "purlins," "plates [laid] . . . firm on the wall" and timber "pins of American pine," to analogize the "fabricating" and ratification of the U.S. Constitution to a team of carpenters raising a roof.[21] Such literary displays of "people who belonged to . . . the rank of urban artisan rather than American farmer" mark for Rigal the appearance of "privileged craft metonyms" for cooperative industry, national union, and cultural development (8, 26). In Sewell's study of similar correlations in France, Agricol Perdiguier's *Livre du compagnonnage* (1839) captures the literary exhibitionism of the crafts in the period. Perdiguier's text broke the seal on artisanal culture, exposing the clandestine rites, institutions, and social networks of journeymen's brotherhoods. Frustrated by the violent battles between members of the three different sects within the system of *compagnonnage*—a secret code of behaviors and alliances that ensured journeymen of lodging, fellowship, and often funds as they travelled from workshop to workshop—Perdiguier revealed its complicated operations to the public. The tactic worked. Reviewed by an array of literary celebrities, including Chateaubriand, Lamartine, and George Sand, the volume became a popular sensation that stabilized artisanal culture; sectarian violence among artisans declined sharply as the first and second editions of the book sold robustly, paving the way for what Sewell describes as a "historical reconciliation" within the trades on the eve of the insurrections of 1848.[22] In the end, this united artisanal front did not endure the upheavals of the era. But in Sewell's instance of the discourses surrounding political revolution, as in Rigal's analysis of the early national period in the United States, the literary history of artisanship offered the reading public an occasion, at least, for thinking about new forms of social organization. The radical possibilities of artisanal culture that the historian Sean Wilentz characterizes in terms of its Whitmanian voice—as the "chants democratic" of tradespeople in early nineteenth-century New York City—echoed, through print, across boundaries of class and nation.[23]

The political mobilization of artisanal lexicons between 1776 and 1848 thus characterizes an emerging culture of craft propelled by a wider panoply of discursive forces than the writing and lecturing of the individual reformers—particularly Ruskin, Morris, and Stickley—who eventually became the crafts movement's most visible spokespeople. Other scholarship supports this view, revealing how the expansion of a language of labor in the period suited the ideological imperatives of nostalgia as well as the interests of the avant-garde. Taking Horace Bushnell's 1851 sermon extolling a prior "age of homespun" as a signal moment in the cultural history of American memory, Laurel Thatcher Ulrich's *The Age of Homespun: Objects and Stories in the Creation of an American Myth* (2001) describes how the celebration of household production spurred nineteenth-century citizens to a kind of collector's passion for their own domestic crafts and for those recovered from the past. The individuals Ulrich describes, from public figures to anonymous citizens who donated family heirlooms to historical societies, collectively emphasized that "objects tell stories. They wrote [these] stories in speeches, memoirs, and poems, and on scraps of paper that they pinned, pasted, or sewed to the things they saved."[24] Ulrich describes an essentially preservative cultural impulse. Miles Orvell's *The Real Thing: Imitation and Authenticity in American Culture, 1880–1940* (1989), on the other hand, focuses on the later nineteenth century to place handicrafts nostalgia among a host of forces that, stressing the authenticity available through objects, "gradually established the aesthetic vocabulary that we have called 'modernist.' "[25] Drawing on a collection of sources that includes essays, periodicals, architectural theory, and design publications, Orvell reveals how the Arts and Crafts Movement tried to articulate a place for the "supposed 'right' use of the machine." Creating a mass-marketable style that also celebrated traditional modes of production, craft partisans instantiate what Orvell unfolds as the culture's more general, and more progressive, adjudication of the imperatives of the imitative and the genuine (158).

Most recently, Beverly K. Brandt's *The Craftsman and the Critic: Defining Usefulness and Beauty in Arts and Crafts–Era Boston* (2009) traces the influence of design critics on one of the premier outlets of the handicrafts movement: the Society of Arts and Crafts of Boston. For my purposes, Brandt's work transforms the historiography of craft's print culture by revealing how fully rank-and-file artisans were asked to participate in that discourse. Members of the Society submitted their works to a jury whose members included such figures as Langford Warren (a Harvard professor and dean, prolific essayist, and editor of *Handicraft* magazine as well as of Vitruvius's *Ten Books on Architecture*) and Charles Howard Walker (a student of the Society's first president, Charles Eliot Norton, and a prominent lecturer as well as a writer for *The Brickbuilder*, *The Craftsman*, and

Architectural Review). Establishing themselves as arbiters of artisanal taste, the members of the jury undertook national lecture tours, founded a library and reading room for the use of artisans at the Society's headquarters, published a bibliography of recommended works about craft, and used their annual reports to remind tradespeople as a class of the necessity of consulting books. Pronouncing on the fitness of objects for inclusion in the Society's exhibition hall and salesroom, the jury addressed individual members in the form of a written report to the object's maker. It is little wonder that artisans, confronted with the full force of Boston Brahminism as it flowed through the crafts movement, sometimes complained—as the metalworker Mary Catherine Knight did—that the "mere saying" of the jury was not the last word on an object's virtue, and that "publishing" an opinion did not make it true.[26]

Horatio Greenough's presentation of his literary career as "bending," to return to the punning name for the author-stonecutter he invented, is thus interpretable not just in the context of his private anxieties but also in the context of his culture's established predilection for talking shop. By 1852, when *The Travels, Observations, and Experience of a Yankee Stonecutter* appeared, craft had developed in the public sphere as a metonymic way of talking about nation-building and political reconstruction. Benvenuto Cellini's *Life* had been translated four times and into three languages since 1771, with the sixth edition in Italian appearing in the same year as Greenough's book. Historical taxonomies of crafted styles were beginning to revolutionize decorative culture, blurring the lines between objects and the tags that labeled them. Horace Bushnell's sermon about the age of homespun rang in the ears of an audience that, the preacher himself worried, might understand his emphasis on the "buzz" of spinning wheels and the "thwack" of looms as "hardly . . . a sermon" in the traditionally exegetic sense.[27] In later decades, craft's renascence flowed even more quickly through channels of literacy, including periodicals, stories, monographs, lexicons, how-to books, lecture tours, juries and their bibliographies, and advertisements for every kind of traditional furnishings. Between the second volume of *The Stones of Venice*, published the year after Greenough's book and featuring Ruskin's famous defense of Gothic detailing as the quintessence of workmanship, and the appearance of the final issue of Gustav Stickley's *The Craftsman* in 1916, the "threads of relation" that Greenough nervously glimpsed between practice and publication became a complicated, tightly woven web.

What I mean to emphasize, in introducing my subject in such broad terms and in so much initial detail, is that my interest lies at the points where those threads of relation are most fully crossed and entangled. This book studies the patterning of artisanship's print discourse less for its discrete aspects—its relevance to politics, say, as described by Rigal and Sewell, or to the Arts and Crafts Movement itself, as described by Brandt—than as a Gordian knot which, in its intricacy, made text the most visible artisanal medium in Anglo-American culture and reconstructed the cultural meaning of workmanship. Even more particularly, my interpretations of authors, theorists of workmanship, artisans, and the things they created stress how they accommodated definitions of handicraft as honest, straightforward, practical, or embodied with a textual apparatus that was representational, fractal, often abstract, and displaced from the hand itself. These strategies vitalized craft against the backdrop of nineteenth- and early twentieth-century industrialization, allowing it to prosper through a series of ideological adaptations and thereby embedding an epistemology of craft for modern culture. I want now to turn to the aspect of my argument that has to do with the axioms of physicality and untranslatability that more customarily define skilled labor, handmade artifacts, and literary as well as cultural theories of craft. For it is only through those axioms that the intense pressures and adaptive logics of workmanship's textual animus, in the artisan's and the author's spheres, become actually readable.

THE ARTISAN'S MEDIUM: CRAFT'S IMMEDIACY

In 1899, Thorstein Veblen complained that the "marks of hand labor"—irregular edges, visible tooling, certain imperfections of execution—were becoming icons of rarity and of expense. For Veblen, such "marks" deflected the meaning of skilled labor to the realm of symbolic conspicuity, establishing a semiotics of artisanship through "propaganda for a return to handicraft and household industry."[28] Veblen's perspective epitomizes the skepticism with which craft's iconicity has been met. The Arts and Crafts Movement has been an understandable focal point of such skepticism. Channeling artisanship through fashionable objects, the movement's "antimodern" potential, as Jackson Lears has put it, collapsed as craft-styled furnishings became an aesthetic type of "bourgeois domesticity."[29]

More generally, craft has been held to the standards of its embodiment, to the standards of tools, workshops, mastery of a single medium, and concrete goals: a long critical tradition establishes the fundamentally discrete experience of labor—practiced by an agent long habituated to the craft's physical and intellectual requirements—as a litmus test of handicrafts authenticity. Craft, in this model, is experiential rather than aesthetic. Its meanings are intrinsic to its actual practice rather than communicable or easily translatable. Plato's *Republic* makes this point clearly. For Plato, craft is a type of virtue because it is a focused and practiced use of one's energies in the service of a single task. A dialogue in the *Republic* between Socrates and Thrasymachus aims to show that a truly workmanlike attitude toward labor depends on the narrowest solicitude for the immediate goal of the work; "the only concern of the craft . . . is to provide what is best for that with which it deals."[30] To the degree that an artisan is motivated by payment, Thrasymachus admits under Socrates' questioning, that artisan is actually practicing a secondary craft (of "wage earning") rather than the true crafts of house carpentry, shepherding, or medicine—properly defined as caring for houses, as caring for sheep, and as caring for bodies (346a-d). For Socrates, craft depends on *telos*, on a goal presented as singularly and incomparably as possible.

Plato uses Socrates' argument to suggest that in the perfect republic each citizen would work in only one medium, and that a ruler, acting as an artisan, considers no personal advantage but only "what is advantageous for his subject —that on which he practices his craft" (342e). What is known to philosophers as the "craft analogy" connects the virtue Plato seeks in the body politic and its leaders to the virtuous specialization—the deep care for the objects under the craftsman's purview—that he attributes to the individual worker. For Veblen, exactly this kind of specialization emerged as an alternative to the semiotics of craft he pilloried in *The Theory of the Leisure Class*. Published fifteen years later, *The Instinct of Workmanship* (1914) lauded craft's animus of "economy" and "efficiency" as the practiced expertise that allows an artisan to exert just the right amount of "muscular force."[31] Such habituation, the "discipline of the handicrafts industry," appears to Veblen as a certain development, disposition, or adaptation of the body to its labor (237); we might visualize what Veblen is talking about—long experience with the medium—in, say, the woodworker's calloused grip, the stained fingers of the textile dyer, or the stonemason's muscular forearms.

Recent critics have worried that craft's teleological virtues have been too exclusively identified with unreflective activity. Turning back to Plato, the philosopher Julia Annas argues that the craft analogy itself presumes a thinking, engaged subject rather than a merely facile enactor of well-established practices. Richard Sennett, questioning his mentor Hannah Arendt's distinction between *animal laborans* (the brutish maker of things) and *homo faber* (the guider or director of ethically sound and politically defensible modes of production), presents a compelling humanistic case for artisanship as engaging the mind as fully as the hands. For Sennett, craft depends on curiosity and adaptation, and in those respects appears as an ideal model for an ethical way of being in the world; the artisan, in Sennett's examples, adjusts to ever-changing conditions and irregular materials, frames new problems as he or she solves present ones, and depends preeminently on "judging while doing."[32] Matthew Crawford echoes the point by addressing not the teleological clarity of Platonic crafts but the uncertainty of the vocations that Aristotle calls "stochastic"—crafts, like medicine or repair, that do not originate the things that are worked on, and may therefore fail to achieve what they set out to do. Stochastic labor, Crawford writes, demands particularly "evaluative attention"; the unpredictability of the bodies or things on which they work means that the doctor or mechanic continually adjusts hope to discovery, joining thinking to practice in the experimental, adaptive ways also described by Annas and Sennett.[33] One of the best results of reframing craft in this way is to expand its interest beyond the private scene of the solitary artisan bent over the labor. As an investigative practice of curiosity, craft in these readings appears socially connective. The achievement of one artisan prompts new avenues of pursuit for another. Diagnostic or procedural questions draw together communities of like-minded practitioners, whether in the same physical space (the scene emphasized by Crawford, whose motorcycle repair shop anchors the narrative) or across much vaster landscapes (the scene emphasized by Sennett when he discusses, for instance, the collective and artisanal nature of open-source computer programming). Paul Greenhalgh's edited collection *The Persistence of Craft* (2003) perhaps represents the most exuberant account of craft's sociability—for the volume places the contemporary practice of craft squarely in the complicated and "interdependent" social and economic systems of modern production and consumption.[34] For the contributors to Greenhalgh's volume, there is a sense of creative *jouissance* in the fact that craft owes its lifeblood and its historically specific forms to patterns of consumer attitudes, advertising, marketing, popular trends in visual culture, and the collaborative or even corporate endeavors of artisans.

These revisionist accounts, however, also reveal the durability of Platonic notions about craft's specialization and, to express the case in terms most relevant to *Talking Shop*, its untranslatability. The purity of concern presumed by Socrates, when he describes "wage earning" as a different craft than carpentry, appears in Sennett's opening definition: "Craftsmanship," he writes, "names the desire to do a job well for its own sake" (9). Even the most radically dispersed community of artisans, the global assembly of open-source programmers who work in public online forums, set the standard of craft in their concentrated attention to the medium. In fact, the programmers studied by Sennett might be said to apotheosize artisanal focus, for—not knowing one another's identities beyond their online handles—their collaboration contracts to the narrow, relatively impersonal point of what each contributor brings to the labor. "What matters," Sennett concludes, is the analysis and action that this or that programmer contributes to the evolving product, such that open source instantiates C. Wright Mills's definition of the "laborer [who] with a sense of craft becomes engaged in the work in and for itself" (27). These are common terms in twentieth-century discussions of artisanship. Crawford contrasts the appeal of "learning to do one thing really well" to the diffuse sense of general capacity that he finds in the managerial economy (19). Skills, he writes, are "inherently situated" in craftwork (164). The "scene of its execution" (208) focuses the "attentiveness" of artisanal labor (82), and craft depends on outcomes measured by the object rather than the subject. In this regard, Sennett's impersonal digital workshop does not differ from Crawford's much more personal repair shop, where despite the bonhomie of mechanics working side-by-side, the "standard internal to the job" (136) appears as the simple question of whether the motorcycle will run.

Most important for my purposes, the predication of craft on internal standards grounds a related presumption: that craft is ambivalently describable because the definitional orientation of craft to its own ends compromises its effective translation. For Crawford, the current "educational regime" has replaced shop class with courses in which knowledge "can be transmitted through speech without loss of meaning." Craft differs from these courses because it "can only be lived," not described—a point Crawford grounds in his own experiences when he describes the impenetrability and frustrating obliqueness of modern service manuals for cars and motorcycles (162). Sennett treats these suppositions in more detail in a chapter on cookbooks. The most effective recipes, he finds, depend on metaphor rather than direct description of processes: because craft really depends on "tacit knowledge" (a phrase also used by Crawford), only a secondhand, figurative, and metaphorical language of "loose" analogies can approximate its practice (185).[35] Whether expert cooks or carpenters, programmers or pianists, artisans "know how to do something" but "cannot put [much of] what they know into words" (94); the instructions offered to the rest of us are most effective, Sennett finds, when they aim to characterize tasks indirectly. What Sennett discovers in his chapter on cookbooks—that the language of craft is a "vexing subject," because, like the cookbooks themselves, "I found myself unable to put clearly into words how hand and eye coordinate" (179)—bespeaks the fault lines of craft and text that, *Talking Shop* proposes, nineteenth- and early twentieth-century culture negotiated. The vexations and improbabilities of rendering craft in language were conditions that authors and artisans in the era knew well and, I assert, tried to soothe. In so doing, they invented a literary language of workmanship and established a durable discourse of craft for modern culture.

As the background for the developments traced in the following chapters, Socrates' abjuration of an exchange motive in the purest forms of craft thus describes an axiom that is textual as much as it is economic; it extends to a quality of rhetorical untranslatability as much as it illustrates a quality of vocational purity. Skepticism about the exchange value of craft further extends, in other recent accounts, to the definition of skill itself. Howard Risatti's *A Theory of Craft* (2007) focuses less on the purity of ends (doing a job well for its own sake, as defined by Sennett and Crawford) than on the purity of means: the artisan, Risatti writes, knows his or her chosen medium so intimately that "technical manual skill acquired in one area usually [does] not carry over to another."[36] Anticipating Risatti's formula, the late Peter Dormer—a central figure in an ongoing scholarly discussion about craft in the United Kingdom that has had surprisingly little transatlantic notice—describes "honest work" as the perfect correlation of plan and result. Crafts skills, for Dormer, hinge on the specialized, experiential mastery of the medium that enables accurate assessment of design and ensures consistency of outcome; deviations from plan belie the teleological standards on which skill, in this line of thinking, is predicated. Dormer does not say that artisans never improvise. Rather, he suggests that acts of improvisation shade into some other definitional territory, marking the limit of the ideal virtues categorized as craftsmanship.

There are other ways of thinking about this, to be sure. The recent critics who stress craft's mental choreography of evaluation and adaptation would strenuously disagree with Dormer's characterization of procedural certainty as an ideal standard of craft. The third chapter of *Talking Shop* describes a line of nineteenth-century thinking in which improvisations around natural variations in the material instead confirm craftedness, proving that artisans—working with media that cannot be shaped to will—do not act like machines. What interests me for the moment, however, are the standards of concentration and singularity of medium shared across the dominant lines of theorizing about handicrafts; these standards tie its meaning closely to the site and to the focal point of the work. Even the most revisionist accounts, the lively essays about the interdependence of craftspeople and consumer culture in Greenhalgh's *The Persistence of Craft*, tend to see the daily processes of artisanship—if not its larger cultural embedding and creative responsiveness to the market—as centripetal forces. The appearance of the artisanal object, the "spirit [that] remains at its core," resides in the "accepted canon of skills" used to make it.[37] While Greenhalgh's collection implies that we might rethink our anxieties about the ways in which craft is beholden to certain impersonal market forces, artisanship continues to signify a "means of asserting personal control" over material in some aspect of the creation (24–25). Handicrafts may be subject to the social, ideological, and financial conditions of the mass market—conditions worth attending as constituent pressures on their design—but those objects are also admirable because they are manifestations of intention. The "easy, accrued knowledge that effervesces from successful objects" is a playful way to put the case of craft's purposefulness (27). But it retains the Platonic commitment to workmanship's focal points, under the aegis of applied skill in a medium, even as it loosens the bonds between craft and rustic or otherwise traditional systems of production.

Talking Shop is aligned with Thorstein Veblen's interest in the semiotics of workmanship, with Jackson Lears's account of craft's popularization, and with Paul Greenhalgh's model of the "persistence of craft" to the degree that I also trace interdependencies of craft and consumer culture, workmanship and the conditions of modernity. But I do so by proposing an account of craft's meaning which, flowing through nineteenth- and early twentieth-century efforts to adapt workmanship to its texts and lexicons, translates more easily to media outside the physical objects on which the artisan's care is exerted. The first two chapters of the book describe how one of the textual outlets of craft, narrative, came to represent the human life of labor—distinguishing it, as story, from the perfect telos attributed to machines and equated with industrial modes of production. Cellini's ready confessions to several murders and his accounts of jailbreaking, poisoning, and prostitution may have scandalized readers, but his desultory narrative also appealed to its canonizers—my subjects in chapter 1—precisely because it located the scope of the craftsman's life outside of the workshop. Cellini's bombastic *Life* presents craft (meaning whatever dexterous activities he is doing, from goldsmithing and sculpture to his chance adventures in street fighting, surgery, or soldiering) as a disposition rather than a learned, merely material relation to a particular medium or material; a similar correlation of craft, identity, and the human voice appears across the many accounts of artisanal production in Nathaniel Hawthorne's fictional corpus, my subject in chapter 2. These examples reveal how literary history promoted an identity-centered alternative to what scholars often call the commodity fetish (as described by Marx, the obscuration of the individual worker behind the products of his or her labor) by embedding the interest of artisanship in the voice or the story of the artisan. But, most relevant to the major argument of *Talking Shop*, the first two chapters also detail the often elaborate strategies by which Cellini's canonizers and Hawthorne adapted the narrative interest of craft to durable ideas about manual labor's vocational specificity, incarnate effort, concentrated focal points, and ethos of results. While celebrating the textual animation of labor, these nineteenth-century figures also staked out the boundaries of craft's narrative attractions; they accommodated their enthusiasm to traditional definitions of workmanship, mollifying the apparent contradictions of translating a physical practice into a textual one. Embedded in a complex of different imperatives, the era's narratives of craft thus demanded as well as drove a definitional flexibility that revised, reframed, and—quite literally—rewrote the axioms of workmanship's cultural appeal.

The aspects of *Talking Shop* concerned with narrative emphasize Hawthorne's work even when that work is not my central subject. Chapter 1, for instance, opens with a discussion of Hawthorne's response to Cellini, while chapter 3 introduces an interpretation of nineteenth-century crafts theory by considering how *The House of the Seven Gables* can be read in the context of a set of ideas we now recognize as "Ruskinian." More generally, the subjects examined in the individual chapters of this book often overlap, aiming to characterize a complex, interlinked, and highly self-referential discourse of workmanship as one of the innovations of the era; for example, figure 1 depicts an advertisement for Cellini's autobiography that appeared in Stickley's magazine *The Craftsman*, which also ran ads for competing periodicals (*Handicraft*, *Building Age*, *National Builder*) and articles on contemporary fiction, poetry, and philosophy that seemed relevant to the handicrafts mission. But Hawthorne appears so often in the following chapters for two more specific reasons. First, his corpus is suffused with artisanal artifacts as occasions for all kinds of speech. Craft—obviously lexical in the case of the embroidered scarlet letter—prompts rumor, speculation, interpretation, public discourse, and musings about the meaning of creation; Hawthorne negotiates and renegotiates the correlations among craft, language, and objects. Second, the depiction of labor in Hawthorne's works invites comparison with theorizations about craft's meaning in the Platonic tradition I have described. Notions of craft's untranslatability stress the gulf between actual, focused labor and the vagaries or abstractions of literary expression. Notoriously etherealizing, the Hawthornian Romance has been read for its revelation of just this gulf. Gillian Brown's *Domestic Individualism: Imagining Self in Nineteenth-Century America* (1990), for instance, argues that "both labor and women are divested of their corporeality" in fiction featuring such domestic heroines and super-capable housekeepers as Phoebe Pyncheon, one of the protagonists in *The House of the Seven Gables*. The labor performed by these women appears not as attentiveness to the job at hand or as an actual exertion but as a kind of "spiritual ministry" that reflects nineteenth-century ideologies of domesticity.[38] Nicholas Bromell's *By The Sweat of the Brow: Literature and Labor in Antebellum America* (1993) concurs, drawing out Hawthorne's investments in

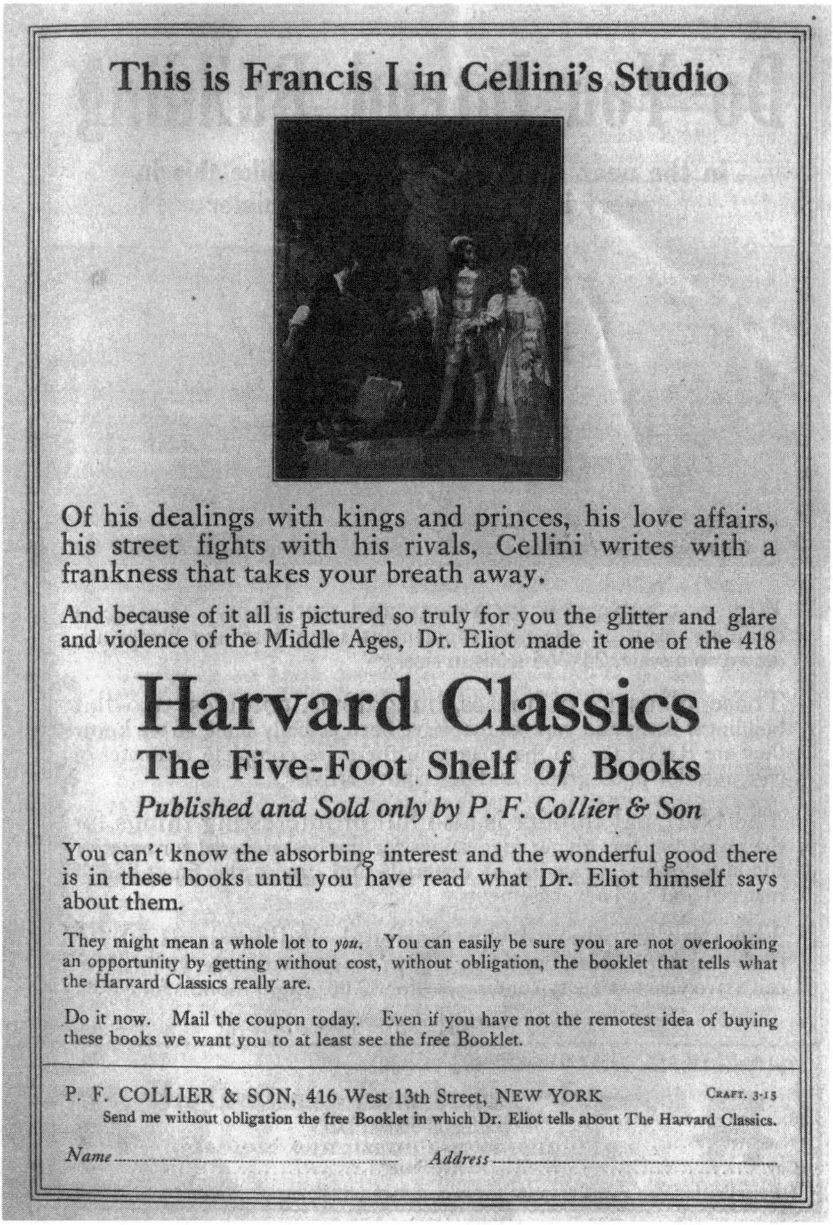

FIGURE 1. Advertisement. (*The Craftsman* 27, no. 6 [March 1915])

essentially bourgeois literary notions about the spiritualization of labor and its elevation of the soul. For Bromell, it is unusual to see people "actually straining their muscles and wielding their tools" in the nineteenth-century canon because the literary culture of the era was preoccupied with the metaphysical meaning of physical exertion.[39] The circumference of manual labor in Hawthorne's fiction reveals its vanishing points when judged by its correspondence to the actual, incarnate experience of work.

Talking Shop in no way seeks to dislodge politically important analysis that reveals the manifold ways in which nineteenth-century culture obfuscated manual work. As scholarship like Gillian Brown's shows, different kinds of labor (whether professional, domestic, skilled, unskilled, urban, or rural) performed by different kinds of laborers (whether slaves, freedpeople, men, women, native-born citizens, or immigrants) offer different thresholds of recognition and visibility. But in arguing that adaptations of labor and text established handicraft as a mainstream cultural value and in certain ways increased—rather than attenuated—its visibility, I do want to notice certain ways in which labor in literature has been judged by the same axioms of work's proper untranslatability as are visible in crafts theory. If the study of Hawthorne's literary corpus offers a specific example, Walter Benjamin's "The Storyteller" represents the general paradigm, for Benjamin names the only conditions under which workmanship and narrative might be viably correlative: when they occur in the same physical space, when stories are told even as work is being actually performed. The Old World workshop, Benjamin asserts, constituted the best home of an oral storytelling tradition. In an era when "the resident master craftsman and the traveling journeyman worked together in the same rooms," stories were transported across geographies and thus embedded orally in the "milieu of work"; they emerged via the "slow piling one on top of the other of thin, transparent layers," with a "perfect narrative . . . revealed through the layers of a variety of retellings."[40] But the rise of the published novel (focused on the protagonist's singular and "incommensurable" experience) and the development of the short story (a streamlined form of single authorship rather than a diachronic accretion of narrative layers) marked, in Benjamin's literary history, the severing of the historical ties between "craftsmanship . . . [and] storytelling" (92). Published and single-authored fiction marks the attenuation of an embodied, spatial relation between literature, labor, and authenticity.

Seeing coincidences between the historical diminishment of the workshop as a center of community life and the historical appearance of narrative forms stressing unique protagonists, Benjamin patterns more recent thinking about writing and workmanship. Michael Denning's *The Cultural Front: The Laboring of*

American Culture in the Twentieth Century (1996), for instance, extends Bromell's assertions about labor's nineteenth-century invisibility into the twentieth century while echoing Benjamin quite exactly in wondering if one of the problems isn't fundamentally generic: fiction comes from "interruptions" to the settled lives of its characters, and thus appears inevitably unsuited to the "repetitive manual tasks of shop and home."[41] "Work itself resists representations," Denning asserts (244), nearly replicating Bromell's statement about "manual labor's resistance to verbal representation" (34) and anticipating Sennett's vexation with the process of trying to explain hand-eye coordination. Denning's claim aphoristically formulates an anxiety about labor's literary evanescence that students of what has been called "work studies" (to distinguish it from the disembodied, sociological, and statistical dimensions of labor history) have variously attempted to redress or, at least, to describe. Focusing on the antinomy of literary idealizations of labor and what appears as its proper or actual sphere of the body, Laura Hapke's *Labor's Text: The Worker in American Fiction* (2001) describes how such writers as Catharine Maria Sedgwick, Susan Warner, Stephen Crane, and William Dean Howells appear to have celebrated work while relying on the "gospel of self-betterment" through labor; these authors "limn workers not as they are but as they should be."[42] One approach to the problem of labor's disembodiment is the methodology adopted by Gillian Brown in her discussion of Hawthorne and other nineteenth-century writers: to explore the ideologies driving the invisibility of the individual worker in canonical literature. Another approach emphasizes a relatively small canon of texts that do represent workmanship more physically, particularly those by working-class writers of the 1930s—a decade crucial to the formation of what Denning calls the "cultural front" of labor consciousness and when, Hapke argues, the celebration of work's physicality finally appeared unsaddled by narratives of moral betterment. In Hapke's narrative, workers appeared "heroic at last" in unvarnished depictions of their actual work.[43]

Literary critics and theorists of artisanship thus evaluate labor by similar criteria of self-containment. A properly embodied practice appears compromised when "interruptions" of routine, fiction's source of interest, drive literature's departure from everyday work (Benjamin and Denning); when mental or moral goals supplant material ones (Bromell, Brown, and Hapke); when excesses of improvisation diminish the pursuit of objective goals (Dormer); when the artisan seeks reward outside the object of the craft itself (Plato); and when artisans try to work in too many media (Risatti). *Talking Shop*, I have said, supports the importance of work's corporeality or skill's telos as definitional values. But I do want to question the impermeability of those standards, the sense that craft is necessarily sui generis, from a historical point of view. In emphasizing correlations between energies traditionally understood in opposition—handmade things and consumer culture, fact and image, embodied labor and print culture—this book studies the adaptation and evolution of values classically associated with a producer-based economy. Historical research in the past two decades has revealed how those values were less split from, than sutured to, mass culture in nineteenth- and early twentieth-century ideology. In an era when Anglo-American culture was aggressively talking shop, craft appears not as insular and specialized, nor as obfuscated, transformed beyond recognition, pushed into cultural pockets, or consigned to a nostalgic world elsewhere.

Against these commonplaces, craft may be best understood as a particularly focused instance of one of the "transit points," to borrow Mark Seltzer's term for sites of ideological adaptation, that recent research has identified as fundamental to the culture of the era.[44] That we continue to negotiate those transit points is evident in the broad spectrum of cultural values craft suggests today. Workmanship is manifestly enjoyable as the practice of local artisans who sell their pottery, woodworking, or textiles in galleries, at festivals, and by commission. But workmanship is also readily consumable as an iconography and language of the mass market, whether presented by Restoration Hardware, Pottery Barn, or Crate and Barrel. Artisans and authors between 1840 and 1920, I will argue, did not acquiesce easily to the definitionally problematic translation of craft into narrative, printed, or stylistically tagged forms. But they could not cleave uncompromisingly to standards of workmanship centered on the body and set in the workshop—and the adjustments they made are manifest in the ways we experience and appreciate craft in our own era.

FIFTH AVENUE ARTISANSHIP: CRAFT'S SALABILITY

In November 1913 the imprimatur on *The Craftsman* magazine read: "Gustav Stickley, Craftsman/Craftsman Building/38th and 39th Sts. East of Fifth Avenue/New York."[45] The address was new. In late October, Stickley had opened the twelve-story Craftsman Building, advertising its centrality to Manhattan shopping on maps that showed the building's location and pinpointed selected other businesses: Bonwit Teller, Lord and Taylor, Gorham Silver, Tiffany and Co., the Waldorf Astoria Hotel. An open invitation to the building's inauguration appeared in the October *Craftsman*, and clearly betrayed Stickley's need to justify the department-store scale of the new endeavor as still relevant to his humbler identity as the "Craftsman":

> For years the dream of my life has been the development of the democratic home—the home beautiful, simple, comfortable, adjusted to the lives of intelligent, artistic, practical American folk. I have written about this home and talked about it and built it; but the utmost that I have been able to do in the past seemed but a drop in the bucket. I felt that I could not reach the great mass of people until I conceived this project of the great home center where people from all over the world would be made welcome, where every phase of homebuilding could be seen and studied, where the practicability of different kinds of building material could be demonstrated and where people could within the four walls of the Craftsman Building plan, design and complete the arrangement for a house suited to their individual needs and their ambitions in the home line.[46]

Positioning the structure as an extension of the populist project, Stickley connects the greatness of "our new home," as he described the building in an advertisement, to the simple, practical homes for which he advocated in the magazine. The side of the Craftsman Building facing Fifth Avenue (fig. 2) visualizes the overlapping of a "home" and a "great home center" in the banner draped along the concrete surface. At the top of the banner, the bungalow offers an complementary roofline to the urban structure. The trees placed on either side of the house mirror the corners of the Craftsman Building, while the bungalow's central gable mirrors what appears to be the smokestack of the building; by such geometrical reflections between the two rooflines, the design of the banner brings the Craftsman's Building's towering height down to earth and domesticates the new endeavor. In the lower left of the banner, Stickley includes his shop mark: a furniture maker's compass surrounding the Flemish text "Als Ik Kan," translated word-for-word as "All I can" but better understood, idiomatically, as suggesting work performed "to the best of my ability." The shop mark, which appeared in various forms on all of Stickley's furnishings, further reduces the scale of the Craftsman Building by identifying it with the items built in the Craftsman workshops. In the penultimate clause of the passage quoted earlier, a probably accidental pun nevertheless reveals the psychological stakes of the company's growth. One might read the word "plan" as it seems to have been intended, as a verb describing the activities conducted by the individual in the Craftsman Building. But it also reads as a noun, describing the prototypical plans for snug and secure bungalows that appeared in every issue of *The Craftsman* and whose design Stickley promoted as a refuge from the pace of modern life. The activities of the shopper in the Craftsman Building in

FIGURE 2. The Craftsman Building. (*The Craftsman* 27, no. 6 [March 1915])

New York are thus further contained by the missionary domestic project of the Craftsman bungalow; the centripetal pull of the "four walls" of the archetypal building "plan" continues to define the endeavor even as the lines between the company's Fifth Avenue home and the consumer's home blur and shift. The seams of the commercial and the domestic could not be clearer than in the closing words of the passage: "ambitions in the home line" is a strikingly entrepreneurial way to characterize the interests of consumers in fitting out their living rooms with the ideal Craftsman furnishings.

Such negotiations, to be sure, became commonplace as handicraft became a mainstream market value. In an 1892 book of photographs of its manufactory, Gorham Silver (one of the retailers whose proximity to the Craftsman Building Stickley cited) presents a pair of views of its "Case Department" that, taken together, narrate the passage of goods from the hands of individual makers to the homes of consumers (figs. 3 and 4). The views are obviously staged: many of the same individuals occupy different workstations in the two images despite the fact that the photographer appears to have pivoted in the center of the room. Theatricalizing the ways in which all manners of cases and containers for Gorham silver are manufactured, the images present an economy of scale as a shop-like atmosphere in which care, not speed, is the dominant value. The postures of the workers are almost uniformly unpressured. In each view of the line of artisan-like laborers against the window, at least one figure stands; others appear at different stages of relatively autonomous crafts processes, with individual sets of tools mounted on the wall between the windows. In the assembly, packaging, and bookkeeping area near the central columns, the pace of labor is even less hurried. The central figure in the south-facing perspective appears to be carefully sealing a box. A man in the distant background waits, apparently for another man to retrieve something from a case of drawers. The standing figure nearest to the columns walks into the area; in the north-facing perspective, the same man, in a different location, departs.

Coming and going, waiting and working, collaborating on the shop floor, the Gorham employees model the steady rhythms of patient artisanal practice. And yet the easy tempo of the manufactory runs no risk of compromising its productivity and the scale of its distribution, literalized in these images as the crafting of the packaging of crafts. The fact that the views do not overlap reveals, between the two, the extent of the room. Some of the easeful figures in the central area are apparently supervisory, particularly the bearded man in a full coat rather than a shop apron. In the south view, he appears to be resupplying the workers with the raw materials for making case linings; in the north view, his gaze rests on the order slips clipped to the surface to the right of his

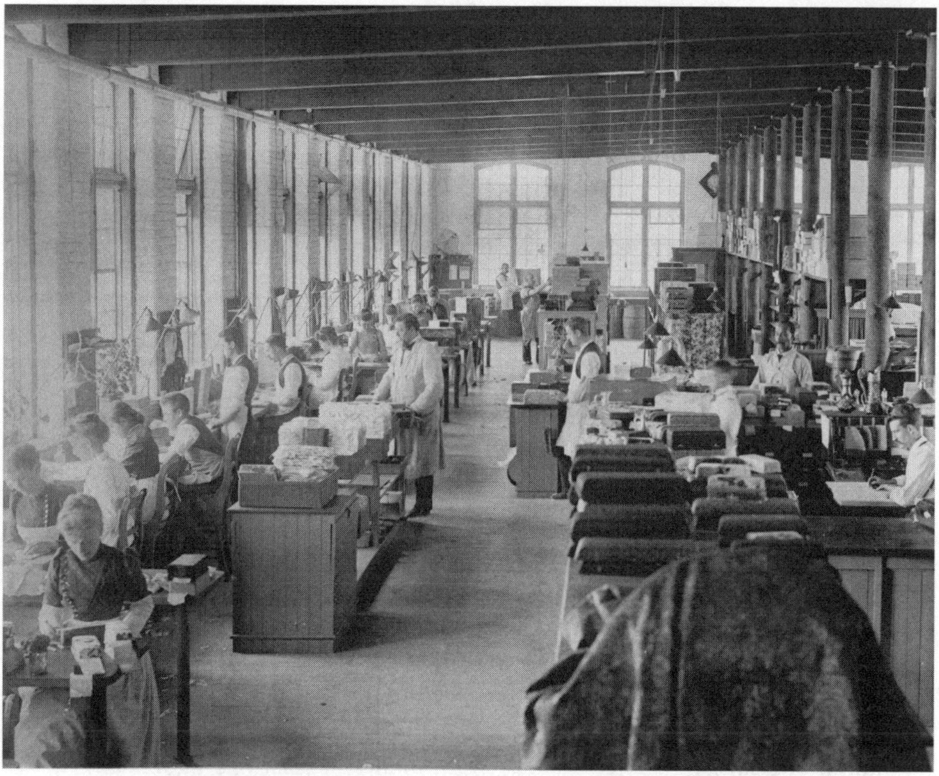

FIGURE 3. Case Department, Gorham Manufacturing Co., section looking south, 1892. (*Views, Exterior and Interior, of the Works of the Gorham Manufacturing Co.*, 1892; courtesy the John Hay Library, Brown University)

hand, and the activity of that hand itself—actuating a bell or other signal—suggests his position as foreman. On both end walls, clocks keep the time of a productive culture that is staged both as an artisanal enterprise and as comfortably matched to the demands of the large market for Gorham silver.

This kind of imagery is legion around 1900. Hundreds of examples depict factory life as something like shop life, and *Talking Shop* rarely focuses on forms of cultural production quite so pointed as Gorham's photographic propaganda. But in tracing the literary and rhetorical contours of the artisanal, I do want to suggest that the accommodations of craft and text in nineteenth-century narrative developed into more and more clearly marketable forms by the turn of the century. For this reason, the following chapters are organized in loosely chronological order; I hope to characterize the diachronic current that eventuates in the negotiated forms of mass-market artisanship visible in the Craftsman Building and in the Gorham manufactory. The first chapter is the main excep-

FIGURE 4. Case Department, Gorham Manufacturing Co., section looking north, 1892. (*Views, Exterior and Interior, of the Works of the Gorham Manufacturing Co.*, 1892; courtesy the John Hay Library, Brown University)

tion to strict sequence, for the popularity of Cellini's autobiography spanned the entire period between 1840 and 1920. And while the final chapter discusses James's packaging of *The Spoils of Poynton* as a craft-centered text in his collected works (1909), that discussion does not take us quite as deep into the twentieth century as the final two sections of the previous chapter—which describe Stickley's Craftsman company just before he declared bankruptcy in 1916. Taken as a whole, however, the sequence of examples in *Talking Shop* aims to tie popular enthusiasm for the crafts to what I see as an ideological condition of such enthusiasm: the increasing facility of Anglo-American culture, over time and outside of the workshop, with the language of craft as it emerged and developed between 1840 and 1920.

The trajectory of the book might also be understood in three argumentative phases. Chapters 1 and 2 depend on close reading to plumb the implicit logic, in central texts of craft's literary canon, that adapted bodily practices to textual media and translated the artisan's attentiveness to the representational dynamics of literary production and reception. Chapter 3 then shifts the discussion into the realm of crafts theory, tracing axioms about technique and assumptions about the nature of artisanship through the middle and late nineteenth century. My central proposition is that, contrary to widespread belief, the era of John Ruskin and the Arts and Crafts Movement did not primarily attempt to rejuvenate traditional canons of skills or to promote ideas about especially adroit manual labor. Indulging in more shifts between types of representational media—texts, objects, decorative surfaces—than anywhere else in *Talking Shop*, the chapter aims to unfold how the communicative dimensions of things meant far more to craft partisans than the actual, technical details of their making or the teleological focus of the maker. What Ruskin called the "expression" of the artisan's subjectivity, an elastic and translatable quality rather than a teleological practice, anchored a theory of craft that emphasized the legibility and representation of workmanship as distinct from the iterative processes of industrial production. Chapter 3 thus embeds the themes of *Talking Shop* in the thinking about artisanal practice done by some of its most outspoken defenders.

The final phase of my argument, Chapters 4 and 5, describes the heyday of handicrafts in the consumer market—roughly between 1890 and 1916—as dependent upon the class of innovations visible in earlier texts, theories, and objects. Stickley, the subject of chapter 4, may be the book's most important example, for no advocate for craft was more devoted to its discursive aspects than the vibrant, enthusiastic entrepreneur who brought the simple, rectilinear designs associated with the American Arts and Crafts Movement to the mainstream. For Stickley, every point on the spectrum joining production to consumption depended on a rhetorical understanding of workmanship's meaning. Stressing the craftsman's sensitivity (an idea he adapted from Ruskin) and identifying the craftsman as a "translator" (an idea he adapted from Emerson's notion of the poet), Stickley articulated how unusual ways of cutting and finishing wood would best realize the qualities of simplicity and honesty he associated with the "very name" of his signature species, oak.[47] The obvious paradox here—that the fundamentally plain qualities of the medium should require relatively elaborate realization to translate properly—reappears throughout the vast discursive complex of the Craftsman endeavor, which extended by 1913 to the *Craftsman* magazine, the Craftsman Farms utopian project (envisioned, in part, as a craft-centered school), the Craftsman Publishing Company, the Craftsman Interior Decorating Department, the Craftsman Restaurant, and the Craftsman Building; at the latter, Stickley enthused, "we should have lectures on home-making, home-building materials, a library . . . [and] a corps of architects fitted to give advice on this most significant subject."[48] Chapter 4 segues to the subject of chapter 5, James's *The Spoils of Poynton*, by concluding with a discussion of how Stickley drew on his foundational accommodations of craft and its translatability—into names, tags, brands, advice, and literary fiction—to defend his company's highly imitative late period designs; these designs included "Colonial Revival," "Jacobean," and "Chinese Chippendale" pieces. At first glance, the interlacing of craft, fiction, and mass-market nomenclatures in Stickley's operation hardly seems relevant to James's interests in *Spoils*. Famously, the antiques at the center of the plot are barely described, and the breathtaking sight of the genuinely old pieces carved by the "hands of rare artists"—working in the "more laboring ages"—cause the novel's characters to fall as silent, as "mute," as the novelist himself (xliii, 14). For James, the ekphrastic use of decorative nomenclatures ran the risk of introducing the "cheaper sound" of the mass market into fiction (xlvi); the silence of the spoils defends against that risk. But, slowly and painfully over the course of the novel, Mrs. Gereth (the original collector of the spoils, now dispossessed of them by an English law denying inheritance to widows) learns to produce a version of that effect that her lost antiques had, using furnishings in reproduction artisanal styles inherited from a dowdy aunt. Through his depiction of the fundamentally dialogic aspects of that effect, I suggest, James charted the novelist's own course to the garrulous culture of craft that the nineteenth and early twentieth centuries invented.

The Spoils of Poynton, in the end, strikes a precarious balance between, on the one hand, the frankly maudlin enthusiasm with which Mrs. Gereth's triumph is celebrated and, on the other hand, what James presents as the frankly haughty desire to preserve the untranslatability of crafted things. More generally, it is probably impossible not to raise our eyebrows at many of the protean efforts traced in *Talking Shop*, just as it is impossible not to see in Stickley's "home center" an anticipation of our own do-it-yourself home centers or putatively "artisanal" mass-market retailers. But I hope to have made clear that I do not see the literary, lexical, and commercial energies of artisanship between 1840 and 1920 as only a hoax on craft's properly untranslatable media and activities. One of the propositions that connects this book's chapters has to do with the good and understandable reason that craft advocates would reorient workmanship toward expressiveness, toward sensibility, and toward its recognizability as narrative: because machines were supremely capable of imitating traditional details, reliably reproducing plans, and iterating teleological activities. Classical accounts of skilled labor, in other words, came to describe the processes of industry as much as those of the craftsperson. Accordingly, emerging ideas about workmanship's meaning veered away from the artisan's authoritative relation with the physical medium and toward an emphasis on the styles, types, and indeed stories of craft that made it compelling in iconic terms and legible as a human practice.

That those developments also fitted craft even more certainly to the market is perhaps less ironic, implying a contradiction, than paradoxical, implying the double imperatives of craft's transliteration: to defend and promote the artisanal while distinguishing it from the merely physical productivity of machines. The crafts movement has been widely critiqued for what one of Stickley's biographers calls its "illustration of craftsmanship" rather than its devotion to actually vernacular methods.[49] It seems today to have hawked images and icons. That, I also argue, it did. But to think of the textual phenomena traced in this book in terms of unbridgeable gaps between the real and the represented, between work and word, between labor and consumption, is to impose incongruities on a definition of craft that was fired in a larger cultural kiln.

CHAPTER 1

THE GHOST WRITER

The Canonization of Benvenuto Cellini

"SUCH HANDS AS THOSE OF BENVENUTO CELLINI"

For nineteenth-century readers, no literary account of artisanship was better known than *The Life of Benvenuto Cellini, Written by Himself in Florence.* Composed mostly in the late 1550s but only printed in its native Italian in 1728 and in English for the first time in 1771, Cellini's autobiography of his life as a goldsmith and a sculptor became a sensation in the period between 1822 (when Thomas Roscoe produced the second English translation) and 1910 (when Robert Cust produced the fifth). Cellini's *Life* epitomizes the transformations of the crafts ideal that *Talking Shop* aims to unfold. Literary critics and theorists of workmanship, I have suggested, have held craft to standards of telos and concentration. But Cellini's text rarely mentions sustained work on a project, and only once—describing his masterpiece, a statue of Perseus—goes into substantial detail about his methods.

More typically, Cellini tosses off references to his often-obscure practices amid a breathless narration of other, more exciting activities: a story about how a priest and his brother swindled him out of a farm, for instance, casually pauses to note that "I did not suspend my labors on the [statue of] Neptune, which was now quite blocked out upon an excellent system, unknown and undiscovered before I used it."[1] With the exception of the work on the *Perseus*, Cellini's labors in the autobiography are taken up, mystified, abandoned, recommenced sooner or later, and finished (if they are finished) with little fanfare beyond his commentary on the public's judgment of them. The onward press of his worldly life absorbs Cellini's craftsmanship, and if the place where craft is performed anchors its meaning in the critical tradition I have described, Cellini's text is notable for moving bewilderingly between locations—Florence, Rome, Padua, Paris—and for rarely saying anything concrete about the various workshops he inhabits. Cellini's representation of himself does not celebrate the singularity of acquired artisanal skills. Instead, the text features its author's instant and intuitive ability to perform whatever craft he tries. Cellini can make large plates better than the established masters of that branch of metalwork. His first effort with steel dies wins him a commission to strike the Pope's medallions. He carves an obscure regional style of Turkish daggers as if the work reflected his own artisanal traditions. His manual skills appear wonderfully useful, and most interesting, for an enormous variety of activities outside of the work in which he was trained. At least as much as his professional work as a goldsmith, Cellini testifies to his manual dexterity by fashioning a clever little key to help him escape from jail; by inventing new surgical instruments to save the diseased hand of a fellow goldsmith's daughter; by remarkable displays of prowess in street fighting; and by the accuracy of vision that allows him to draw a bead on invaders from the ramparts of the Castel Sant'Angelo.

The autobiography is so exciting, and so famously narcissistic, because its energies are so capacious. It is the subject of this first chapter in *Talking Shop* on the same grounds. I am interested in how Cellini's nineteenth- and early twentieth-century canonizers—translators, advocates of artisanship, fiction writers, and art critics—created an account of artisanal sensibility that cohered around the example of his range and charisma. And yet the imperatives of craft's classic standards (purpose, focus, specialization, habituation) did not vanish; Cellini became the era's "artist-craftsman *par excellence*" in part because the energies of the *Life* were also framed to accord with durable standards of artisanal exertion.[2] Cellini's *Life*, the following pages suggest, appears as the hub of converging standards of workmanship. In what ways, I ask, did the era that discovered Cellini negotiate the imperatives of craft's teleological standards and the appeal of the freewheeling, garrulous, multifocal autobiography? What are the points of contact, if any, between Oscar Wilde's praise of Cellini's *Life* as an instance of the dazzling literary imagination before the "decay of lying" and John Addington Symonds's insistence that he was a "most veracious man," possessing "the qualities of a consummate craftsman, not those of an imaginative artist"?[3] How did Cellini's canonizers settle his fame around the "labor of his craft" and what he did with his "own hands"—a phrase often associated with Cellini—despite the fact that relatively few of Cellini's physical works are well known and despite the fact that his periphrastic and peripatetic book presents few scenes of labor per se?[4]

Cellini's *Life*, these questions are meant to suggest, holds various places in the western canon and exemplifies a spectrum of ideas about workmanship. The Rabelaisian *Life* appeals because it fits romantic ideas about the hurly-burly workshop of the Old World—and prompted the crafts advocate Elbert Hubbard to declare, in 1911, that Cellini was a "man who trod the borderland of sanity."[5]

But the text also suggests to Richard Sennett what it did to Symonds: that Cellini "hewed to the traditional craft value placed on truthfulness" in his labor, at least to the point of declaring his opposition to gilding and other ways of imitating genuine material.[6] Sennett's Cellini also hews closely to the value of untranslatability which, I have suggested, defines thinking about craft and literature; the autobiography, Sennett suggests, was written "for himself," and not intended for publication (69). Not all scholars, in fact, see Cellini's intentions as so modest. In 1559, he submitted the manuscript to the editorial eye of the historian and poet Benedetto Varchi; citing the letters to Varchi, Michael Cole suggests that Cellini used his writing to defend the viability of the vocation —metalwork, and specifically bronze-casting—through which he "knew . . . that his fame would live."[7] These different accounts of Cellini and his *Life*, one suggesting that it was a private document and the other that the author imagined it in public terms, do not just frame a scholarly question about the manuscript and its purposes. They also reveal the margins of the attitudes about craftsmanship that are the subject of this chapter. From one point of view, labor involves a centripetal concern with the objects under one's care: the craftsman's solicitude, described at length in Plato's *Republic* as the purity of the relationship between artisan and material, appears as Cellini's refusal to dissimulate solid gold and as the private experience of labor recorded in the *Life*.[8] From another point of view, Cellini's enormous popularity involves his representation of Old World craft *as* a representation, a narrative account of a uniquely dexterous way of being cohered around the larger-than-life persona he constructed. Those two standards inform readings of Cellini today, but they were negotiated most explicitly—and, I think, with the greatest stakes—by the nineteenth-century translators, writers, and critics who brought the *Life* to prominence in the first place.

The worker's hands, Janet Zandy writes, are "indicators of capacity [and] skill."[9] Trained in the task and in many cases shaped (or deformed) by repetitive toil, the hands are the "embodiment of knowledge" (xii), a register of the "physicality of labor" (2). But the literary history of Cellini's hands—their representation in the nineteenth century—presents a curious pattern, in part because the physicality of the artisan's touch was compromised a priori by the narrative basis of Cellini's fame. Patterns of reference to Cellini's hands offer a focal point for the issues of specialization and range, bodily telos and the more general iconicity of the artisanal sensibility, that I have outlined as instrumental to his canonization. Moreover, Cellini's hands appear everywhere in nineteenth-century renditions of his meaning. His touch defines his fame, even as he—unlike, say, Michelangelo—is not well remembered for very many of the actual results of his manual exertions.

Nathaniel Hawthorne's oeuvre exemplifies the pattern: Cellini, in Hawthorne's writing, is regularly characterized by his hands. He first appears in "Rappaccini's Daughter" (1844), wherein a "vase wrought by the hands of the renowned Benvenuto Cellini" contains the apparent antidote to the poisonous engineering of Dr. Rappaccini, which makes human touch fatal.[10] The fiction of the later 1840s and early 1850s does not name Cellini, but the notebooks Hawthorne composed during his visit to Italy in 1858 and 1859 contain a number of representations. Describing a visit to Florence's Uffizi Gallery in June of 1858, Hawthorne slips into a room, the Cabinet of Gems, which happens to be open for a special tour; there, he imagines "such hands as those of Benvenuto Cellini" carving magnificent cups and setting gems in crystal vessels.[11] On that same visit to Rome, ascending "at a venture" a staircase in the Palazzo Vecchio, Hawthorne and his family ascend "flight after flight of stairs," wandering "through passages, and peeping into doorways" until he arrives at the Hall of Audience—where he finds a statue of St. Sebastian and a vase said to be by Cellini, as well as other objects "that might well have been wrought by his famous hand."[12] A few years later, now reminiscing about his travels in England in *Our Old Home* (1863), Hawthorne again describes gaining access to an obscure room, in this case private apartments above a bookseller's shop; the bookseller shows him drawings "in chalk or pen-and-ink by Giordano, Benvenuto Cellini, and hands almost as famous."[13] Cellini, the maker of "elaborate handiworks," appears in *The Marble Faun* (1860) when the sculptor Kenyon produces an exquisitely wrought box "of Benvenuto's school" that contains a sculpture of a "beautifully shaped hand."[14] That sculpted hand, housed in a box typifying the most famous hands Hawthorne could think of, is itself a laboring hand—the painter Hilda's, watched furtively "at its work" by the lovestruck Kenyon (106).

Hawthorne's imagery typifies mainstream associations of Cellini and his hands, his handiwork, and his touch. Harriet Spofford's "In a Cellar," published in the *Atlantic Monthly* in 1859, anticipates Hawthorne's novel quite exactly by identifying Cellini's style with the crafting of a hand; the story describes a saltcellar in the form of a "tiny hand," with curves and lines attributed to Cellini.[15] In an 1885 address to the Worcester Free Industrial Institute, Daniel Coit Gilman, the first president of the Johns Hopkins University, named a "shield by Cellini" as a generic instance (alongside "a statue by Michelangelo") of work "marked by the artisan's own touch" rather than by the blade or burr of a machine.[16] Cellini's name, the decorative historian John Culme demonstrates, emerged as a metonym for traditional handiwork shortly after 1840: the tag "Cellini" became a "measuring-rod of craftsmanship" against which jewelry and metalwork were judged.[17] One can see what Culme means in, for instance, Balzac's *Unconscious Comedians* (1846), wherein a goldsmith appears as a "modern Benvenuto Cellini."[18] References to Cellini as a standard of artisanship abound in literary descriptions of collections, rarities, and objets d'art—as, for instance, when Thackeray names the splendid workmanship of a silver service as the "Benvenuto Cellini pattern."[19] By the turn of the century, Cellini had been fully taken up as an authority on technique, in part because his writings that actually were technical (unlike the *Life*) had been published in Italian in 1858 and in English, as the *Treatises on Goldsmithing and Sculpture*, in 1898. His elaborate style rarely appealed to prevailing taste for a putatively workmanlike straightforwardness, but Julia deWolf Addison's *Arts and Crafts in the Middle Ages* (1908) strikes a common note: Cellini appears as a technician whose "ability as a craftsman" and command of manual processes outstripped the historical significance of designs that were too stylized and, in keeping with the era's moral recoil from Renaissance mannerism, considered too indulgent.[20] Elbert Hubbard's *Little Journeys to the Homes of Eminent Artists*, published by his Roycroft Press in 1902, includes a chapter on Cellini that mirrors Addison's view: "so exquisite is the workmanship," and so "skillful" was the man, Hubbard suggests, that his hand effectively mitigates his decadent designs and his narcissistic personality.[21] In 1898, when William Morris closed the Kelmscott Press, another craft reformer, C. R. Ashbee, bought the printing equipment; it was Ashbee who translated and printed the *Treatises*, issuing them as the first imprint of his new Guild of Handicraft Press. Ashbee's translation was intended "for the workshop."[22] He introduced it by praising Cellini's "graphic touch" (ix) and dedicated the book to the metalworkers of the guild—"for whom," Ashbee declared on the frontispiece, "I have set my hand to this work" (iii).

If Hawthorne's emphasis on Cellini's hands thus reflects a nineteenth-century commonplace, the curiosity of the pattern, and the point I wish to draw out in broader cultural terms, is that so much of Hawthorne's language is subjunctive. Rhetorically speaking, that is only true in the Hall of Audience, where Cellini's famous hands "might well" have wrought this or that, and in *The Marble Faun*, where the "skill and elaborate fancy" of the Cellini-like box "would by no means have discredited [Kenyon's] word" if he had "thought fit to say that Benvenuto Cellini wrought this precious box" (105). But the narrative effects of the subjunctive—of uncertainty, projection, and judgment—apply to every episode. As envisioned in the Uffizi, Cellini's are "such hands" as perform great work. Those hands are the standard for an artistic school in *The Marble Faun*, and an emblem for "other hands" during the visit to the bookseller's collection in *Our Old Home*. The fact that Hawthorne refers to "drawings in pen-and-ink or chalk by Giordano [and] Benvenuto Cellini" in the bookseller's huge and disordered collection actually obscures rather than specifies Cellini's contribution, for Cellini, unlike Luca Giordano, was not known for drawing.[23] Cellini's name, in all cases, appears more as a generic referent for handcrafted rarities than as an identifier for the creator of specific things.

The evaporation of Cellini's works *behind* his hands—the curiously inverted relation of object and touch suggested by Hawthorne's references to Cellini's generic class of hands—is also marked by the physical settings of the episodes I have named. Hawthorne locates Cellini's works behind closed doors and in galleries reached by the most bewildering routes. In the Uffizi, he thinks about Cellini only because he happens to be there when the Cabinet of Gems is open. He is not one of the "privileged party" to which the gallery has actually been made available, and so the encounter is circumstantial and lucky, exactly like the visit to the private chambers of the bookseller's shop. The jewelry in the Uffizi anticipates the remoteness of the Cellini drawings in *Our Old Home*: the drawings are an obscure genre of Cellini's in the first place, and they are tucked away in an upstairs room "veiled behind the unostentatious front of a bookseller's shop, in a very moderate line of village businesses" (*Our Old Home*, 190). Similarly, Hawthorne reaches the Hall of Audience in the Palazzo Vecchio by a spontaneous "venture" up a staircase. The labyrinthine route takes him up "flight after flight of stairs" and a sequence of passages; the statue of St. Sebastian and the vase by Cellini are, in an architectural as well as a narrative sense, obscurely situated. They are equally obscure in history. Hawthorne records the attribution of the statue and the vase as the opinion of an official his family meets once in the Hall of Audience; in fact, Cellini is not known to have made a statue of St. Sebastian, and so Hawthorne's compunction in presenting the attribution as hearsay is likely well-founded. The disappearance of the objects of the hand behind the idea of the hand, however, may be best exemplified by the sculpture of Hilda's hand in *The Marble Faun*. It originates in Kenyon's secret study of the original ("She never knew it! . . . I stole it from her" [106]), and it remains tucked away in the box that is *like* Cellini's work but not actually by him. Despite the prominence of the piece as the embodiment of Kenyon's desire, and despite the obvious symbolism of the "stolen" hand in a novel about how artists use one another (and in some cases exploit their models), the sculpture, as quickly vanishing as the other objects associated with Cellini in Hawthorne's corpus, never reappears in the novel. "The hand," Kenyon says, "is a reminiscence." Miriam's response to that assertion reveals the dynamics of Hawthorne's obfuscating references to Cellini's hands as much as it, more explicitly, addresses the novel's love plot: "May you win the original some day" (106).

Creating his own "reminiscence" of the artisan's hand in the pattern of his references to Cellini, Hawthorne buries the actual objects associated with Cellini's hands in obscure places, complicated narratives, and doubtful provenance. This predilection epitomizes the history of Cellini's canonization. Despite the emphasis on his touch, Cellini's popular reputation was formed largely around two works: the *Perseus*, shown in figure 5 and discussed later in this chapter, and a gold saltcellar made for Francis I. (The saltcellar—undoubtedly the source for Spofford's association of Cellini, a hand, and a saltcellar—has a peculiar twenty-first century notoriety because it was stolen from the Vienna Kunsthistoriches Museum in 2003 and recovered, through a bizarre chain of events, three years later.) Many of Cellini's works have been lost, but enough remain—including a bas-relief at Fontainebleau, a bust of Cosimo de'Medici, a crucifix at the Escorial Monastery in Spain, and an assortment of medallions—to suggest a pattern to Cellini's canonization: that the actual pieces made by Cellini's hands were less highly praised than one might expect given all the energy poured into celebrating his touch. The bust of Cosimo de'Medici, Symonds wrote, is "an unsympathetic and heavy piece of portraiture," and he went on to say that Cellini's "most substantial title to fame rests, and must always rest, upon his Perseus" (xliv–xlv). But even the *Perseus* appeared secondary to the fact that "we have first to regard Cellini as the composer of one of the world's three or four best autobiographies" (xxxv). "His fame," the *Encyclopedia Americana* echoed in 1918, "rests largely on his autobiography"; the *Encyclopedia* names only a few works indisputably by Cellini, devoting most of the entry to reviewing his life story and making reference to the many works "ascribed to him."[24] Thus, the appraisal of Julia deWolf Addison and Elbert Hubbard—that Cellini should be canonized as an icon of the highest skill rather than for the particular objects of that skill—seems to have been more or less borne out. Hawthorne's references to a school, a standard, and a classification bespeak Cellini's representative status—a point Hawthorne himself suggests, intentionally or not, by framing each episode to suggest the indistinctness of the physical works even as he celebrates Cellini's artisanal iconicity.

My point in correlating Hawthorne's pattern of casual references to Cellini with the history of his canonization is simply to suggest that Hawthorne registers the paradox that other writers, the ones considered in what follows, negotiated in more explicit and more highly pressured ways. Cellini's hands become

FIGURE 5. Benvenuto Cellini, *Perseus*, 1545–1554. Bronze. Loggia di Lanzi, Florence. (Photograph by Fredrik Posse/Stryngford, Sweden)

paradigms of workmanship, "reminiscences" of the craftsman's body even as, dissociated from actual objects, they operate outside what Zandy describes as the pure "physicality of work"—and, more generally, outside the traditional standards of craft's embodiment and its orientation to the objects and results of labor. This has to do, I will suggest, not just with the fact that Cellini's fame was founded on his narrative, but with the particular ways in which that narrative depicts workmanship. One final instance of Hawthorne's invocation of Cellini will, I think, draw the subject toward the patterns of literary representation that constitute my subject in the remainder of this chapter. On another visit to the Uffizi, a month after the one I have already described, Hawthorne catches another glimpse into the Cabinet of Gems, once more presented as a lucky encounter: "On our way towards the door of the gallery," he writes, "we saw the cabinet of gems open, and again feasted our eyes" (375).

This time, however, he clearly identifies Cellini's handiwork: "two crystal cups, with engraved devices, and covers of enameled gold, wrought by Benvenuto Cellini, and wonderfully beautiful." Hawthorne offers no more details, but here his teasing obliquity is more fully explained: he draws back from recording further specifics about the objects because "it is idle to mention one or two things, when all are so beautiful and curious; idle, too, because language is not burnished gold, with here and there a brighter word flashing like a diamond, and therefore no amount of talk will give the slightest idea of one of these elaborate handiworks" (375). This explanation contrasts Hawthorne's craft as a writer with the craft before his eyes. Viewed negatively, Hawthorne is describing a failure: at the limits of ekphrasis, words and handicraft appear incompatible. But viewed positively—as a guide to what Hawthorne's words *do* accomplish in the other episodes that invoke Cellini's touch, and as an anticipation of what later writers derive from Cellini—the passage gives another dimension to Hawthorne's penchant for obscuring Cellini's things at the moment he seems to assert them. "No amount of talk" is compatible with the physicality of craft. Accordingly, Hawthorne offers us Cellini's hand and his handiworks as the *mood* of Old World workmanship. Impromptu ventures, happenstance encounters, uncertain origins, and glimpses into "Benvenuto's school" compose the narrative impression of a celebrated but unspecific culture of craft. Tactility, the apparent subject of Hawthorne's stream of references to Cellini's hands, becomes a general effect rather than only a physical touch; craft's icons—the things that Hawthorne says he cannot adequately render—become its iconicity. Because "language is not burnished gold," the textual romance of workmanship appears predicated less on practical skills and particular objects than as diffused into the larger, hazier collective of "such hands" as craftsmen are celebrated to possess. This way of thinking does not mean that Old World workmanship cannot be represented or that craft and language are fundamentally incompatible, as one might think reading this passage outside of the context provided by the entirety of Hawthorne's references to Cellini. It means, on the contrary, that Old World workmanship constituted a narrative subject understood, for Hawthorne, in typological terms. The universal, generic appeal of Cellini's hands reflects the standards of the body and the represented culture of craft that the nineteenth century concurrently invented, questioned, promoted, and defended.

DI MIA MANO: CELLINI'S NARRATIVE TOUCH

Cellini's full title for the autobiography projects the centrality of his physical hands to his later iconicity. *La Vita di Benvenuto Cellini, Scritta Da Lui Medesimo in Firenze* stresses authorship as a manual act: the word *medesimo* makes the subtitle translate literally as *Written By His Very Same Self in Florence.* But the very first thing one learns from the book is that he did not write it himself. Cellini moves much more abruptly than Hawthorne from the standard set by the hand to the evaporation of the work done by the hand, as revealed in this introductory note to the *Life:*

> I first began writing this Life of mine in my own hand, as can be seen from some of the odd pages attached here, but it took up too much of my time and seemed utterly pointless. So when I came across a son of Michele Goro, of Pieve a Groppine, a young boy of about fourteen who was in a poor state of health, I set him to the task. And while I worked I dictated my Life to him, with the result that as I quite enjoyed doing this I worked much more keenly and produced a good deal more. So I left the burden of writing to him and I hope to carry on with the story as far as my memory allows.[25]

The introductory note appears in the major nineteenth-century source for the Italian text, Brunone Bianchi's *Vita* (1866). It was sent to Benedetto Varchi along with a poem when Cellini submitted the nearly complete manuscript for his review.

It does not appear, however, in the most important nineteenth-century translation of Bianchi's *Vita*, John Addington Symonds's *Life* (1887–88)—even though the second edition does include the poem sent to Varchi that is also part of Bianchi's front matter. Symonds's translation went through three editions in twelve months, the last of these a less expensive, single-volume issue marketed to a general reading public eagerly consuming both the *Life* and the idea of craft itself. In this context, it seems obvious why Symonds would have suppressed the note. For the contradiction between the title and the confession is reinforced by the first sentence of the autobiography proper, which claims that everyone who has done something important ought to write the story of his life *di lor propria mano*, "with their own hand"; the note admits that this manuscript is mostly written in the hand of a sickly boy.[26] The first lines of the introductory poem, included with the second edition, announce that "I write" *(io scrivo)* the *Vita travagliata*, the "hard life" or, more literally, the "labored life." Yet the labor of the hand thus celebrated did not actually produce the autobiography's pages. In the story, Cellini's superior dexterity again and again wins him commissions in goldsmithing and sculpture against the vicissitudes of favoritism and the biases of patronage. To an old friend who refuses to recommend him to a new master, for instance, Cellini lashes out: "My hands are such that without aid from you they will declare what sort of a fellow I am" (26). The hand appears throughout the narrative as a standard against which authority is tested. What Cellini does *che le mane mia*, "by my own hand," those around him fail to do; Cellini is repeatedly frustrated which a king, pope, or duke breaks a guarantee made *di sua mano*, "with his own hand."[27] But the independence born of one's own hands, celebrated in the nineteenth century as Cellini's "own touch," is not physically embodied in the manuscript that invokes it. Recent scholarship has introduced us to the journals and autobiographies of Old World tanners, textile workers, goldsmiths, glaziers, and furniture-makers.[28] The most famous of these opens by abandoning the first bit of handiwork it sets out to do.

We might, of course, put the problem of the introductory note more sympathetically: the craftsman enjoys talking about his life of handicraft more than doing the handiwork announced in the title of a *Life, Written by Himself*. This is not surprising when it comes to penmanship, an obviously tedious activity on which to found handiwork authenticity—especially in light of the life that follows. The rest of the *Life* bears out a notion of handicraft less as a single activity than as a narrated way of being that shifts quickly between all kinds of different activities. Cellini barely describes his apprenticeship, despite the fact that the sixteenth-century system for training goldsmiths was long, programmatic, and generally understood as the background required of those, like Cellini, who aspired to make bronze sculptures as well as jewelry and coins.[29] The testaments to his manual dexterity and craft skills extend across the range of media I have already described and to activities that are much more exciting than work: making wax nails to help in escaping from prison, inventing a special kind of gunpowder for long-range shooting, soldiering, inventing new surgical instruments, street fighting, and, he says, particularly dexterous lovemaking. In the context of the entire autobiography, the introductory note involves not so much the abdication of artisanal authenticity as its relocation to the craftsman's whole life. A physical achievement becomes a narrative achievement of memory and character. The *Life* immediately redefines its opening proposition of crafts autonomy—writing *di mia mano*—to refer to the account of his life rather than to the physical manuscript.

A matter of the hands becomes a matter of narrative and character. Labor transposes into lifestyle. A specific manual task diffuses into the account of unsettled artisanal capacity that does everything so well. Cellini averts the threat that literature and the routines of labor are incompatible by predicating his account on the transference of his skills across various trades. I will have more to say about this transference in the final section of this chapter, but for the moment I would like to draw out the nineteenth-century response to the friction between workmanlike purpose—the craftsman's ideally teleological orientation to conclusions and ends—and the predication of a narrative of universal capability on "heedless animated talking" (Symonds, liv). Suppressing Cellini's confession about the amanuensis even as he did acknowledge that the *Life* was dictated in his own introduction, Symonds recoiled from the stark contrasts between the title, the introductory note, and the first sentence. He may also have projected, or imagined his readers projecting, late nineteenth-century anxieties about outsourcing, exploitation, and the division of labor. Cellini celebrates producing "a good deal more," employs a weak youth to take on the "burden" of the work, and immediately divides labor that formerly (as recently as the title, in the *Vita*) belonged to one man.

But the disappearance of Cellini's touch behind his voice did not only involve the specific problems posed by the introductory note. It also involved the long-windedness of the autobiography itself. When he wrote the part for Cellini in his verse drama *Michael Angelo*, Henry Wadsworth Longfellow—who claimed to own a Cellini cup and who almost certainly read the text in Bianchi's Italian edition—implicitly rejected Cellini's claim that he could produce "a good deal more" while spinning his story.[30] Instead, holding Cellini to the mirror of traditional standards of craft's untranslatability, Longfellow suggested that Cellini likely produced a good deal *less* because he was so inclined to speak about his accomplishments. Benvenuto, as he is called in Longfellow's play, is characterized above all by his prolixity, and one of the major questions raised by the play concerns the compatibility of talk about craft with craft itself. In the first scene that features Benvenuto, he visits Michelangelo while the elder artisan is at work on St. Peter's Basilica. The setting alone is loaded with meaning, for Michelangelo worked on St. Peter's until his death, and his refusal to give up the task became a nineteenth-century icon of what Ralph Waldo Emerson describes as Michelangelo's workmanlike "dignity of purposes." "Is there not something affecting," Emerson asks, "in the spectacle of an old man, on the verge of ninety years, carrying steadily onward," transforming "his poetic conceptions into progressive execution?"[31] Asking readers to consider the appeal of sequential labor, concluded only by death, Emerson's rhetorical question invokes the teleological mandate of craft and the artisan's sovereign devotion to his intentions. Longfellow's Cellini, however, strides into the play with the express hope of turning Michelangelo from his dignity of purpose, as signified by St. Peter's. Benvenuto desires that the two men travel together to their hometown. Michelangelo refuses, citing that city's very beauties as a distraction: "Whenever / I think of anything beside my work, / I think of Florence."[32]

Benvenuto misses the point about constancy, commitment, and focused labor, and the exchange turns into a contrast of voice as much as of place. Benvenuto tells Michelangelo two famous stories from the *Life*, the longer of which Michelangelo cuts short. More than any other episode in the autobiography, the interrupted story reveals how Cellini ties his extraordinary accomplishments not to telos, training, or purpose but to the rhythms of a desultory life and to his universal artisanal capacity. The story is set during the Sack of Rome in 1527, and Cellini has been persuaded to go observe the fight between the papal and French armies from the ramparts of the Castel Sant'Angelo. He begins demonstrating how to shoot a certain kind of arquebus, and happens to descry a dim figure through the smoke. Cellini fires. "It was the Constable of France," he tells Michelangelo in Longfellow's version of the story, "the Bourbon, / That I had slain" (106). Cellini's announcement is striking because he is both so hapless, wandering into the battle, and so extraordinarily instrumental. He kills Charles III not because he commits to the task of fighting but because when he does take up the gun, his inherent dexterity—the subject of most of the autobiography—transfers so easily to skills even "better than those of my own art."[33]

Longfellow's Michelangelo, who represents the reverse values, will have none of it. His devotion to place, purpose, and plan is not unlike that of Longfellow's most famous artisan, the village smithy. ("Week in, week out, from morn till night, / You can hear his bellows blow; / You can hear him swing his heavy sledge; / With measured beat and slow.")[34] For Michelangelo, like the blacksmith, things are made by concentration, practice, acquired technique, and "patient doing"; "stone rests on stone, and wanting the foundation / All would be wanting" (156). He interrupts Benvenuto twice, on the first occasion by congratulating him: "Rome should be grateful to you," Michelangelo interjects. Cellini responds quickly, concluding Michelangelo's thought ("But has not been. You shall hear presently") and plowing ahead with his narrative. Twenty lines later, Michelangelo cuts Cellini off with a curt phrase: "Now let us speak of Art." Cellini's response is breezy ("Of what you will"), but the episode as a whole makes the same point—that Cellini should discipline his voice and turn to his work—in a variety of ways. To Benvenuto's urging that he return to Florence, Michelangelo opposes the "fever to accomplish" the work of the moment, demanding that Cellini "speak not of it" and asserting that Rome has a certain charm that "no man can describe" (103–4). Silence appears a workmanlike value: the true artisan works "right on through censure and applause" (108). Michelangelo's reminiscences of Florence are not of stories but of things: the "marvelous dome of Brunelleschi, / Ghiberti's gates of bronze, and Giotto's tower; / And Ghirlandaio's lovely Benci" (105).

Through Michelangelo, Longfellow thus critiques what the American art critic Royal Cortissoz described, in 1906, as Cellini's major flaw: that he "talked too much" to produce really great works.[35] But the question of Cellini's volubility had another side, for Longfellow and Symonds, as it also did for Hawthorne. Old World workmanship appealed because it suggested a culture of the hand and because that culture could be imagined in typological terms; craft appeared as an effect as much as a physical practice. Consider, to begin with, Symonds's attitude about the amanuensis—an attitude I will explore in the remainder of this section before turning, in the next, to the denouement of Longfellow's play. If Symonds censored the introductory note because it appeared too baldly incompatible with the artisanal values of patient labor and work performed *di mia mano*, he also confessed that the dictation gave the *Life* some of its most authentically workmanlike textures. One of the major interests of the *Life*, Symonds asserted, could be found in its vernacular rhythms. For one, Cellini's unedited technical vocabulary and his rich lexicon for "works of art or handicraft or armory now obsolete" constituted features of narrative color rather than practical interest (liv). For two, the romantic sound of craft's archaic language conjoined with Cellini's "Florentine slang," his penchant for shifting from one story to another, and his use of a bewildering cast of characters to suggest the vitality of the Renaissance workshop. Symonds read such vitality as a symbol of the unstandardized nature of pre-industrial production. Imputed to the life of the tradesman, Cellini's vulgarities—which Symonds tried to reproduce to the degree allowed under Victorian publishing standards—seemed the proper idioms of an era during which, Symonds reminds his readers when discussing Cellini in *The Renaissance in Italy*, "things were not bought, machine-made, by the gross in a warehouse" (825).

Drawn to Cellini's voice as the authentic sound of workmanship, Symonds faced the double bind that the unsequenced work he was translating seemed to sell short artisanal telos, as Longfellow asserted, and to represent, as a compelling effect, the improvisatory energies of a pre-industrial mode of production. A passage in which Symonds describes the difficulty of translating Cellini reveals his effort to accommodate the associative, unintentional rhythms of Cellini's story and the consummate, focused quality of artisanship. The passage is shot through with the fault lines of Victorian attitudes toward the labor of the hand and, more particularly, toward the translation of that labor into text:

> The truth is, that to translate Cellini's *Memoirs* taxes all the resources of the English language. It is, in the first place, well-nigh impossible to match that vast vocabulary of vulgar phrases and technical terminology. Some of Cellini's most vivid illustrations owe their pungency and special coloring to customs which have long passed out of current usage. . . . In the next place, his long-winded and ungrammatical periods, his suspended participles, his vehemently ill-conjugated verbs, his garrulous anacolutha and passionate aposiopeses, his ingenious recourse to repeated pronouns and reiterated adverbs for sustaining a tottering sentence, his conversational resumption of the same connective phrases, his breathless and fiery incoherence following short and incisive clauses of a glittering and trenchant edge, all these peculiarities, dependent on the man's command of his vernacular and his untutored talent for expression, offer stumbling-blocks at every turn to the translator who wishes to preserve something of the tone of the original while presenting a continuous discourse to modern readers. (liv)

The sentence after the ellipsis opens by noting Cellini's "long-winded and ungrammatical periods." Long-windedness initially appears as the text's unsystematic construction. Like Cellini's manual labors, his prose is variously "suspended" and taken up again; his volubility is mimicked in the sentence describing it, and constitutes the aspect of Cellini's personality that Longfellow's Michelangelo thought least compatible with his workmanship. Eleven clauses later, however, Symonds has talked himself into a somewhat different position. Cellini's composition looks more and more rhetorically deft as Symonds begins teasing out its classic rhetorical constructions: anacolutha, aposiopesis, and his "effective resumption of the same connective phrases." Behind his "ill-conjugated" verbs and "untutored" vernacular, in other words, Cellini's prose is "ingenious." Traditional in an apparently accidental way, the language of the *Life* appears skilled and even technically masterful; the description of Cellini's "command" of the vernacular seems to transform careless talking into a craft, formulating a play of exertion and error that is also present in the near-oxymoron of something "vehemently ill-conjugated." All of this is to say that Cellini's rhetoric, in Symonds's description of it, dodges all over the place and yet seems not unlike the mastery of his professional craft—moving toward a "glittering and trenchant edge" that calls to mind nothing so much as his goldsmith's skills and tools. Cellini ends up displaying remarkable "command" of expressive devices and "sustaining" what might totter, just as he must in his delicate metalworks and sculptures. Spiced with the "technical terminology" of his own craft as well as with the ancient rhetorical devices named by Symonds, Cellini's narrative offers the overall impression of a heedlessness that is in fact good workmanship or, to formulate the same effect in reverse, a mastery of rhetorical craft and traditional forms that is also unconstrained by them.

While celebrating Cellini's vigorous and unlearned style, Symonds's insistence on the actually "trenchant" edges of the *Life*'s prose—its "glittering . . . edge"—marks his effort to discipline Cellini's free-wheeling model of authorial and artisanal workmanship. Symonds's importance to Cellini's canonization lies more broadly in his insistence that Cellini is less interesting for his roguishness than for his craftsmanship. As revealed in his translator's introduction to the *Life* and in the third volume of *The Renaissance in Italy*, Symonds's Cellini figures preeminently as a "consummate craftsman" (xlii), an "adept in all the technicalities" (xlii) of metalworking and an icon of "prodigious skill" (xliii). More subtly, Symonds's accomplishment in discussing Cellini connects the "very qualities which render his life-history dramatic" (his "lack . . . of reserve," that heedlessness represented above all by the spoken rhythms of his voice) to the "externality of his nature" that also made Cellini such a good craftsman. Symonds does not find Cellini possessed of very much fineness of feeling; his sculptures lack the religious elevation and the "moral and intellectual elements" that the Victorians habitually identified with the art of the earlier sixteenth century (xliii). But Symonds produces a Cellini for the crafts revival whose double appeal—for his impetuosity and for the excellence of his manual labor—is legible in the style of the *text* to the degree that Cellini's language is at once untutored, because dictated, and technically exemplary. The image of the translator faced with the "stumbling-blocks" of Cellini's unstable prose gives a sense of the anxiety raised by the very source—the unstandardized vitality—of the *Vita*'s interest. In the context of Cellini's autobiography, "stumbling-blocks" constitute a particularly sculptural figure of clumsiness; Symonds, we have seen, did not think Cellini a great sculptor. But the translator promises to bring "continuous discourse" to the raw vigor of Cellini's relationship to material (in this case, the manuscript and its "stumbling-blocks")—and Symonds begins, I have suggested, by teasing out the actually traditional virtues of the text's rhetorical design and by eliminating the jarring introduction of the amanuensis even as he praises the dictated, spontaneous quality of the composition. To read his translation of the *Vita*, Symonds seems to be suggesting, is to see the consummation of craftsmanship at the same time as it is to encounter a methodology that does not depend on teleology, constancy, or patient relations to the medium.

This paradox—that consummation, a teleological virtue of arriving at something, becomes indistinguishable from Cellini's spontaneity, a quality not dependent on training or experience—is significant in the broadest terms because it reveals the double imperatives of craft's meaning in the late nineteenth century. The era's most famous artisanal text, depicted and described *as* a text by Symonds, allies a celebration of craft as traditional skills to the spontaneous and even spasmodic habits figured as an alternative to the "machine-made." The Cellini described by Symonds suited the craft revival's stress on charisma, subjectivity, vitality, and (to borrow Jackson Lears's formulation of the movement's aims) the energetic "revitalization" of an inhumane and overstandardized machine culture.[36] But Symonds also essayed to accommodate Cellini and the *Life* to traditionally technical definitions of craft, arriving at a formulation in which elements of instinct and elements of consummation flowed together. Cellini's "breathless and fiery incoherence" become indistinguishable, in the passage describing the original Italian text, from "the man's command" of his craft.

THE VOICE OF THE WORKSHOP: CELLINI'S *PERSEUS*

In this regard, Symonds offered an account of Cellini's *Life* that appealed to the same values as the episode in the *Life* that his nineteenth-century canonizers most particularly loved. Because that episode features certain statements of Cellini's own about the *literary* interest of his workmanship, it concerns the relays of craft and narrative in a double sense: the episode describes the moment when Cellini seems to realize that his life had interest as a story, and it became an endlessly retold anecdote—by poets, essayists, and opera composers—in its own right. Mirroring Symonds's beliefs about the style of the text he popularized, and Hawthorne's translation of Cellini's hands into an impression and an effect, the episode was the most eagerly consumed element of Cellini's career in the nineteenth century. It concerns the casting of Cellini's magnum opus in metal, the statue of Perseus holding the head of Medusa. I am interested in it because the episode also concerns the casting of Cellini's magnum opus in words, the *Life* itself.

The dramatic center of the story about the *Perseus* occurs when Cellini, lying ill on what he presumes is his deathbed, suddenly leaps in perfect health to oversee the pouring of the alloy into the mold for the statue. The occasion for the instant recovery is Cellini's overhearing, through the fog of his sickness, that his apprentices may have botched the job. The mere thought of these "ignoramuses" infuriates him so deeply that Cellini feels "vigor fill my veins," and he strides into the workshop to "conduct my work in person," "roar[ing] out first to one man and then to another." He shouts orders to gather wood to stoke the flames; to stir the liquid metal; to keep the rain out of the open-sided workshop by hanging boards and carpets around the perimeter; to correct the composition of the alloy by throwing in hundreds of pewter dishes and platters; and to fill the mold. The performance of having "helped with my own hands" is thus a vocal as much as a manual one. "Now here, now there," Cellini rushes around the workshop, orchestrating the performance by demanding both the "aid of hand and hearing" (386–87). The *Perseus* is saved through this synthesis, and it immediately enters the realm of legend; Cellini, recounting it, "indulged a boastful humor." His rivals, anxious to prove that only the devil's intercession could have saved the statue, tell the story to Cellini's "mortal foe, Messer Pier Francesco Ricci"—who translates the story again, writing a version for Cosimo de'Medici "far more marvelous and full of thrilling incidents than what they had narrated" (388). Thus does the moment of Cellini's greatest autonomy as a craftsman, when he must cast his own statue, become indistinguishable from his public voice, shouting in every direction, and from the story about him that instantly enters circulation and begins to echo through Italy; it becomes yet again "more stupendous and astonishing" when Duke Cosimo and the Duchess, Eleanora di Toledo, "heard it from my own mouth" (390).

All of the vocal energies cohered around the episode thus suggest the *Life* as well as the *Perseus*. When he rises from his bed, Cellini declares that "before I die I will leave such witness to the world of what I can do that as shall make a score of mortals marvel" (385). By "witness" *(saggio)*, Cellini seems to mean the statue; he won't die, his exclamation suggests, before reclaiming the work from the incompetence of his assistants. But *saggio*, derived from the word for "wisdom," also means a written essay, a textual display of knowledge—and indeed Cellini prefaces his avowal to leave such witness of himself with the claim that the *Perseus* has been intentionally sabotaged by an "act of treason" against his craft itself *(un tradimento fatto ad arte)*, and that he will "sift it to the bottom" (385). The "witness" or *saggio*, then, comprises both the statue and the projected results of his investigation—the latter clearly enough imaginable as the *Vita* itself, for the text is nothing if not a record of all of the enemies, conspirators, and circumstances that the ever-embattled Cellini must overcome in his work. When he utters the vow, moreover, Cellini doesn't actually know if the *Perseus* can be saved. And yet throughout the *Life*, Cellini always defends the certainty of what he promises; one way or another, by the statue or by the text (and, as it happens, by both), Cellini's guarantee to leave witness to his labor will go fulfilled.

The episode of Cellini's casting the *Perseus*, then, turns on the same relation as the composition of the autobiography; putting his own hand to the work becomes an exercise of voice, dictation, narration, or command. Symonds translates the string of verbs Cellini uses to describe his activities in the scene—*comandavo, aiutavo, e dicevo*—in the spirit of the episode's weaving together of bodily and rhetorical labors: "I . . . gave orders, helped with my own hands, and cried aloud" (387). Collapsing the statue and the text into his *saggio*, Cellini renders act and voice indistinct and blurs the lines of bodily exertions and words—just as he does when he freely transitions between the admission about the amanuensis and the injunction that lives be written by persons of note *di lor propria mano*, "with their own hand" (1). As Cellini tells it, the origins of the *Life* (both as a dictated text and as conceived at the moment of the near-disaster with the *Perseus*) lie in the freewheeling voice and the centrifugal authority that confirm his skills as a handicraftsman. What really interests me here, however, is how Cellini's nineteenth-century interpreters managed the shifting boundaries of body and voice, craft's focused manual exertions and its multifocal appeal as a narrative, in the *Perseus* scene. For the variously retold story of Cellini's flying around his workshop shouting orders and vowing to leave his *saggio* appears as the centerpiece of almost every later account of his career. This "most celebrated passage in Cellini's *Life*," as John Pope-Hennessy puts it, might be seen as the epicenter of nineteenth-century translations of workmanship into narrative.[37] In his chapter on Cellini in *Little Journeys to the Homes of Eminent Artists*, the craft advocate Elbert Hubbard quotes a full third of his text directly from Cellini's account of casting the *Perseus*. Katharine Gibson's *The Goldsmith of Florence: A Book of Great Craftsmen* (1929) takes Cellini as the titular figure and the central voice, quoting almost the entirety of the chapter on Cellini directly from the same section of the *Life*; the stories of other master artisans in the book, by contrast, are told by Gibson in the third person. If "no better taste of the man's quality can be given than by letting him tell his story himself," as Hubbard puts it (115), the *Perseus* episode ties Cellini's inimitable voice (his telling of his own story) to his wide-ranging vocal authority as a craftsman (his orchestrating the casting of his own statue when the assistants botch the job).

And yet if that authority is predicated on Cellini's centrifugal energies, one can also see in references to the *Perseus* episode a mirror of Symonds's efforts to settle and focus Cellini's dictated prose. The endeavor to discipline Cellini's voice by stressing consummation and conclusion—what Symonds calls the "continuous discourse" glimpsed through rhetorical shifts and breaks—is dramatically rendered in what was surely the most theatrical nineteenth-century version of the *Perseus* scene. Hector Berlioz's opera *Benvenuto Cellini* was first performed in 1838 as a comic work; the hurly-burly of Cellini's *Life* seemed a perfect match for the episodic construction, burlesque digressiveness, and quicksilver repartee characterizing the opera buffa style in which Berlioz and his librettist originally worked. Berlioz's *Cellini* failed, drawing enough interest to sustain only eight performances. But when Franz Liszt resuscitated the moribund work in 1852, he gave its protagonist a teleological sensibility lacking in the original version, eliminating digressive asides and compressing the timeline so that the plot would move more surely toward the consummating scene: the casting of the *Perseus*. Liszt's adaptations defined the score and the staging of *Cellini* in the era when the *Life* and its author became increasingly iconic representations of Old World workmanship. When the opera was performed at Covent Garden in 1853, for instance, the *Perseus* scene was performed not as sounds and commands heard offstage, as in the 1838 version, but with the visual spectacle of the huge statue, "red and incandescent," revealed as the mold was broken away.[38] Just as the new libretto settled the digressive dialogue of the opera buffa version, Liszt's version turned the vocal and aural emphasis of Berlioz's treatment of the scene to its physical results; the adaptation of the text and staging in that sense parallels Symonds's work with the Italian original. Breathing new seriousness into the opera, concentrating its energies, and celebrating artisanship's manual dimensions, the new score included a hymn to their work sung by goldsmiths, closed with a song celebrating handiwork, and was publicized by Liszt himself in a press release that boldly incarnated the craftsman's labor: "Honor to master metalworkers! Make way for the beautiful things!"[39]

Transcribed verbatim by Hubbard and Gibson, retold in operatic form by Berlioz and Liszt, and discussed in virtually every nineteenth-century rendition of Cellini's life, the *Perseus* story was oriented to the voice and to its own canonicity from the moment Cellini dictated it. Dramatizing the self-sufficiency guaranteed by Cellini's "own hands" (rather than those of his incompetent assistants), the episode expresses the craftsman's autonomy as a performance of vocal representation and thus reflects the rhetorical dynamics of Cellini's canonization more generally. And yet the suppression of the introductory note,

Symonds's description of his goals as a translator, and Liszt's operatic adaptation also suggest how the era resisted the *excesses* of Cellini's garrulousness—or, to put the same case more positively, how Cellini's canonizers pushed his rendition of craft as instinct and spontaneous narrative back toward the artisan's hands, objectively "beautiful things" (like the statue itself), a "trenchant edge," masterful metalwork, and teleological effort. This latter description, of Cellini's volubility settled into workmanlike purposefulness, in fact describes one of the dramatic developments in Longfellow's *Michael Angelo*. Cellini first appears, I have suggested, as the obverse of Michelangelo's understated constancy; Michelangelo must curtail Benvenuto's prolixity. But Benvenuto also appears in a second scene, near the end of the play. He returns to Michelangelo's workshop and, as in the adaptation of Berlioz's *Cellini* performed at Covent Garden, it is the *Perseus* that appears to have focused his labor. Here is how Longfellow's Benvenuto describes saving the statue:

> I straightway opened all the sluices
> To fill the mould. The metal ran like lava,
> Sluggish and heavy; and I sent my workmen
> To ransack the whole house, and bring together
> My pewter plates and pans, two hundred of them,
> And cast them one by one into the furnace
> To liquefy the mass, and in a moment
> The mould was filled! (157–58)

Michelangelo, hearing this description, congratulates Cellini for having "turned your vices into virtues" (158). Cellini's vices, we know from the first scene between the two men, involve his distractibility. Those vices become virtues, for Michelangelo, to the degree that the casting of the *Perseus* turns the centrifugal into the centripetal. Cellini's impulsive and spasmodic habits cause him to leap on the spigots and to decisively command the workmen; Benvenuto's lines have a gathering effect, describing how he causes the assistants to rush through the whole house, collect everything pewter, and bring it all to the workshop. Constellating rather than sidetracking, "my impatient, wayward nature," Benvenuto says, "now has served me / Where meekness could not, and where patience could not" (155). Benvenuto, not served by patience, remains the representative of a kind of artisanship still distinct from Michelangelo's. In Longfellow's description of the metal-casting, Cellini indeed continues to embody fluidity: his craft is literally one of liquids, and the context of the scene is that Cellini has come "in haste" from Florence to beg Michelangelo, once more, to return to that city (153). Refusing again, Michelangelo reasserts the "patient doing" of things

(155). The stone of St. Peter's, laid piece by piece over months, and the molten bronze of the *Perseus*, poured into the mold in a single night, are the material correlatives of each artisan's unchanged personality.

But the difference between this scene and the first is that Benvenuto's vigor has become intentional and that his quicksilver intuition has been directed. The image of the filling mold literalizes the containment of Benvenuto's liquid personality—and its channeling into the kind of productive work that Michelangelo, in the earlier scene, had found Cellini dodging. Most significantly for my purposes, Benvenuto has also acquired rhetorical self-awareness. Whereas Michelangelo, in the first scene, stops Cellini from talking too much, Benvenuto now edits his own account, wondering aloud: "Wherefore do I prate of this?" (159) Longfellow also organizes Cellini's words to accord him a sudden poetic facility. Cellini speaks in iambic pentameter throughout *Michael Angelo*, but the excerpt quoted above is more inventive than the rest of his part. Beginning with a nine-syllable line before the sluices are completely opened, the meter accrues substance even as the mold fills: the next six lines are eleven syllables, only settling back to proper pentameter after the molten bronze has been poured. ("Sluggish" is also a trochaic inversion, the stress on the first syllable of the line rather than the second jamming the metrical pace as Benvenuto describes the insufficient liquidity of the metal.) The creative prosody is significant insofar as it reflects the vocal command that the goldsmith, we come to realize over the course of the scene, now possesses. To Michelangelo's request that Benvenuto "tell me of France," where Cellini has been working for Francis I, Benvenuto offers a contained version: "It were too long a tale / To tell you all," going on to give only the details that will "suffice in brief" not to distract from the other things he wishes to discuss (153). Those things, as it happens, are themselves centered by language that is not Benvenuto's own. The two men first confer about the content of a letter written by Michelangelo. Benvenuto then goes on to advise Michelangelo on how to interpret a letter written to the latter by the pope. Cellini now seems to be the master of language whereas, in the first scene, he had appeared unable to manage his own speech.

Benvenuto is a minor character in *Michael Angelo*. But his development between the two scenes in which he is scripted reveals the grounds of Cellini's emergence as the voice of workmanship in the late nineteenth century. Crucially, I think, the occasion for the maturation of Cellini's voice is not his capitulation to the values of craftsmanship asserted at the beginning of the play. Instead, Cellini reasserts an artisanal style that, although different from Michelangelo's, is still sufficiently disciplined to suggest the purposive skills also accorded to Cellini by Symonds and Franz Liszt. The nineteenth century embraced Cellini's *Life* precisely because his instinctive ability to do every craft and his peripatetic narrative, set in cities all over Italy and France, did not depend on the constant relations to medium and place celebrated in Michelangelo's work on St. Peter's; to recur to Symonds's description, Cellini's appeal was the appeal of inconstancy itself, an alternative to the extreme constancy of the "machine-made." Cellini's "incoherence," to borrow another characterization from Symonds, suggested the "incommensurable" aspects of handicraft that Walter Benjamin also praised—and that Benjamin saw as the element typically *unavailable* to modern narratives of manual labor, once "traveling journeymen" ceased carrying stories from shop to shop.[40]

If work and its textual representation appear poorly compatible in the critical discussion extending from Walter Benjamin—because unalleviated labor, in effect, seems too boring for narrative's purpose—Cellini circumvents that problem by establishing an authorial relationship to craft on the basis of having put his hand to many things, in the *Life* as a whole, rather than on the basis of fidelity to a single medium. The artisanal narrative and the craftsman's labor become congruent because neither is tied to a single material or to a distinct branch of applied mastery. Cellini hardly represents the image of the artisan patiently bent to his habitual task. And yet if a certain incoherence of place, labor, and literary style bespoke the appeal of Old World workmanship as unstandardized, the scenes most identified with his voice (the work's dictation as well as its origin in the casting of the *Perseus*) also channel Cellini's inconstant relations with physical media into certain outcomes. Symonds, Longfellow, and Liszt presented nineteenth-century audiences with Cellini's dual achievement: he was reactive and yet teleological, instinctive at the same time as exemplary in his results. Turning vices into virtues, the consummating achievement of Cellini's two masterworks marks his canonization along the entire scale of workmanship's meaning in the age of machines.

THE *LIFE* AS LIFESTYLE: PURPOSE AND ECCENTRICITY IN THE AUTOBIOGRAPHY

When Michelangelo, in Longfellow's play, stops Cellini from telling the whole story of killing Charles III, he intervenes in the fundamental correlation on which the interest of the *Life* is predicated. The autobiography features the easy relations between happenstance and instrumentality, epitomized when the sightseeing tour of the ramparts turns (thanks to Cellini's capacities in everything dexterous and involving sharp sight) into the most important accomplishment of the papal army during the Sack of Rome. In silencing Cellini's narrative of this episode, Longfellow's Michelangelo—like, I have suggested,

Emerson's—stands for a perspective used defensively. The "progressive execution" of Michelangelo's labor, as Emerson put it, runs against the alternative notions of craft as spontaneity that, this chapter argues, the nineteenth century incarnated in the literary persona of Benvenuto Cellini (231).

Read against the Platonic heritage of telos represented by Michelangelo's labor on St. Peter's Basilica (or, to take a more recent definition, against Peter Dormer's celebration of the habitual practices that keep artisans to the "sticking-point" of a clearly projected outcome), Cellini's *Life* appears a hoax or an assault on craft's true interests.[41] But an equally compelling standard of subjectivity and intuition, I have suggested in the preceding discussion of Cellini's voice, emerged in the nineteenth century as a mirror for durably Platonic models of craft. By dislocating his skills from the primary site of the workshop or the technicalities of the process (neither of which is described in very much detail in the *Life*), Cellini stretches his appeal as an artisan from the teleological specialization of vocation into the texture of his universally dexterous life. In the remainder of this chapter, I turn from the form of the *Life* and from its representation of the artisan's own voice to its more general representation of the artisan's character, analyzing how the text became an icon of craft's emerging fashionability by reframing traditional artisanal standards of plan and result. The period of Cellini's canonization saw craft's emergence as an idealized lifestyle able to be experienced outside of the daily sweat and toil of the professional workshop: artisanship was translated onto the page for the pleasure of armchair artisans; promoted as a consumer style by enterprises ranging from Gustav Stickley's Craftsman company to Montgomery Ward; and discussed in periodicals ranging from *Decorator and Furnisher* to *House Beautiful*. Mutatis mutandis, Cellini's more vigorous lifestyle correlated with these transformations, all of which are discussed in detail in later chapters of *Talking Shop*. For despite Cellini's continual efforts to get paid—and paid well—for his work, his workmanlike way of being in the world, the example of his artisanal range and charisma, abetted the emergence of craft as a character-building hobby rather than just a profession. The super-capable persona presented in the *Life* further supported emerging associations of craft with sturdiness, a phenomenon literalized by the massiveness of Arts and Crafts furniture. And Cellini's character offered a compelling subject for general readers, epitomizing a print culture of craft that would extend well beyond the exploits of the Florentine goldsmith or the specific interest of traditional methods in the trades.

The appeal of craftsmanship as a way of being, a temperament rather than just a learned set of skills, is exemplified by a well-known essay of Martin Heidegger's. Heidegger traces the etymology of the modern German *bauen* (building) to Old High German *buan* (dwelling). The correlation of building and dwelling typifies what Heidegger describes as a "venture in thought [that] does not view building as an art or as a technique of construction"; rather than a learned practice defined by "activities of cultivation and construction," by things "accomplished," Heidegger's essay experimentally proffers building not as a means to an end but as an organic response to environmental and spiritual conditions.[42] Shaped by traditional skills but not beholden to their technical reiteration, craft has to do with "the manner in which mortals are on the earth"; the situational etymology of "building" suggests an identity-centered notion of workmanship (326). And yet Heidegger's cautiousness in framing his essay as a "venture in thought" bespeaks some of the opposing pressures on his model. Rendering labor contextual and positing the appeal of workmanship outside of the work itself, building-as-dwelling runs counter to the teleological principles of single purpose and reproducible outcome durably associated with artisanship.

The problem of craft's purposefulness appears to Cellini himself when he is forced to explain his quicksilver shifts from his professional practice to, in Heidegger's term, the "manner" in which he lives as an artisan. Indeed, a sustained uncertainty about his purpose and his subject define the opening episodes of the *Life*. Wishing "to keep space and words for my art, which has been my chief inducement to write," Cellini, for instance, forebears to "add further particulars" about a fight that he has with a soldier (44). But he qualifies almost every such statement, and—without Michelangelo to cut him off, as in Longfellow's drama—spills out a series of details and stories; "Since I am writing my life," he allows, "I must from time to time diverge from my profession" (42). Suggesting that "I might enlarge at great length" about his dealings with the curiosity hunters who bring him ancient gems from the Roman ruins, Cellini first cuts himself off ("I will refrain from fear of being prolix") and then, in the very next sentence, indulges himself further: "I must return a little way [in the story]" (47). Shortening episodes "outside my art, the which is the real object of my writing," and resisting any impulse "to ornament my biography with such matters," Cellini backtracks: "There is only one more circumstance which, now that the occasion offers, I propose to record" (75).

Such equivocation appears over and over again in the first third of the *Life*, as Cellini talks his way into his subject. But he ends up justifying his digressions with as little anxiety as he gives up his stated commitment to writing *di mia mano*. One example may suffice to suggest how Cellini typically accommodates his fidelity to his profession and the equally compelling narrative of his way of living—and how, in so doing, Cellini differentiated himself from other models of Old World artisanship that the fifteenth and sixteenth centuries offered to the nineteenth century. To escape the plague, Cellini journeys to some Roman ruins "while I was still a young man of about twenty-three" (45). The trip looks clearly enough like an element of his professional training, for studying ruins was considered one of the ideal foundations of the artisan's development—and indeed the account of the trip strikingly mirrors a story told about the youthful Filippo Brunelleschi and Donatello by Vasari, whose *Lives of the Artists* was known to Cellini. In that episode, one of the most famous in the *Lives of the Artists*, Brunelleschi has just persuaded a panel of judges *against* choosing his design for the door panels of the baptistery of San Giovanni in Florence. Realizing that the work of Lorenzo Ghiberti in bas-relief surpasses his own, Brunelleschi declines sharing the commission with Ghiberti on the grounds that he would rather become "first in a single craft," architecture.[43] That important phrase *(primo in una sola arte)* is loaded with the standards of professional singularity and specialization that Brunelleschi also accords to Ghiberti's skill —by suggesting that he, Brunelleschi, not win the commission—and that Vasari uses to characterize Brunelleschi's freedom from jealousy over the superior capabilities of another.[44] With his friend Donatello, himself laboring to hone an "expert skill" in sculpture matched by "no other artisan," Brunelleschi journeys from Florence to the Roman ruins (147). For Vasari, the trip to the ruins thus becomes the agent of specialization for both aspirants; they "studied them continually," digging out old fragments of columns or sculpture and becoming known as the "treasure-hunters" by the Romans, who think that they are seeking precious gems (117). The fact that they do find a few precious gems enables them to finance such intensive study of their individual crafts of sculpture and architecture.

The episode in Vasari, in short, features narrowness of calling as its primary virtue. No artist of the Renaissance is more associated with care for a single object than Ghiberti, whose entire professional life after winning the commission was devoted to the enormous doors for the baptistery. These are the doors that Michelangelo praises as the "gates of bronze" in his first discussion with Benvenuto in Longfellow's *Michael Angelo*, and that Michelangelo named the "Gates of Paradise" for all posterity. Leaving Ghiberti to this life work, Brunelleschi and Donatello each develops his own "single craft" by haunting the Roman ruins. Cellini begins his own account of the trip he takes to Rome, to escape the plague, by mirroring the celebrated activities of these two men. Studying ancient methods, he sketches ancient buildings and molds copies of their details in wax; he, too, like the treasure hunters, finances his days with unearthed gems.

But studying becomes less interesting than shooting the pigeons who hang about the ruins and taking healthful exercise away from the plague-ridden city. Cellini addresses the probability that readers may think their author is wandering from his craft, the same problem that appears in the introductory note and that saturates the opening third of the *Life*. He is half-apologetic that "this exercise bid fair to withdraw me from my art and studies" (46)—thus distinguishing how he spent his days from the story of Brunelleschi and Donatello, and explicitly addressing the attention deficit that Symonds, for instance, essayed to smooth over in his translation of Cellini's spoken language. Cellini's answer to those who would worry about his commitment to his craft is that hunting "gave me more than it deprived me of, seeing that each time I went out shooting I returned with greatly better health, because the open air was a benefit to my constitution" (46). This constitutes an argument for craft (rather than against working too hard) because, in the *Life* as a whole, Cellini's constitution matters more than his training, and recreation thus becomes the agent, not the antithesis, of narrative and artisanal purpose. Here is how Cellini describes learning to enamel: "To this branch [of craft] I devoted myself [and] . . . in spite of all its difficulties, it gave me so much pleasure that I looked upon them as recreation; and this came from the special gift which the God of nature bestowed on me, that is to say, a temperament so happy and of such excellent parts that I was freely able to accomplish whatever it pleased me to take in hand" (45). Attaining one's "object" and succeeding in a craft depends on disposition, temperament, and an attitude about good workmanship as the "gift" of a certain constitution. The significance of the scene at the Roman ruins, accordingly, is to assert the difference between Cellini and the model celebrated by Vasari, and to suggest—as explicitly as anywhere in the *Life*—that nothing can really draw him away from his trade because his life and his work are so intertwined. Indeed, elements of Cellini's workmanship saturate even the activity of shooting pigeons. Cellini uses a fowling gun "which I have made myself" (like the manuscript, it is described as *di mia mano*), and which is polished so well—in this respect exactly like the jewelry he sells—that it appears "as bright as any mirror." "Mirror" is Symonds's translation for *specchio*, which also has the sense of "specimen" or "example," and Cellini indeed goes on cataloguing a list of things he handcrafts. The gunpowder he uses, he tells us, is "also made with my own hands," in this case by "secret processes" he discovers. Shooting the gun he has made, with the gunpowder he has invented, further testifies to his "pure skill in the art" of doing everything and anything requiring care and coordination (46).

Thus, casually shooting pigeons is, in a narrative and representational sense, very much *on* the subject of his craft. Escaping a city in the grips of a plague from which "many thousands" died each day, and then putting down his sketchpad and modeling wax to take up his sporting piece, Cellini pulls craft away from the standard of both its ancient models—the ruins themselves—and its careful study (45). That his gun models his craft draws the point that his life and his labor are really the same. The episode's antinomy of sickness (the plague) and health (his sport) reinforces the same antinomy in the introductory note, wherein a sickly boy does the tedious job while he works. It also reinforces the same antinomy in the story of the *Perseus*, wherein Cellini leaps up from his sickbed, tapping his inherent vitality in order to save his craft. Workmanship is joined not to history or study but to a general state of health. In a further turn from the story about Brunelleschi and Donatello, the "treasure-hunters" in Vasari's account, Cellini *meets* "treasure-hunters" while he wanders through the ruins looking for pigeons; the story turns into an account of his transactions with these well-connected traders, who bring him commissions "with nearly all the cardinals of Rome" while selling him emeralds, sapphires, topaz, diamonds, and rubies. Thus Cellini, like Brunelleschi and Donatello, is supported by the gems of ancient Rome, but with the difference that his profit comes from days spent rambling around the ruins rather than from actual digging into the past. As a result, the circle between the craftsman's labor and the craftsman's vital life closes even more tightly: invigorated and financially supported from hunting, Cellini says, "I found that I could work better and with far greater mastery than when I spent my whole time in study and manual labor" (46).

The text thus justifies its digressions with ease, forging relays of healthy living and productive work that drove the appeal of the *Life* in the nineteenth century. Circulating around the ruins rather than delving into the ancient traditions of his craft or honing his expertise in *una sola arte*, Cellini offered a model of artisanship that could not have been more clearly distinct from the division of labor or the specter of iterative production. But if Cellini easily negotiates the standards of telos and eccentricity, those standards came under heavier pressures in the culture that canonized the *Life* than they do in the *Life* itself. A difficult piece C. R. Ashbee wrote about Cellini for the *Art Journal* of 1894 reveals, exactly because it is so difficult, how an advanced industrial culture put particular demands on the dual imperatives that also drove Cellini's iconicity and the suitability of his narrative to nineteenth-century interests. The essay, "Cinquecento Jewelry," opens by defining what it calls the "point of view of the craftsman" in metalwork.[45] That point of view was epitomized for Ashbee by Cellini's *Treatises on Goldsmithing and Sculpture*, the technical documents Ashbee translated in an edition "intended for the workshop."[46] Taxonomizing and separately treating eight branches of metalwork, the *Treatises* are first held by Ashbee to model the true artisan's regard for acquired expertise in clearly defined and differentiated techniques; Cellini's careful approach to the acquisition of skills marks this text's "right healthy contempt . . . for anything approaching to dilettantism" (153). Expertise was signified by "how far labour was subdivided in the workshops of the Cinque-cento" (153). Metalworkers pursued specialties. If they excelled in more than one branch of the craft, the skills required appeared as discrete lines of accomplishment. Cellini himself, Ashbee tells his readers, claimed that most metalworkers could master no more than two branches. At this point in "Cinquecento Jewelry," Ashbee leaves out the fact that Cellini habitually made that sort of statement to distinguish himself, as a master "equally versed" in all "the various departments of art," from the typical metalworker (*Life*, 51). In Ashbee's celebration of Cellini's Old World artisanry at the outset of the essay, the subdivisions of craft appear sui generis, learned from the ground up and on their own terms rather than from the lateral exchange of skills between them.

Ashbee's initial reading of the *Treatises* in "Cinquecento Jewelry" typifies the aspect of Cellini's canonization that celebrated his manual skills and stressed values of culmination, focus, and accomplishment. The *Perseus*, I have suggested, is the centerpiece of this way of presenting Cellini's life and his *Life*. But more casual references also name similar virtues. Gustav Stickley's magazine *The Craftsman*, to take one example, features Cellini as an icon of intentionality in various articles on jewelry, pottery, and Old World workmanship. In one issue, an essay by Louise C. Chard idealizes the "singleness of purpose," founded on "much study and observation," of traditional craft. The essay concludes by implying an association between these virtues of singularity and the intentionality put into every piece by the celebrated goldsmith of Florence: "We cannot all drink from Cellini's goblets," Chard writes, "but we can have our objects of decoration few—even a single one—but good."[47] A different piece praises the "student-like" approach of a designer for Tiffany & Co., whose exuberance is enough tempered by thorough study that he would appear to be working "from the inspiring reading of Cellini's treatises."[48] Cellini, other essays suggest, may be a "fiery spirit," and full of "eagerness," but reading the *Life* can be recommended for its insight into "the care, the struggles, the methods undertaken to assure success"—even if one must "study calmly and critically the . . . honest and wise effort" behind a text that more compellingly depicts "inspiration."[49] Perhaps most tellingly, an article by C. Valentine Kirby on clay modeling "as a means to develop skill in craftsmanship" links Cellini with Michelangelo as well as with two of the artisans whose highly specialized skill, I have suggested, Cellini explicitly and implicitly *rewrites* in the *Life*—Ghiberti and Donatello, whose study of the Roman ruins Cellini abjures.[50] The "consummate skill of a Ghiberti, a Donatello, a Cellini, or a Michelangelo," Kirby suggests, was founded on a careful process that began with modeling in clay and wax (490).

In the link with Donatello, Ghiberti, and Michelangelo, Cellini appears to Kirby as equally "consummate"—a word, from Latin roots suggesting something brought to the superlative degree, etymologically loaded with standards of workmanlike telos. I have already described how Cellini appears a "consummate craftsman" to Symonds (who brings "continuous discourse" to his prose), to Longfellow (who depicts the channeling effect of the *Perseus*), and to Ashbee (who praises his "subdivision" of workmanship into discrete purposes and nontransferable skills). But the problem Ashbee faces, and the interest of "Cinquecento Jewelry" for me, is that noting "how far labour was subdivided" in Cellini's era also places Renaissance craft on the dystopian trajectory of history summarized by Karl Marx as the "division and subdivision of labor" and culminating in the mechanization of formerly artisanal tasks.[51] Shortly after defining the craftsman's interest in focused and narrow skills, Ashbee tries to distinguish the subdivision of labor suggested by Cellini from the "present day of subdivision of labor, one workshop or group of men and machines producing one portion of a piece of work, and another, another" (153). If specialization looks appealing from the craftsman's point of view, it looks threatening once Ashbee starts to think in relation to industrial modernity. This paradox makes "Cinquecento Jewelry" a confusing and volatile essay. Asserting the appeal of artisanal concentration, as manifested by the branches of metalwork described in the *Treatises*, Ashbee ends up writing his way toward the wide-ranging Cellini of the *Life*: the second half of "Cinquecento Jewelry" celebrates how "even Cellini finds difficulty in keeping to his classifications" (152) and, like the autobiography, praises diverse abilities in "chasing, embossing, engraving, enameling, filigree, [and] casting" (154). But it is not just his panoply of metalworking skills that suggests Cellini's overtopping of the very principles of focused labor that he simultaneously, for Ashbee, models. Cellini's autobiography, I have suggested, argues that living healthily manifests his universal dexterity and reinforces the quality of his professional labor; by this logic, stories about life "will not be off the subject" of his trade. "Cinquecento Jewelry" takes up this argument by claiming that Cellini's desultory literary habits "help to reveal the methods of the workshop": stories about arguments, patronage, practical jokes, and relations with other craftsmen constitute "all the many touches of sixteenth-century life" that made work and life "indivisible," and thus refreshingly unlike the alienation of the worker under industrial models (152).

As a laborer tested in relation to traditional ideals of workmanship, Ashbee's Cellini represents an argument against dilettantism and an icon of specialized, concentrated, and singular process. But as a storyteller about work analyzed in relation to the "division" of labor attributed to industrial culture, Ashbee's Cellini represents the universal capacity, untrammeled lifestyle, and wide-ranging situational prowess idealized as belonging to the crafts. Beholden to both histories, "Cinquecento Jewelry" appears as a kind of stream-of-consciousness about Cellini that floats through instances of the situation of workmanship under pressures from both classic and emerging meanings. But if the essay reads with difficulty, its equivocal position on Cellini's narrative exuberance can be read as a blueprint for the reception of craft as a literary subject in the nineteenth and early twentieth centuries. For Ashbee, Cellini's predilection for storytelling transforms his own discrete methodological "classifications," making him unable "to talk about goldsmithing without linking it to the other arts and crafts of Italy" (153). Such prolixity is both good (because it reveals that wider, synthetic capacity that was part of the idealization of craft in the nineteenth century) and bad (because it departs from the standards of professional specialization durably associated with the meaning of workmanship). That the issue should turn on Cellini's enthusiasm as a storyteller, in particular, suggests the centrality of print media to the emergence of workmanship as a cultural style of greater vigor and personal vitality.

Representative of the craft movement's textual vitality and its orientation to the "manner" of the craftsman's living, then, Cellini's *Life* was implicitly understood by Ashbee as testing the limits of workmanship as a narrative subject and cultural style. The instability of "Cinquecento Jewelry" marks Ashbee's harnessing of craft's various standards. Royal Cortissoz, the art critic who commented that Cellini "talked too much," took an explicitly dimmer view of the artisan's eccentricity. Cellini "did not concentrate his energy" or "send it through the right channels" of consistency; he was "not steadfast enough to reach perfection in any form of art."[52] When Cortissoz claims that Cellini never felt the "voiceless whisper" of inspired labor, the implication yet again is that Cellini is too loud: the purposeful pursuit of ideal ends ("fate had done all that could be done to place models of what sculpture should be before Cellini" [xvi]) is waylaid by the gusto of his narrative. The ideal "models," in this instance, refer to individuals Cortissoz names: Ghiberti and Donatello, of course, as well as Andrea del Verrocchio and Antonio del Pollaiuolo. But Cortissoz also draws out his point in terms of Cellini's relation to one of his own physical models, the comparatively small wax figure he made of the *Perseus* before making the full-size mold (figure 6). Because the craftsman's sources are so central to the standards of workmanlike purpose with which the nineteenth century wrestled, I would like to close this chapter by focusing on what the relations between the wax model and the eventual bronze sculpture make visible for Cortissoz: the flow of energy between Cellini's plans and his results. Looking at how two turn-of-the-century figures deeply concerned with art—Cortissoz and Henry Adams—thought about Cellini's designs reveals the dual axioms of purpose and adaptation, standard and circumstance, under which the nineteenth-century culture of craft operated.

According to Cortissoz, the difference between the wax model of the *Perseus* and the eventual statue is one of grace: the lithe forms of the model vanished in the clumsier, heavier final rendition, indicating that "the sculptor lost his grasp on the original idea as the work went on" (xxiii). There is no question that the model is slighter physically, and perhaps even egoistically: the wax Perseus looks down and away, in an attitude of comparative humility, while the bronze gazes down but forward. The bronze, moreover, stresses the potency of the subject as the grotesquerie of the decapitation, and (signed "Benvenutus Cellinus" on the strap across the torso) likens the triumph of Perseus to that of Cellini himself. Whatever one thinks about Cortissoz's aesthetic preference for the more demure statue, its significance for my purposes has to do with Cortissoz's claim about how easily the statue can be misread. We would do well, Cortissoz suggests, "to put out of mind the whole dramatic story of its casting"—for the difference between the better model and the inferior final product, he holds, can only be appreciated if the narrative does not "affect our view of the matter" (xxiii). The most famous episode in the autobiography obfuscates our impartial view of the correspondence between intent and outcome; Cortissoz, in effect, cautions the autobiography's audience—an audience that loved the narrative of the *Perseus*—not to lose sight of one of the established benchmarks for evaluating workmanship. The argument literalizes the tensions between the textual narratives of craft and traditionally teleological standards of performing what one sets out to do.

The curiosity, however, is the context Cortissoz chooses for describing the attenuation of teleological standards (Cellini's failure to make the product he modeled) and the distraction of the narrative for viewers of the stature (a narrative which, he feels, is itself too distractible). For he makes these points when introducing a new edition of Cellini's text. Cortissoz chooses a strange

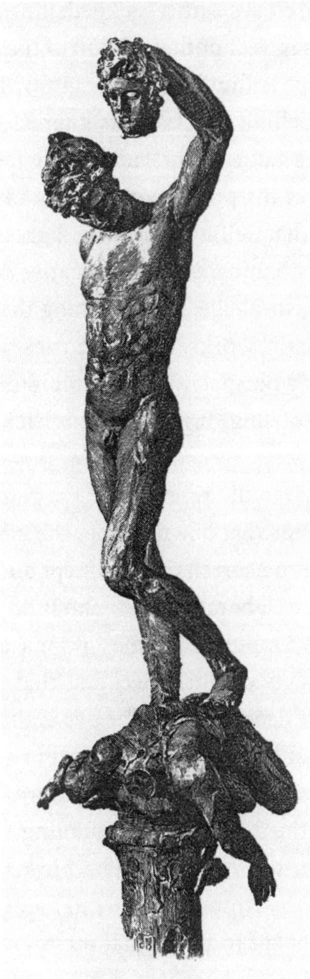

FIGURE 6. Cellini, wax model for *Perseus*. As engraved in Royal Cortissoz, "Benvenuto Cellini: Artist and Writer." (*The Life of Benvenuto Cellini* [New York: Brentano's, 1906], xxii)

venue for asserting that talking about craft is a poor substitution for doing it, that reading about craft runs the risk of submerging our proper judgment of it, and that the ideal craftsman responds to a "voiceless" calling. One hears, in these evaluations, an echo of Plato's sharp divisions of labor—between, say, writing and working—and a preview of later scholarly suspicion about the compatibility of literature and labor. But Cortissoz's forum virtually mandates a more complex position: his introduction to the *Life*, already a legendary account of the craftsman's existence when Cortissoz wrote his introduction for Brentano's Publishers in 1906, closes with a backpedalling analysis of why, given the cautionary tone of the essay, yet another edition of the autobiography should be issued. The first argument is familiar. "To begin with," Cortissoz claims, "in interesting the world in Cellini, [the *Life*] has interested the world in his works, and has thus fostered the fame of the latter" (xxiv). Cellini's own position is that wandering away from his profession actually made him a better artisan, and Ashbee's position is that Cellini's narrative digressions reveal the wider life of the cinquecento craftsman as a vital alternative to the deadeningly "subdivided" labor of the industrial age. In suggesting that the *Life* will bring more attention to Cellini's material works, Cortissoz tries out a similar accommodation in terms of the *reader*'s perspective: the autobiography, because its "air . . . of movement" is so compelling, brings readers back toward, not away from, the true craft (xxiv).

Cortissoz seems to be rapidly reversing his argument about the *Perseus*. In that discussion, he contends that one must put the narrative out of mind to see the material object fairly; the correlation of intent and outcome, craft's classic standard, is obfuscated by elaborate stories about how things come to be. But when Cortissoz turns to enumerating the "points of view from which this famous book appears in a good light," he claims that the narrative immerses us in the physical work more deeply (xxiv). The two claims are not entirely incompatible: one might say that the *Life* draws interest to Cellini's craft, which then must be seen independently of the prompting story. But the circularity of the discussion characterizes the difficulty of accounting for craft as a popular narrative subject, circa 1900, while guarding its physical media and preserving classic standards of workmanship. Cortissoz in fact goes on, at the end of the essay, to describe Cellini's *Life* in terms that move swiftly between textual and manual registers. Cellini's reminiscences come in an "extraordinarily tangible form," narrated "with a generous hand" (xxx). Those reminiscences move quickly between episodes, but any given episode is told "without a superfluous touch." The most tautly strung sentence in the essay asserts that "this maker of literature was never a literary man" (xxviii). In "making" a decidedly tactile literature, Cellini appears as the master of a narrative that embodies and represents the physicality of his trade; the *Life* for Cortissoz may not be good enough to qualify Cellini as a "literary man" (he does not possess the "professional . . . instinct of the man of letters"), but it does appear to have a workmanlike, vigorous quality as a literature of the body. And yet, at the same time, Cellini's actual, manual craft does not signify the mute purpose that Cortissoz (like Longfellow when describing Michelangelo) attributes to the best workmanship. Cellini is thus neither a great artisan nor a great writer. As a "maker of literature," he is an author-artisan whose two identities interweave excitingly but who is a true master in neither calling.

Cortissoz toes a fine line. He disallows Cellini, on account of his garrulous narrative, from becoming an icon of the truest or best workmanship; craft in this respect is defined by a Platonic clarity about purpose, intent, and result, not by the contingencies revealed in Cellini's dramatic account of ever-changing circumstances and quick adaptations. But Cortissoz simultaneously whips up enthusiasm for the text as a legitimate record of the artisanal, and a viable instrument of craft revivalism, by reading it as a stimulus for public interest in Cellini's works and as an account textured by the artisan's skilled but not masterful hand. Alongside Ashbee, Cortissoz is representative. The canonizers of the *Life* held Cellini to a standard of telos and found his intentions weak and his results poor. But they also held him to other standards—of situational mastery, a wider way of life, and printed narrative—and, by these measures, they accepted him as the "maker" of an "extraordinarily tangible" and paradigmatic artisanal legacy.

That legacy appears just as complex and equivocal for a figure not at all instrumental to Cellini's canonization, but who described his own autobiography as a kind of crafting. Inverting the interest of the artisan-as-author for Cellini's popularizers, Henry Adams grappled with what Cellini meant for the author's imagination of himself as an artisan. Adams's goals in *The Education of Henry Adams* (1907) appear workmanlike in the classic, teleological sense. Presenting his own life as a way of studying the imperatives of his era, Adams seeks to "run direction through space," to "arrange sequences," to correlate "cause and effect," and to give well-wrought shape to cultural history.[53] The autobiography, he writes, is a study in the "mechanics" of cultural change and an attempt to record the physics of historical force: "Did it pull or push? Was it a screw or thrust? Did it flow or vibrate?" (435, 342). Adams was, accordingly, drawn to metaphors of craft. "The pen," he writes, "acts like a hand" (389). The labor of the cultural critic is to "model . . . the plastic material over and over again" (389), so that the *Education* appears as a piece of "workmanship" and its author as a "tailor" who uses his autobiographical persona—the "manikin"—as the form on which to drape the literary and historical garments he crafts (xxvii–xxx).

Given Adams's artisanal desire to "mix narrative [with] didactic purpose and style," to give teleological and certain shape to his experiences, his equivocal response to Cellini's *Life* as a model for his own artisanal narrative is not surprising.[54] Adams's letters thrice refer to the *Life* alongside the *Confessions* of St. Augustine and Rousseau. But of this triplet of autobiographies cited by

Adams as inspirational, the craftsman's narrative—Cellini's—does not best model the craft of narrative, the literary workmanship of pressing "discipline through freedom" to which Adams aspires (12). "Of them all," Adams writes, "I think St. Augustine alone has as idea of literary form,—a notion of writing with an end and an object."[55] The ability to model what he saw, the artisanal charge Adams associated with his self-presentation as a manikin in various crafted garments, was not reflected in the *Life*.

Adams thus reads Cellini's text as did the nineteenth and early twentieth centuries more generally: as a work that did not exemplify the constancy of purpose and the enactment of design classically associated with craft. But consider how a passage in the preface sets up another, different standard of literary workmanship in pitching the *Education* as an artisan's autobiography: "At the utmost, the active-minded young man should ask of his teacher only mastery of his tools. The young man himself, the subject of education, is a certain form of energy; the object to be gained is the economy of his force; the training is partly the clearing away of obstacles, partly the direct application of effort. Once acquired, the tools and models may be thrown away" (xxx). To be sure, Adams's invocation of the historian's "mastery of his tools," the "economy of his force," and the particular "object to be gained" aligns the passage to some degree with traditional models of workmanship; the phrasing anticipates the "animus of economy" Veblen attributes to the craftsman's process.[56] But the passage also teases out a different view of the young man's artisan-like education—a view matched elsewhere in Adams's writing by a complementary regard for Cellini's "form of energy." For if on the one hand, the passage suggests workmanlike teleology, on the other hand, the "object to be gained" is not the outcome toward which the energy is directed (what Veblen calls the "object of [the craftsman's] solicitude" [33]) but rather the *ability* to direct energy itself. The craft metaphor in this sense involves no particular "mastery." It involves the habit of mind characteristic of artisanship. The startling idea that the tools and models might finally be "thrown away" suggests the emphasis on character and temperament toward which workmanship was increasingly oriented. My later chapters will draw out this point, but it is worth saying here that Adams's figuration of the young man's education exemplifies the principles of a popular Swedish system of craft instruction called *sloyd*. Very popular in the United States in the decades surrounding *The Education of Henry Adams*, *sloyd* depended on instructional models and asserts the limited role of the teacher; the standard curriculum asked students to work on conventional models (a letter opener or soup ladle or ax handle) that could be carved with a knife. The purpose of the "*sloyd* system of models," wrote the superintendent of a New

York school, was "formal" rather than "material": "materialists believe in giving a knowledge of the actual things met with in life, while the formalists lay stress on the cultivation of correct habits."[57]

Sloyd would have appealed to Adams's vigorous commitment to "self-education," and the description of instructive models and disposable tools perhaps refers explicitly to the system. Reading the passage in this way detaches artisanship from narrow purposefulness, dissociates craft from its tools, and—the point with which I will conclude—mirrors a view of Cellini in *The Education of Henry Adams* that praises rather than rejects his lack of sequentiality. In the widely known chapter "The Dynamo and the Virgin," Adams discusses how the sculptor Augustus St. Gaudens experiences the historical and artistic force of the Virgin—for Adams, the embodiment of creative energy associated with mystery, feeling, and sexuality—as a spark that does not quite catch flame. For St. Gaudens, Adams believes, the Virgin is known primarily as "taste," a stylistic predilection of art history for Madonnas and for scenes of passion. In general, St. Gaudens emerges in the chapter as materialistic, as too concerned with the outward, technical perfectibility of art; he cannot seem to find a deeper trust than the "usual contradictory suggestions of brother sculptors," and puts "interminable last touches" on his work (385). St. Gaudens seems to Adams the nineteenth-century artist with the finest spirit, but his obsession with the material progress of his labor is stifling:

> In mind and person, St. Gaudens was a survival of the 1500s; he bore the stamp of the Renaissance, and should have carried an image of the Virgin round his neck, or stuck in his hat, like Louis XI. . . . St. Gaudens was a child of Benvenuto Cellini, smothered in an American cradle. Adams was a quintessence of Boston, devoured by curiosity to think like Benvenuto. St. Gaudens's art was starved from birth, and Adams's instinct was blighted from babyhood. Each had but half a nature. (387)

The "quintessence of Boston" in Adams, he makes clear across the *Education*, is his desire to corral all force into a "channel," to work out the economies and directions of history. The alternative to this model, and to St. Gaudens's "interminable" labors, is to "think like Benvenuto"—to experience sculpture as instinct, to create not according to the laws of material or the certainty of result (predicated on "such order as seemed rigidly consequent") but from the wellspring of the "occult," the "irrational," and the unsequenced "revelation of mysterious energy" (383).

St. Gaudens is a starved child of Cellini to the degree that his work *almost* taps a wellspring of feeling, of self-trusting creativity that operates instinctively and also knows when to stop trying to seeking perfect form; Adams, we should recall, likewise presents his own education as a literary artisan as ideally consummated when he throws away his tools and models. But like St. Gaudens, whose interminable last touches reveal his materialist notions of perfectibility, Adams cannot suppress his own predilections to keep hammering away at his life and its relation to the history of his era. The massive *Education of Henry Adams* famously replays, again and again, a maddening struggle. The artisan-historian tries always to keep going, to make sense, to "arrange sequences"; "if he could not reach [comprehension] by one method, he would try as many methods as science knew" (382). But Adams is also beset by an "avalanche of unknown forces" typifying the modern age (461); "after ten years' pursuit," Adams writes, "he found . . . his historical neck broken by the sudden irruption of forces totally new" (382). My interest in this dialectic, discussed in some form or other by virtually everyone who writes about the text, has to do with how it structures Adams's response to Cellini as a model of workmanship. On the one hand, as an instance of the force associated with the Virgin and as an icon of the kind of energy Adams wishes he could see more fully realized in his friend St. Gaudens, Cellini appears as a compelling artisanal alternative to notions of craft as telos. There is no better literary instance of a craftsman who breaks with canonical methods and is more willing to throw away the tools he mastered as an apprentice. Acting not along lines of sequence but of instinct, moving from this craft to that craft, Cellini adapts instantly to ever-changing circumstances. Adams is "devoured by curiosity" about a figure whose neck would never be broken by inexplicable forces.

On the other hand, however, Cellini is a counterexample for Adams's workmanlike desire to advance, like St. Augustine, toward an "end and an object." Cellini, by this standard, does not model the actual craftsmanship of the *Education* as a study in the "order" of forces (12); only St. Augustine, Adams avers, understands "literary form." Adams's birthright of practical construction may be smothering, as he says in the passage quoted earlier. But it structures, nonetheless, his notion of how the pen, acting "like a hand," crafts a "form [that] is never arbitrary." Instead, the well-wrought text is a "sort of growth like crystallization," dependent more on "the sequence of the main lines of thought, than on their play or variety" (389).

Adams's occasional references to Cellini offer a microcosm of what this chapter has tried to draw out as the complicated legacy of his narrative. The major point I have argued is that variously compatible standards of workmanship converged on the *Life*. For Adams, Cellini puts the craftsman-historian's partiality for cause and effect to the test; Cellini's narrative offered an alternative to which Adams was drawn but to which his teleological notions of craft could not be fully adapted. Adams, accordingly, offers his *Education* as a failure, because the craftsman-historian can neither control force nor "think like Benvenuto." For other writers considered in this chapter, however, Adams's partiality—for sequence, technique, and purpose—composed a standard to which Cellini's narrative could be deliberately and carefully accommodated. As narrative, for instance, the Italian text appeared to its major English translator as an unsequenced, ungrammatical nightmare. And yet the closer Symonds looks, the more he finds himself able to draw out the "glittering and trenchant edge" that makes Cellini's prose an actually ingenious instance of traditional rhetorical devices and workmanlike composition.

Symonds, to be sure, explicitly aimed to offer readers a translation expressive of the hurly-burly, improvisational artisanal life before the dominance of the factory and of what he called the "machine-made" standard. The *Life* in that regard fit an emerging model of the craftsman's experience as a subject of wider compass than the extremely narrow calling described, for instance, by Plato. But Symonds, just as much, desired to reveal Cellini as a "consummate craftsman" in metal and in prose. The interlaced imperatives of garrulousness and concentration, range and specialization, define the legacy that Longfellow and Liszt, Ashbee and Cortissoz, tried to ensure. Benvenuto, as Longfellow calls him, comes of age when he casts the *Perseus*. His empty boasts are initially contrasted to Michelangelo's workmanlike silence. But they evolve through the masterwork into a triumph of productive craftsmanship that is vocal and energetic—the story of the casting, Cellini himself insists, bears "witness" or *saggio* to his skills—without being, when Cellini tells the tale to Longfellow's Michelangelo, undisciplined or prolix. Liszt's restaging of Berlioz's opera buffa performs a similar transposition of Cellini's character, also using the *Perseus* to signify the consummation and intentionality of his metalworking prowess. The craftsman's devotions may be ideally "voiceless," as Cortissoz puts it, and ideally focused by traditional crafts specializations, as Ashbee claims. But both writers, like Cellini's other advocates, place him in the more delicate position mandated by the nineteenth-century context of Cellini's popularization. Under the pressures of modern subdivisions of labor, his quicksilver movements between crafts, cities, and callings look as compelling, as instances of the artisan's more vigorous life, as they are threatening, as contraindications of the artisan's virtuous specialization.

The broadest questions suggested by these various imperatives are framed by Hawthorne's confused, subjunctive, and abstracting pattern of references to Cellini's hands and to the objects of Cellini's handiwork. As artisanship became a cultural style, figures like Hawthorne wondered how the immanence of actual crafted things related to craft's general iconicity. What, Hawthorne's references to Cellini's *class* of hands suggested, are the lines of an individual's labor and the generic interest of the artisanal lifestyle? How should readers test the narrative appeal of workmanship against its material dimensions? Are there lines of compatibility between, on the one hand, the embodied appeal of handicrafts labor and, on the other, the ghostliness of Cellini's actual touch, as represented by Hawthorne and by the vexing fact that a ghost writer actually penned the text advertised as having been written *di mia mano*?

Cellini himself, characteristically, had ready answers to these questions. Hiring the son of Michele Goro allowed him to work harder, turning what looks like an abdication of his *propria mano* into a defense of it. Going shooting at the ruins pointedly breaks with the model of artisanal devotion epitomized by Ghiberti and Donatello, but it actually causes him to win commissions and find stones to set, and enables him to return to his work with redoubled focus. The nineteenth century did not answer the questions posed by Cellini with such easy assurance, but with a harder and more tortured set of theories, interpretations, and adjustments. The next chapter opens an extended discussion of Hawthorne's fiction by investigating one of the only objects he did clearly attribute to Cellini's own hand: the vase by Cellini in "Rappaccini's Daughter," I will argue, stands for that story's vigorous interrogation of the relations of craft, body, touch, and narrative. But I would end here with a comment of Henry Adams's that speaks for the difficulty as well as the appeal of the *Life* as the era's preeminent artisanal text. Likening the pen to a hand, as I have said, Adams was "devoured" by his interest in Cellini's freedom from excesses of sequence. But "too often," Adams went on in the metaphor of the pen and the hand, the labor of the author-artisan "runs into side-paths and shapelessness, loses its relations, stops or is bogged." Lost relations, side-paths, and shapelessness were just the problems Cellini's canonizers saw in his prolixity. Adams's projection of a solution is also one they embraced in trying to bring sequence and linearity to Cellini's artisanal narrative: the craftsman's pen, Adams wrote, finally must "return on its trails, and recover, if it can, its line of force" (389).

CHAPTER 2

LEGENDS OF LABOR

Nathaniel Hawthorne and the Voice of Craft

WEBS OF WORKMANSHIP: "RAPPACCINI'S DAUGHTER"

The previous chapter argued that Cellini's canonizers accommodated the purposeful application of the body, a traditional standard of artisanship, with the narrative appeal of Cellini's free-floating dexterity, peripatetic life, and universal capability. In this context, I suggested, Nathaniel Hawthorne's categorical references to "such hands as those of Benvenuto Cellini" typify a culture of craft in which the artisan's body was both emphasized and abstracted, at once incarnated and generalized. The current chapter traces the circumference of manual labor's literary dimension in a wider corpus of Hawthorne's writing than the notebooks, memoirs, and sketches in which he repeatedly names Cellini. I want to suggest that Hawthorne's early fiction in particular, centered around crafts from embroidery and house-building to carving and watchmaking, might be understood in terms of its emphasis on artisanship.

More specifically, I analyze how the crafts worker's touch in Hawthorne's early work appeared in specifically narrative forms: as tales told within tales about the incarnating power of labor; as crafted objects marked by their textuality; and as a language of workmanship beholden, like Cellini's *Life*, to represent both the artisan's habitual, durable practice and the inimitability and contingency of an unstandardized life. Hawthorne used all of these forms to test the compatibility of craft's emerging interest, as story and text, with craft's traditional virtues as physical practice and material results. This chapter emphasizes Hawthorne's early career. I discuss a selection of stories about artisanship from *Mosses from an Old Manse*, as well as *The Scarlet Letter;* the latter text, Hawthorne's breakthrough novel, itself looks back to his earliest literary efforts, rewriting an account of engraving that first appeared in the self-published *Fanshawe*. These works interest me because the author's struggle to establish mastery of his own medium—print—seems to have made him uniquely aware of the relations between craft and story. Famously, "The Custom-House" describes a writer who has not yet confirmed his vocation. When new literary work does come his way, in the form of the scarlet letter he discovers, Hawthorne sets the scene in a room whose condition mirrors the author's unconsummated labors: the "brick-word and naked rafters" of the attic room had "never been covered with paneling or plaster," appearing "still to await the labor of the carpenter and mason."[1] Likening his authorial charge to the artisanal charges of the carpenter and mason—all of which appear as only partially completed—Hawthorne's meditations in his early fiction tend to recur to the questions involved in understanding text as craft and craft as text. The next chapter extends the case for craft's animation as a narrative subject in Hawthorne's fiction to the novel composed immediately after *The Scarlet Letter.* But that novel, *The House of the Seven Gables*, raises questions about the nature and representation of skill that are better understood, I argue, in the context of theories expressed by A. W. N. Pugin, John Ruskin, and the Arts and Crafts Movement; Hawthorne's third major novel, *The Blithedale Romance*, is even more obviously oriented to the dynamics of handicraft as part of a formal utopian project. The early fiction treated in the following pages instead comes back again and again to the more general case, testing the implications for corporeal standards of workmanship when artisanship refracts into stories, projections, and narrative effects.

"Rappaccini's Daughter" (1844) is a revealing place to begin, for it lodges these concerns in a handmade artifact that initially seems to have little to do with the literary medium or storybook atmosphere of craft. On the contrary, the magnificent vial "wrought by the hands of the renowned Benvenuto Cellini" (the only object by Cellini in Hawthorne's corpus that is unambiguously able to be accessed, handled, and attributed) promises to restore tactility to a world that imperils it. The vial contains what is thought to be an antidote to the poisonous engineering of Dr. Rappaccini—whose daughter Beatrice, one of his experimental subjects, kills whatever she contacts. The antidotal potential of the Cellini vase, given to a young man who passionately desires the daughter, is thus touch itself; Cellini's handiwork, uniquely presented by Hawthorne as the actual work of the goldsmith himself rather than "such hands" as his, symbolizes the reverse of Rappaccini's disembodying science. Rappaccini's threat to craft becomes symbolically unmistakable when Giovanni, the young man in love with Beatrice, also begins to suffer from the effects of the scientist's engineering. The first thing killed by Giovanni's chemically poisoned breath is a "small artisan," a spider working on an intricately "interwoven" web near another icon of craft, the "antique cornice" of the old building. The insect "suddenly ceased its toil" when Giovanni exhales, its web vibrating "with a tremor originating in the body" of the minute workman (121–22).

Read along these lines, "Rappaccini's Daughter" can be plausibly interpreted as detailing the menace of science and technological manipulation to handicraft and to the bodily dimensions of workmanship. Dr. Rappaccini indeed seems like a perversion of the very idea of touch. He appears on the one hand as a kind of perverse craftsman, cultivating his plants "with his own hands" (100), tending "what his own hands caused to grow" (96), and nurturing a garden repeatedly associated with "the own hands of Signor Giacomo Rappaccini" (94). The irony, as it develops, is that Rappaccini "defended his hands with a pair of thick gloves" from the plants that he has made poisonous to his "actual touch" (96). That irony defines the whole story, which is suffused with references to hands even as it is about a threat to touch. Hands appear as instruments of craftsmanship (the vial "wrought by the hands" of Cellini); as a metaphor for contests of power ("thou hast fallen into his fearful hands" [107]); as the first revelation of Beatrice's condition (the beautiful "Beatrice handled . . . several of the plants which her father had most sedulously avoided" [97]); and as the dominant, recurring image of forbidden desire ("there had been no seal of lips, no clasp of hands . . . he had never touched one of the gleaming ringlets of her hair" [116]).

Through the agency of the Cellini vase and its contents, the story seems as if it might overcome the problem that so many of the hands it presents cannot handle anything. But if craft and touch thus appear as the standards to which the story might return, Hawthorne finally presents such hopes as no more than idealizations. For the antidote fails. Rather than being restored to the realm of the corporeal, Beatrice dies when she drinks from the vase. Her nature turns out to have been so altered that "as poison had been life, so the powerful antidote was death" (127–28). By this turn of events, the vase appears like all the other examples of Cellini's handiwork in Hawthorne's corpus: it suggests the promise of touch without its fulfillment. As in the Uffizi or the bookseller's shop, Cellini's work demarcates the fault lines of the actual body and the story told about it. The goldsmith's own story indeed suffuses "Rappaccini's Daughter": both Roy Male and Mary Cappello have noted that "Rappaccini's Daughter" is textured by references to Cellini's *Life* beyond the explicit attribution of the vase, primarily in that the surnames of the story's characters correspond loosely to certain figures mentioned in the autobiography.[2] If the story is thus something of a meditation on Cellini, the gap between all the references to Rappaccini's laboring with his own hands and his "actual touch" (blocked by his thick gloves) might even be taken to refer to the composition of the *Life* itself; Cellini's text, advertised as having been written by his own hands but in fact written by an amanuensis, seems clearly enough echoed by Rappaccini's garden, advertised as the work of his own hands but in truth untouchable by him.

Hawthorne would likely have read Cellini's *Life* in the 1822 translation by Thomas Roscoe, which included in the appendix the introductory note confessing to the amanuensis.

Regardless of whether Hawthorne was thinking about the specifics of the autobiography's composition, however, the central interest of the *Life* as a document in crafts history—that it presents little account of sustained physical labor—appears as the failure of Cellini's artisanship to turn the tide of Hawthorne's story back toward the "actual touch" of the hand. Most important for my purposes, this pattern correlates with the unique framing of the story, through which Hawthorne comments on his own authorial craft. Naming the story as authored by one M. de l'Aubépine, whose name and literary productions are Hawthorne's own, translated into French, Hawthorne teasingly anticipates the tale's questions about the maker's authority. As performed by the "small artisan" of the spider, craft is destroyed by Giovanni's breath. As performed by Rappaccini's "own hands," craft is ironically detached from physical touch. And as represented by the literary labors attributed not to Hawthorne but to a stand-in, Aubépine, craft marks an actually ambiguous artisanal provenance; nobody touches anything directly in this text, not even the author. The hinted connections between Rappaccini's garden, Cellini's manuscript, and Hawthorne's authorship of the tale—all of which are marked by equivocations attending the creator's own hands—cannot be overcome.

Rather than restoring the experiences of the hand, the Cellini vase, acting on Beatrice's altered state, thus operates in the pervasive context of scientific manipulation and evanescent touch that it putatively opposes. The vase insists, moreover, on the *narrative* basis of Cellini's fame as an artisan. For the vase in "Rappaccini's Daughter" appears as a prop in a revenge plot that mirrors the dozens of contests that the ever-embattled Cellini describes in the *Life*. The vase is given to Giovanni by Rappaccini's archrival Professor Pietro Baglioni, who appears at a window at the end of a story to deride his nemesis "in a tone of triumph mixed with horror" (128). It is unclear if Baglioni surmised that the dram could kill Beatrice, but the vase appears at best as merely ineffectual (for Beatrice, not for the semitriumphal Baglioni) and at worst an agent in the ongoing contest between the two men. In the *Life*, almost every craft Cellini describes is framed by a narrative involving the "considerable jealousy" between Cellini and "those who thought they were capable of matching [his craft]" (*Life*, 88). The vase in "Rappaccini's Daughter" reflects a condition of Cellini's workmanship that Hawthorne's reading of the autobiography—which we know to have occurred two or more years before he wrote the story—would have clearly revealed to him: the narrative focal point is not Cellini's tactile relationship with material or medium but the often invidious culture of claim and counterclaim in which that craft is set.[3] Indeed, if it is true that Hawthorne derived the names for his characters from his reading of the *Life*, then Pietro Baglioni, recalling Cellini's interactions with the military leader Orazio Baglioni, hints at the dynamics by which the skill of the hands is loosened from particular achievements and particular objects. Orazio Baglioni appears in two scenes in the *Life*. In the first, he challenges Cellini to demonstrate his accuracy by shooting at a tavern sign. Cellini hits the sign dead center, dropping it among the important citizens dining at the tavern—and prompting the politic Baglioni to feign murderous fury at Cellini and later, in private, to beg Cellini to deny that he was present when the goldsmith fired the gun and imperiled the patrons (72). In the second scene, Baglioni, now general of the Florentine army, makes Cellini one of his captains. Cellini's elderly father begs him to refuse the commission on the grounds that "I ought to pursue the noble art in which I had labored so many years and with such diligence of study" (78). Both scenes thus feature craft denied, an activity of the hands devalued. In the first case, Baglioni divorces himself from the very skill that he asked Cellini to demonstrate; in the second, he appears as the agent of the mutability of vocation which, I have suggested, worried Cellini's nineteenth-century canonizers and that Cellini's father, in this scene, resists. The antecedent of Hawthorne's Pietro Baglioni, whose idealization of Cellini's handicraft masks slipperier motives, is a man who threatens to draw Cellini away from his labor of goldsmithing and who (in this respect quite precisely anticipating Hawthorne's Baglioni, whose vial is a lie) ends up distancing himself from the skills of the hand that he himself idealizes.

What Hawthorne presents in "Rappaccini's Daughter," then, is exactly that lateral motility of craft for which Cellini preeminently stood. Invoking certain fault lines associated with the translation of craft into a narrative rather than a singular calling, and featuring the misleading *fiction* that the Cellini vase will restore an unmediated culture of the hand, Hawthorne addresses a problem of representation; what looks like a story founded on apparently straightforward antipodes of artisanal touch and scientific engineering turns out to be a story about the inseparability of craft from its untrustworthy figurative forms. To trace Hawthorne's anxieties about the fate of craft to its growing appeal and animation as narrative (rather than to the attenuation or disappearance of traditional workmanship under the pressures of science, industry, and technology) is to offer an account of the relation between Hawthorne, labor, and modernity that differs from the established scholarly discussion of that topic. A brief excursion into the history of scholarship on manual labor in Hawthorne may be most interesting to readers of *Talking Shop* who are literary historians. But the excursion will serve more generally, I hope, to characterize the stakes of Hawthorne's realization that artisanship could not be best described as simply imperiled in industrial culture; instead of disappearing, it was transforming and indeed expanding in the public consciousness, reverberating through the age as stories and accounts celebrating the work of the hands.

This subject in general—the relation of narrative to real things and actual bodies—centers critical debate about labor in Hawthorne's corpus. Several decades of excellent and highly influential scholarship on Hawthorne and the modern marketplace have illuminated how Hawthorne's definition of literary Romance, wherein the "Actual and the Imaginary may meet," relates to emerging modes of production and consumption that operated in vaporous, unsubstantial ways (*The Scarlet Letter*, 30). The notorious "ethereality" of Hawthorne's world comprises everything from impalpable technologies (daguerreotypy, electricity) to the obscure or dissimulated motives of persons, and appears as a response to the modern marketplace along two divergent lines.[4] Michael Gilmore's *American Romanticism and the Marketplace* (1985) represents one perspective. In Gilmore's study as well as in more recent analysis by, for instance, Alan Trachtenberg (who studies the "dodgy" qualities of photographic representation), Hawthorne inhabits a culture of spectacle in which "appearance matters more than substance"; Hawthorne's fiction reveals and critiques a modern commercial marketplace predicated on conspicuity, representational finesse, and the manipulation of appearances.[5] Walter Benn Michaels's influential reading of *The House of the Seven Gables* in *The Gold Standard and the Logic of Naturalism* (1987) represents the other perspective. For Michaels, "impalpable" property in Hawthorne's novel (including a plot of land that has never been visited by its owners and Hawthorne's representation of the novel itself as a "castle in the air") constitutes less an instance of the modern economy than a way of resisting its vaporous, ever-shifting quality.[6] Ethereal possessions appear as aristocratically remote, signs of a type of ownership isolated from exchange, trade, and capitalistic fluctuation.

What matters for my purposes is the influence of these studies, one of which stresses the lines of correspondence between Hawthornian Romance and emerging technologies of representation and the other of which positions Hawthornian Romance as a defense against the vicissitudes of an emerging economy in which everything is for sale. Critical approaches to the narrower topics of work and manual labor in Hawthorne's corpus tend to reflect the economic perspectives of *American Romanticism and the Marketplace* or *The Gold Standard and the Logic of Naturalism*. In her introduction to the recent collection

Hawthorne and the Real (2005), for instance, Millicent Bell describes the character of Priscilla in *The Blithedale Romance* as an icon of modernity's threat to traditional workmanship: "Priscilla knits little purses by hand but looks like a mill girl from Lowell," Bell writes, going on to posit that Westervelt's exploitation of Priscilla as his mesmeric medium makes the girl into "a representative of the new slavery of the factory which bound thousands like her to mechanized needlework under the rule of . . . the male factory manager."[7] In this reading, the apparent hypnotism of Priscilla by Westervelt combines with her waifish aspect to make her craft look ironic; her handiwork actually epitomizes the vanishing, enervated, and zombielike (or, in Hawthorne's language, mesmerized) nature of modern factory labor. Bell's axioms here, correlating the emerging mainstream of labor with mesmerism, suggest Gilmore's perspective on the nineteenth-century marketplace as spectral, dehumanizing, and predicated on the "mystification of human agency"; the failure of Priscilla to represent handiwork, despite her practice of it, mirrors Gilmore's comment that Hawthorne's "essentially artisanal" fantasies were "fated to be disappointed" in commodity culture.[8] Other commentators on manual labor in Hawthorne's corpus focus instead on how the work he depicts mostly aims at what Nicholas Bromell calls his penchant for "spiritualizing matter," or on how such metaphysical operations become, under certain conditions, viable models of unalienated labor. Gillian Brown's *Domestic Individualism* (1990), for instance, identifies women's work in particular as a practice that, because it is represented as spiritual or unworldly, operates outside the mainstream economy. Echoing Walter Benn Michaels to the degree that she identifies a certain kind of immateriality as *insulation* from the market—rather than, as for Gilmore and Bell, an instance of it—Brown describes how women's work becomes a kind of moral ministry signified, for instance, by the apparently magical nature of the housework by which Phoebe exorcises the ghosts from the House of the Seven Gables. Phoebe's work never appears onerous. As "magic and play," it looks not unlike the aristocratic model of possession described by Michaels: Phoebe's housework, Brown writes, constitutes "a sphere secure from the [industrially alienated] processes work signified in the nineteenth century."[9]

In mapping the viewpoints of Bell and of Brown onto the perspectives of Gilmore and Michaels, my aim is to suggest that readings informed by two influential and quite different models of Hawthornian modernity share a perspective about manual labor in his fiction as vanishing or otherwise evanescent. The difference between these critical approaches has to do with the degree of complicity or resistance discovered between the ethereal nature of labor and the modern market, rather than with the metaphysics of Hawthornian labor itself.

It is fair to say, I think, that Hawthorne's insistence on the imaginary and "phantasmagorical" nature of his own authorial labors structures his representation of the labors performed within his fictions, and that scholarship has therefore bent its interpretive energy, explicitly or implicitly, to the vanishing points of craft.[10] Carolyn Maibor suggests that Hester Prynne's needlework offers her a private exercise of her fancy and a public exercise of her sympathy: in returning to again take up her needle in Puritan New England, at the end of the novel, Hester chooses sympathetic involvement in a community of women within which she operates as a "sister of mercy."[11] Echoing Brown's reading of Phoebe's "spiritual ministry," Maibor's interpretation stresses Hester's handiwork as an affective practice; the tactile quality of handiwork vanishes by virtue of becoming what Maibor calls a "substitute" for Hester's feelings (70). The "invisibility" of Hawthornian labor is also Cindy Weinstein's subject in *The Literature of Labor and the Labors of Literature* (1995). For Weinstein, the nineteenth-century literary mode epitomized by Hawthorne can be described as an "economics of allegory"—that is, a relativistic practice in which symbolization, like financial capital, is unstable, subject to "incessant circulation," and "alienated" to the degree that no clear correspondences can be drawn between literature and the "work" of making meaning that it performs.[12] By contrast, Weinstein posits, John Bunyan's *Pilgrim's Progress*, a classic archetype of allegory, offers "visible" literary labor: characters or situations have a one-to-one correspondence with the meaning they are designed to convey. In Hawthorne's much less stable notion of signification, in which many interpretations may be derived from one symbol, literary work is obfuscated (and therefore appears a correlative for nineteenth-century anxieties about the alienation of human labor from its products) because the text itself never reveals what, precisely, it is actually doing.

Thus, the major critical issue concerning Hawthorne and work has turned on how, and in what contexts, we should read his dematerialization of toil: is it aristocratic or capitalistic? Oriented to the factory or the home? Exemplified by Priscilla as a model of the Lowell "mill girl" or by Phoebe as the magical housekeeper? An instance of what Weinstein sees as an unstable, circulating economy of work or what Maibor sees as a retreat from that economy into the stable community ultimately embraced by Hester Prynne? The following pages aim to contribute to this discussion by considering how Hawthorne's attitudes about artisanship presume the narrative modality which, I have posited, craft developed in the nineteenth century; like other readers, I am interested in how Hawthorne depicts and interrogates work that is not physical or very literally embodied. But I also want to question the correlation of this pattern with the deferral, evanescence, diminution, marginalization, or vanishing of craft. For Bell, Priscilla represents how the "new slavery of the factory" threatened traditional handiwork; for Maibor, the refuge of craft appears as the coterie of women who gather at Hester's cottage on the outskirts of town, where labor translates into sympathy. Brown and Weinstein both identify Hawthornian work as variously concealed, whether because Phoebe's labor appears secretive, shuttled into the private and unseen realm of domestic labor, or because the authorial labor of Hawthorne's novels is marked by its untraceable designs. *Talking Shop* as a whole, and this chapter in particular, makes the opposite case: I mean to stress the explosive vitality, not the evanescence, of craft within new channels of textual practice. Hawthorne's fiction, I think, might be read not just for the ways in which the dematerialization of labor reflects (or resists) the modern economy and the emerging market. It can also be read for the ways in which craft, one of Hawthorne's most visible subjects, bears the mark of a whole host of modern pressures, appearing as an idea that Hawthorne continually pressures and tests. Nineteenth-century anxieties about the fate of handiwork and the attenuation of touch in industrial culture inform the entire arc of Hawthorne's career, but these anxieties would be legible to a contemporary audience—reading Cellini, beginning to understand historical details of workmanship within an encyclopedic grammar of ornament, and increasingly oriented to the representation of craft within a consumer society—at moments other than those when craft seems to disappear, labor becomes alienated, or handwork turns into an ideal private ministry. Anxieties about the fate of the artisan's touch would also be legible, perhaps particularly so, in the very structure of talking about it and representing it in words. For it was in talk about workmanship, one of Hawthorne's major themes, that the question of craft's modern life was most pointedly relevant and, for the nineteenth century, most recognizable.

"Rappaccini's Daughter" is therefore my opening example because it so clearly features craft as a represented idea and a story told by one character to another. To be sure, the tale involves the threat of modernity, in the form of genetic engineering, to touch; Dr. Rappaccini's necessarily gloved hand marks a perversion of workmanship. But the story's conclusion, I have argued, reveals its anxieties as having to do as much with the misleading figuration of craft's promise by Pietro Baglioni. The attribution of the vase to Cellini (whose voice was so loud but whose output was comparatively slight) and the allusion to the Florentine general Orazio Baglioni (who appears in Cellini's *Life* as a hypocritical idealizer of the goldsmith's skill) clearly place the story's concerns in the realm of the values advanced, but not actually defended, through workmanship. Hawthorne thus registers something more than the poisoning of the "small artisan" by the breath of modernity, even as that language for the spider's death does suggest the peril for the local artisan in the technological culture represented in the story. For "Rappaccini's Daughter" is as much about a nineteenth-century aspect of craft, as narrative, predicated on anything but its diminution. Consider again, as a correlative for the story told by Baglioni about the Cellini vase, the preface attributing the story to M. de l'Aubépine. I have already claimed that the preface serves to confuse the matter of the story's artisanal provenance, effectively hiding the author's hand within a story that is largely about hidden hands and the ambiguities of touch. The preface is also noteworthy, however, for representing Aubépine's "indefatigable prolixity" as an enormous corpus of writing. Translating his own name and the names of his works into French, Hawthorne also lengthens them into multivolume novels rather than short stories. "The Celestial Railroad" appears as *Le Voyage Céleste à Chemin de Fer* in three volumes; "Fire-Worship," in fact a very short sketch, appears as *Le Culte du Feu*, a "folio volume of ponderous research." In the Latin lexicon of publishing abbreviations, the preface visualizes Aubépine's collected works as a materially complex assortment of works in "3 tom.," "1 tom.," "2 tom. 8vo," "5 tom. 4to," and the folio-size *Culte du Feu* (92). All of this is an inside joke for a writer who had self-sponsored the publication of only one unsatisfactory novel, *Fanshawe*, and who always felt his authorial production to be slighter, and to come less easily, than he hoped.

But the prolixity of Aubépine also suggests how craft dilates as Hawthorne, in "Rappaccini's Daughter," begins talking shop. Aubépine's "slight embroidery" of reality in his fiction becomes a "startling collection of volumes," themselves the doubles of Hawthorne's own writing. The preface, setting up "Rappaccini's Daughter" as a "translated specimen," spins out layers of text; Hawthorne's story becomes Aubépine's, one of a huge oeuvre, which the reader, if he or she gets the joke, then translates back into the names of Hawthorne's works (91). Doubling and redoubling, the author's craft anticipates the fate of the "little silver vase" by Cellini. For in both cases, craft turns out to represent neither the immediacy of workmanship nor the directness of touch, but representation itself—the system of translation, that is, in which craft is embedded. When Baglioni brings the vial to Giovanni, he first "chat[s] carelessly about the gossip of the city," and then goes on to recount a "marvelous tale," an "old fable," about Alexander the Great's inability to touch a lovely woman who, like Beatrice, had been "nourished with poisons from her birth upward" (116–17). Seeing Giovanni's situation as a revivified myth, he produces the vase as an antidote, a promise that Giovanni need not play the part of

Alexander the Great in the reenactment of the story. But the vase, a prop in Baglioni's own tale about craft's salvific promise, also turns out not to make reality any different from the old legend; by dying, Beatrice remains untouchable, and thus the correlative of the woman in the episode involving Alexander the Great. Fact and fiction, object and narrative, become indistinguishable; like Hawthorne's reduplicating authorial craft, the vase "wrought by the hands of the renowned Benvenuto Cellini" enters the realm of repeated and replayed narrative that it is initially offered to forestall. Artisanship, to return once more to the spider, only seems to have been pushed into the cornice of Giovanni's apartment and then annihilated by his chemical breath. As legend, craft reemerges neither as antidote nor as casualty, but very much like the spider's artisanal web—as an "artful system of interwoven lines," "crossing and recrossing" as artisanal objects become props in stories or old fables, and as the author's craft, correlatively, expands and widens into the narrative matrix that craft, in the 1800s, was rapidly becoming (121).

THE LETTER A, GULES; OR, THE ENGRAVER'S TEXT

The most famous translation of workmanship in Hawthorne's corpus comprises heraldic instructions to a gravestone engraver: "On a Field, Sable, the Letter A, Gules."[13] On stone, the heraldic colors "gules" and "sable," red and black, were represented by different patterns of incision: parallel vertical cuts for gules, cross-hatching for sable. The scarlet letter is thus monumentalized not only as a remnant of moth-eaten embroidery or as a faded engraving, but more durably as a *language* of craft: the letter is a letter described in a novel, and its funerary form appears in the novel's final line as a transcription of artisanal practice. The trajectory of *The Scarlet Letter* as a whole—meaning both the narrative and the "Custom-House" introduction—indeed suggests Hawthorne's preoccupation with the condition of artisanship as text. Embroidered by Hester Prynne, the physical A found in the Custom House attic has become the subject of many more letters, growing first into Surveyor Pue's six pages of explanatory manuscript and then into Hawthorne's imaginative expansion of the tale. The novel itself concerns the rumor and speculation prompted by an artisanal object and concludes, in its final words, with a written code for producing crafted things.

My broadest purpose in the analysis that follows is to suggest that Hawthorne's representation of the scarlet letter as various arcane crafts—a herald's code, a mysteriously stitched letter, and an ancient engraving—has to do less with the sixteenth-century setting of the novel than with the nineteenth-century pressures of its composition. Just as the "herald's wording" of the gravestone engraving serves to summarize his "now concluded legend," Hawthorne's frequent materialization of crafted objects as readable "legends" emphasizes the relays of text and bodily workmanship that the nineteenth century promoted (204). A "legend," of course, refers to an unauthenticated story. But its etymological roots are from the Latin *legenda*, a participle with imperative force; it describes things that require reading. Hawthorne's interest in the translatability of skilled labor into representations of itself (including instructions, icons, stories told by one character to another, and Hawthorne's own fiction) makes workmanship legendary in the root sense of the word. As a pattern that will help make sense of the heraldic code in *The Scarlet Letter*, consider first how artisanal objects that become interpretable legends populate Hawthorne's fiction. The obvious examples are the works of master artisans—an embroiderer and a carpenter—that center *The Scarlet Letter* and *The House of the Seven Gables;* both artifacts present difficult-to-read histories, appear as the titles of the novels in which they feature, and are described by Hawthorne as "legends."[14] But more occasional Hawthornian crafts also feature the dynamics of giving voice to workmanship and of crafting textual surfaces, a fact that seems to encode the storyteller's reflections on himself as an artisan. In "Chippings with a Chisel," a story I will consider in detail at the end of this chapter, Hawthorne uses the craft of gravestone engraving to interrogate the boundaries of traditional sentimentality (the conventional verse inscribed by a stonecutter on innumerable headstones) and originality (the spontaneous expressions, direct from the mouths of the bereaved, that the narrator believes the stonecutter should reproduce). The question about whether inscribed monuments are better predicated on universally accessible or individual phrases suggests Hawthorne's lifelong ambivalence about the writer's dependency on public appetite as well as on his incommensurable, one-of-a-kind artistry; the dialogue about engraving, in "Chippings with a Chisel," thus describes the writer's craft as well as the stonecutter's. Similarly, in *The House of the Seven Gables*, Holgrave—the representative of a family of tradesmen defined by their "diligence at handicrafts" (25)—appears as an artisanal combination of engraver, writer, and photographer. His name and his artisanal genealogy connote his photographic work of "mak[ing] pictures out of sunshine" and his tradesman-like labor of working up the history of Alice Pyncheon for the popular magazine *Godey's Lady's Book* (91).[15] Aptly named, Holgrave en-graves the story of Alice "in the form of a [written] legend" (186), and the "legendary" curse of the Pyncheons in the form of a daguerreotype showing a dead and bloody Judge Pyncheon (240). Holgrave's missionary artisanship—in the novel as a whole, he works to re-enfranchise the

Maules—thus reflects correlations of writing, craft, and representation. In the story "The Great Stone Face," time itself appears as the artisan who inscribes, engraves, and composes the legendary. The "wrinkles and furrows" on the face of the story's protagonist "were inscriptions that time had graved, and in which [time] had *written* legends of wisdom" (emphasis added).[16]

Such associations of engraving and writing, of legends and craft, suggest Hawthorne's understanding of his authorial effort in terms of the tradesman's and, more generally, his imagination of workmanship as a way of narrating and representing history. The heraldic inscription in *The Scarlet Letter* puts enormous pressure on the pattern, for craft appears as a text of *uncertain* durability and extraordinarily ambiguous representational content. The instructions are arcane and, as Lawrence Buell has recently observed, likely allude to the "esoterica" of sources in Andrew Marvell (whose poem "The Unfortunate Lover" closes by describing "In a Field *Sable* a Lover *Gules*") and in Sir Walter Scott (whose introduction to *Waverley* describes history as a contest of energies "colored gules" and those "tinctured sable").[17] For Buell, the ending is critically "underexplored" (86) in part because it is "teasingly oblique" (74). Certainly, thinking about the relation of craft to language in the novel's conclusion presents something far more ambiguous than Holgrave's craftsmanlike ability, as a writer and practitioner of "my own trade" of daguerreotyping, to counter the dispossession of his artisanal forebears (*House*, 91). For the physical letter actually worn by Hester ends up deeply abstracted: the text closes with an occult representation (the textual instructions) *of* a representation (the engraved escutcheon), itself a code (via the patterns of incision) for how we are to imagine color on a gray surface. The engraved letter, moreover, appears as only a "semblance" of its own original form (204)—a fact that might be taken to refer as much to the Russian-doll layering of signs in the novel's final paragraph as to the timeworn gravestone itself. If Hawthorne imagined his own craft as engraving, as I have suggested, the passage concluding *The Scarlet Letter* seems to parody the distance between texts and physical things. Just as the promise of touch attributed to the Cellini vase in "Rappaccini's Daughter" evaporates behind Baglioni's deceitful story, *The Scarlet Letter* closes with a web of representations that pulls us farther and farther from the material dimensions of workmanship and its objects.[18]

Or so it seems. Considering the final paragraph of *The Scarlet Letter* in light of a passage that rehearses its imagery—the description of a grave in Hawthorne's first novel, *Fanshawe*—offers a way of thinking about story's conclusion that does not make it seem quite so oblique, when it comes to the relationship of craft and language, words and things, the novelist's medium and the tradesman's. The villain in *Fanshawe*, a kidnapper, loses his hold on a cliff he is trying to scale. He is interred at its base:

> The body was buried where it had fallen, close by the huge, gray, moss-grown fragment of rock—a monument on which centuries can work little change. The eighty years that have elapsed . . . have, however, been sufficient to obliterate an inscription, which some one was at pains to cut in the smooth surface of the stone. Traces of letters are still discernible; but the writer's many efforts could never discover a connected meaning. The grave, also, is overgrown with fern bushes, and sunk to a level with the surrounding soil. But the legend, though my version of it may soon be forgotten, will long be traditionary in that lonely spot, and give to the rock, and the precipice . . . an interest thrilling to the bosom of the romantic wanderer.[19]

The natural stone marking the kidnapper's grave anticipates the rocks that serve as the only headstones for the titular characters in other short stories by Hawthorne, including "Roger Malvin's Burial" and "The Ambitious Guest." But the scene, in which no new stone is erected for the deceased, also anticipates the interment of Hester Prynne's body under Dimmesdale's already-established monument—a circumstance that begins to figure the similarity between the burial sites of the kidnapper, in *Fanshawe*, and the adulterous lovers, in *The Scarlet Letter*. Like the "sunken" grave in the later text, the kidnapper's grave in *Fanshawe* has "sunk" into the earth. Like the faded engraving of the scarlet letter that the "curious investigator may still discern," "traces of letters" remain just "discernible" in *Fanshawe*. Like the "now concluded legend" of Hawthorne's tale of Hester Prynne, the "legend" of his first novel is also memorialized by a worn, half-legible marker.[20]

Most important, however, is how Hawthorne *rewrites* the passage he draws upon in the later novel, and how the differences between the scenes in *Fanshawe* and *The Scarlet Letter* complicate the attribution of too much obscurity to the heraldic, textual version of the embroidered A. In *Fanshawe*, we experience the labor of inscribing stones as the "pains" taken by "some one" to memorialize the kidnapper. The identity of the carver is not revealed, and the anonymity of that figure marks the anonymity the youthful Hawthorne projects, in the passage, for his own work. Unable to read the meaning of the inscription—despite his "many efforts"—and convinced that his own "version" of the legend is likely to be soon "forgotten," the writer likens his text to the stonecutter's. The labors of inscription come to naught when Hawthorne describes time's erasure of the laboriously carved words on the stone, confesses to wasting his own energies trying to interpret one of the source texts for his novel (the engraving), and concludes that the durability of that novel is—in the long term—therefore futile. Moreover, how the stonecutter might have eulogized or identified the kidnapper in an inscription remains unimaginable for the reader. All we learn is that he was an occasional childhood companion of the once-dissolute innkeeper Hugh Crombie (who may or may not have carved the monument); he appears as "angler," "villain," and "guide," but never by a proper name even after he is revealed as the son of the Widow Butler. That we cannot imagine what name might be carved on the monument mimics the condition of the novel itself—for Hawthorne published *Fanshawe* anonymously. Both media, novel and stone, appear as labors of equal and profound obscurity.

Against this extreme instance of textual evanescence, the conclusion of *The Scarlet Letter* looks downright certain of the writer's workmanlike authority, and the figuration of the writer's craft as funerary engraving appears far more sure of the correlations between labor and its texts than its representational obliquity—to borrow Buell's term—would at first suggest. Twenty-two years after the publication of *Fanshawe*, the final paragraph of *The Scarlet Letter* revisits much of its imagery and language while shifting the burden of interpreting the engraving from the writer to the reader, famously invited to "perplex himself with the purport" (204). Rather than describing his own inability to discover a "connected meaning" in an all-but-obliterated text, as in *Fanshawe*, Hawthorne in *The Scarlet Letter* allows that the "curious investigator may still discern" the iconography on the stone (204). The novel closes, correlatively, with a text—the herald's code—that, while arcane and oblique for most readers, also works as a traditional form of *preserving* names, genealogies, and lineage; with the code, another artisan could re-engrave the letter. Transformed from the victim of time to the agent of the monumental, and presenting a funerary text to the curiosity of the reader rather than the writer, Hawthorne shifts the responsibility of historical memory. In the context of the novel's closing insistence on what the reader takes from the "now concluded legend" (rather than on how the writer's "version" of a legend will soon be absorbed into the general obscurity of the "traditionary"), Hawthorne relocates the letter, initially discovered as a moth-eaten rag, to an engraving on stone and thence to the "motto and brief description" that enables, in perpetuity, the artisanal reproduction of that letter. We know from "The Custom-House" that Hawthorne imagines himself recovering a story rather than, the theme of the engraver's inscription in the anonymous novel *Fanshawe*, losing one. Using heraldry to represent the letter through a language of craft—heraldic code was equally useful for emblazoning coats-of-arms on stone, textile, wood, stamps, and metal—Hawthorne acts against the "eighty years of exposure" that erase the similar legend in *Fanshawe.* That the legend becomes textual and conventional, turned backward toward heraldry rather than forward into the obscurations of time, is reinforced by a description of the scarlet letter at the beginning of the final chapter. The letter thought to have been seen on Dimmesdale's chest is described as "imprinted" there; it is recognized by the "deep print" it has left in "undesirable distinctness" in the author's mind (200). Excesses of durability constitute a familiar Hawthornian theme, materialized throughout his fictions as the vampiric hold of the past on the present. But the endurance of the scarlet letter in its printed and imprinted form also marks how assertively Hawthorne refigures his artisanal relation to letters and to language between his first and second novels. The exposure that rubs out the monument in *Fanshawe* cannot work against the tombstone in *The Scarlet Letter* precisely because the mature writer, acting again as an engraver, is much surer of his texts.

On the one hand, then, the obscure language that concludes *The Scarlet Letter* caps the decay of the embroidered letter's physical form as it becomes the novel's "mystic symbol" and its famously reassignable and variously refigured text. On the other hand, reading the tombstone against its model in *Fanshawe* suggests that Hawthorne imagined the final sentence of *The Scarlet Letter* as an assertion of artisanal security; the engraving encodes not the evanescence of letters—Hester's A and his own fiction—but their durability within a traditional language of craft that allowed coats-of-arms to be accurately reproduced.[21] Between *Fanshawe* (1828) and *The Scarlet Letter* (1850), however, Hawthorne did not just gain confidence as a writer. He also worked on both sides of modern commerce: as a measurer of coal for the Boston Custom House (1839–41), as Surveyor of the Salem Custom House (1846–49), and as one of George Ripley's corps of Arcadian farmers at Brook Farm (April–November 1841). (In *The Blithedale Romance,* the fictional rendition of his experience at Brook Farm, Hawthorne encodes his move from the city to the country as a specific abandonment of the commodity, coal, that he spent his days measuring in Boston: the novel's narrator, Miles Coverdale, contrasts the "artificial temperature" of urban coal-fires with the "cheery . . . blaze" of oak logs he finds upon arriving at the utopian commune [145, 9].) The nineteenth-century appetite for craft as a *modern* value, an idealized condition contrasted with emerging patterns of production and consumption, appears as the central subject in several well-known stories of the 1840s and, preeminently, in "The Custom-House" introduction to *The Scarlet Letter.* I want to turn in the next several pages to Hawthorne's invention of a language of craft not as a reflection of his authorial hopes (as in the rewriting of

Fanshawe) but as that language related to the conditions of commerce in his era. The double aspect of craft's transliteration in the heraldic engraver's code—concretizing at the same time as it depends on representational "obliquity"—becomes legible not only in the context of Hawthorne's ideas about his own craft but also as a register of the more general imperatives of workmanship that Hawthorne identified in the decades between the novels. Three stories of 1844 and "The Custom-House" constitute, I think, good examples of Hawthorne's complex meditations on craft's meaning as he contemplated the different economic systems represented by the Custom House and by Brook Farm.

I have already discussed one of these stories, "Rappaccini's Daughter." Interlacing the appeal of an actual object of Cellini's handiwork with misleading stories about that very appeal, "Rappaccini's Daughter" epitomizes the pattern whereby craft becomes both an icon of a restored relation with the body and a misleading, dodgy narrative. A false promise about craft's potential to incarnate, to vitalize, also appears in two other stories about workmanship that Hawthorne published in 1844: "Drowne's Wooden Image" and "The Artist of the Beautiful." The first is about a carver of nautical figureheads who crafts a particular figurehead so beautifully that it seems to the townspeople to come to life, appearing on the streets. But the disappointment occasioned by the Cellini vase (that craft's promise to enliven the body cannot hold) mirrors the disappointment occasioned by the wooden carving. For we learn in the final paragraph that the figure walking the streets is in fact the actual woman who modeled for Drowne, an elegant Portuguese visitor taken for a crafted image made animate; beauty, the story suggests, originates in living people and only secondarily in the inspired "genius" of the artisan's labor, and Drowne returns to his uninspired style of carving wooden "blockheads" once the woman sails back to her home in the Azores.[22] Craft, in "Drowne's Wooden Image," thus promises animation that it cannot deliver, a point also dramatized in "The Artist of the Beautiful." A watchmaker, Owen Warland, appears like Drowne to have joined craft and life, materializing their union in a mechanical butterfly. But in attempting to reproduce life, Owen has manifestly missed it, for he loses the woman of his dreams, Annie Hovenden, to the stolid blacksmith Robert Danforth. Owen may have "won the Beautiful into his handiwork," but Robert Danforth has the greater satisfaction, in life itself, for having the smaller creative ambition.[23] In the final scene, the infant son of Robert and Annie crushes Owen's butterfly. The icon of handiwork's incarnating potential is pulverized into miniature metal parts.

Later nineteenth-century utopian movements promoted craft as "the art that is life."[24] The three stories of 1844, written after Hawthorne's return from his own utopian experiment in manual labor at Brook Farm, instead describe craft as the art that is not life: craft fails to restore a culture of touch, to incarnate wooden carvings, or to vitalize the artisan who, like Owen Warland, lives for the "delight in beauty" that William Morris would celebrate in 1878 as the elevation of the "lesser arts."[25] The stories seem clearly enough to caution against imputing too much vitalizing force to the trades. Artisanship is either practical and unimaginative, like Robert Danforth's iron hardware or Drowne's conventional nautical figureheads, or it is visionary in its aspirations and potential to give life but deflated by the irony of the stories, like the Cellini vase, Owen Warland's butterfly, and Drowne's carving of the woman. Drawn to the elevation of labor as a fictional subject and through his own ambivalent participation in the Arcadian experiment at Brook Farm, Hawthorne was disinclined to spin abstractions about work's virtues: "What delusion can be more lamentable and mischievous," he wrote to his future wife from Brook Farm, "than to mistake the physical and material for the spiritual?"[26]

One might read Hawthorne's caution against such "delusion" as an instance of what Nicholas Bromell calls his "traditional preference" for the latter term, the spiritual, over the former terms, the physical and the material; Hawthorne's depictions of labor, Bromell posits, originate in a bias for "the mental over the bodily" (101–2).[27] The stories of the early 1840s have been read more generally as depictions of the "artist's struggles" to transform matter into higher registers of meaning (Gilmore, 53). Owen Warland's brief creative transcendence *over* his merely practical vocation, one of Hawthorne's recent biographers states, confirms "what the artist knew all along: he is different from the rest."[28] But the frustrated yearning of "Rappaccini's Daughter"—to protect a culture of touch and of the "small artisan" threatened by Rappaccini's scientific engineering—also frames Hawthorne's interest in the culture of craft as it was developing against industrial culture; the stories of 1844 involve not just the originality of the artist but the potential elevation of the trades as promoted by such enterprises as Brook Farm. To be sure, the transcendence of the material associated with the "artist's struggles" is not categorically different from the idealized values often attributed, in the nineteenth century, to manual labor. Historians and literary critics have documented how efforts to reclaim the laborer from "industrial occupations," as Charles Fourier put it, stressed the metaphysical or otherwise elevating rewards that would flow from working with one's hands.[29] Fanny Wright's Nashoba commune in rural Tennessee is an extreme but archetypal example. Slaves purchased by Wright and brought to Nashoba could buy their freedom by work and study, representing what the architects of many midcentury utopian labor communes tried to convey: that labor was the route, even the precondition, to elevation and betterment of the self. A complicated matrix of cultural values, flowing in part through the evangelical dimensions of labor advocacy and in part through wariness that the hand could become like a machine (my subject in the next chapter), tended to keep advocates of manual labor from praising manual skills as desirable or appealing in themselves. Instead, the value of handiwork appeared aspirational, oriented toward a higher condition rather than an earthly one.

Hawthorne's craft-centered stories of 1844 can be read, I think, as an interrogation of this point of view. The delusion he described to Sophia reveals the Brook Farmers as mistaken in their presumptions about labor's salvific force, and introduces a viewpoint—that manual labor has become a false idol—that we might see as Hawthorne's attempt to *protect* craft from the etherealizing, abstracting, and idealizing operations of nineteenth-century utopian ideals. Consider "Drowne's Wooden Image." There is no denying that Drowne's day-to-day labors appear uninspired and prosaic when juxtaposed with the visionary accomplishments that are the main themes of the stories; none of Drowne's customary figureheads "seem as if the wood were imbibing the ethereal essence of humanity" (310). But that apparent demerit, after all, may be one only of perspective. The presumption that craft's standard should be "ethereal essence" appears to the reader of "Drowne's Wooden Image" *as* a perspective to the degree that it is articulated so insistently by a character in the story. The painter John Singleton Copley represents the voice of art's standard, and while most readers have tended to identify Copley as an interpretive authority, he is in some ways the most wooden figure in a story of wooden figures. Copley has one theme, and states it again and again: the ideality of art and the craftsman's accession to "the very spirit of genius" (313). The cadence of the story is kept by Copley's confirmation and reconfirmation of his perception, presented by Hawthorne in most cases as an inference: what "the painter fancied" (311) and "could not help imagining" (314) seems to "imply a genius" previously unknown in Drowne (311). Copley, moreover, is defined by acts of watching, glancing, and "look[ing] earnestly" at the woodcarver (314). He stands for the voyeuristic qualities by which Drowne's craft seems to be vitalized for the townspeople: "Do you see it? Do you see it?" one of them cries. "Drowne's wooden image has come to life!" (316). What I have been describing as Hawthorne's unique sensitivity to the appetite for legends of craftsmanship in the nineteenth century appears in "Drowne's Wooden Image" as the circulating account of the woodcarver's transcendence: "The narrative," we are told, "had formed itself into one of the most singular legends that are yet to be met with in the traditionary chimney-corners of the New England metropolis, where old men and women sit dreaming of the past, and wag their heads at the dreamers of the present and the future" (315).

The old men and women remember the story of Drowne as a legend of craft uplifted. The "dreamers of the present and the future" on the same topic (of craft uplifted) suggest the Brook Farmers or, more generally, a metropolitan public whose appetite for the handmade and interest in artisanship grew throughout the nineteenth century. But the story in fact resists the very idealization of workmanship that it features as a projection, a legend, and an inference. For when the carving proves to have been done from life, channeling the loveliness of a living Portuguese woman, the putatively visionary nature of Drowne's workmanship settles back toward his practical skills of mimicry; those skills may have been put to use with more passion than ever before, but they are not different in kind from the "imitation of the human figure" for which Drowne has always been celebrated (307). Read in this way, "Drowne's Wooden Image" appears to be about the ideality *imputed* to craft rather than the struggle of the creator to emerge from the limitations of his everyday vocation. Copley's ceaseless moralizing forces the reader to consider how the legend of the craft-made-flesh depends on idealizing projections that the story's denouement—revealing the woman who stood as the model—calls into question.

None of this is to say that Hawthorne does not distinguish between the tradesman and the imaginative artist. The visionary aspects of craft are deflated in the story—just as they are in *The Blithedale Romance*, when Miles Coverdale finds that work is so tiring that "the clods of earth, which we so constantly belabored and turned over and over, were never etherealized into thought. Our thoughts, on the contrary, were fast becoming cloddish." (66). But what I mean to suggest, additionally, is that "Drowne's Wooden Image" figures in Hawthorne's corpus as another story about the story of craft. Thus, while set in colonial-era Boston, it is as much about the "dreamers of the present" and the projected virtues of craft in the nineteenth century; the "celebrity" of the oft-retold legend about how a tradesman gave life to a carving recalls the story about craft's incarnating potential that Baglioni tells Giovanni in "Rappaccini's Daughter." When Hawthorne asserts that craft does not reinvigorate touch, incarnate wooden carvings, or replace the human vitality represented by Owen Warland's lost fiancée, he not only registers his ambivalence about the potential of creativity and his awareness of the "artist's struggle" but also satirizes the promise of craft—naming it, in effect, as a fiction of the Baglionis or Copleys of the world. Compare, in "The Artist of the Beautiful," Owen Warland's desire to vitalize and incarnate a crafts object with Robert Danforth's actually incarnate craft, his bodily labor of "main strength" (449). For Owen, the idea of bringing a craft to life is founded in legend and derived from texts. He speaks "at wearisome length" about "marvels of mechanism that he had read about in books." His oldest example of such a mechanism is itself a speaking object; Owen's references to the "Man of Brass, constructed by Albertus Magnus, and the Brazen Head of Friar Bacon" refer to the same legendary marvel, a brass head said to answer any question put to it. Robert Greene's sixteenth-century *Friar Bacon and Friar Bungay* correlates the talking head with the echoing nature of myth itself: "I tell thee, Bacon," says an Oxford scholar, "Oxford makes report, / Nay, England, and the court of Henry says, / Th'art making of a brazen head by art / Which shall unfold strange doubts and aphorisms, / And read a lecture in philosophy."[30] The double voice of Bacon's brazen head, a talking head that is much talked about, epitomizes the structure of Owen Warland's artisanal aspirations. A reader and a "babbler," he goes on to cite stories of automata, of a mechanical duck, and of an insect of steel and springs that—quite like Owen himself—"buzzed about the ear" (465).

Robert Danforth's prosaic workmanship, by contrast, is described not as chatter about how craft gives life but as his own "strong voice" (452). He speaks "in such a hearty volume of tone that it made the artist shrink," recasting Owen's inherited and ventriloquized ideas about legendary incarnations into the stronger acoustic reverberations of the present (449). And if the projected nature of vitalization through craft links the three stories I have been discussing—incarnation, that is, appears as the imputed or presumed virtue of Drowne's wooden image, of the Cellini vase, and of Owen's labors—Robert Danforth's workshop unites body and voice not as project but as fact. Annie and her father, a watchmaker who was Owen's master during his apprenticeship, pass by the blacksmith's open door:

> Within was seen the forge, now blazing up, and illuminating the high and dusky roof, and now confining its luster to a narrow precinct of the coal-strewn floor, according as the breath of the bellows was puffed forth, or again inhaled into its vast leathern lungs. . . . Anon [Danforth] drew a white-hot bar of iron from the coals, laid it upon the anvil, uplifted his arm of might, and was soon enveloped in the myriads of sparks which the strokes of his hammer scattered into the surrounding gloom.
>
> "Now, that is a pleasant sight," said the old watchmaker. "I know what it is to work in gold, but give me the worker in iron, after all is said and done. He spends his labor upon a reality. What say you, daughter Annie?"

"Pray don't speak so loud, father," whispered Annie. "Robert Danforth will hear you."

"And what if he should hear me?" said Peter Hovenden. "I say again, it is a good and a wholesome thing to depend upon main strength and reality." (448–49)

Hawthorne synthesizes the worker, the workshop, and the voice of work in this passage. Annie and her father have just come from Owen's shop, where Annie's request for silence—"Hush, father! He hears you"—had been heeded rather than, as on Robert Danforth's stoop, rejected; the pair passes between the two locations "without further conversation" (448). But in refusing to accede to the request when confronted with the image of the blacksmith's muscular toil, Peter Hovenden draws the lesson of the forge. The workshop appears as an echo chamber and an amplifier of an actual, rather than a legendary, voice. Peter Hovenden will "say again" what he thinks about the blacksmith's "reality." Robert Danforth actually *does* overhear the man and his daughter on his threshold (" 'Well said, uncle Hovenden!' shouted Robert Danforth"). And the workman's voice makes "the roof reecho," much as the sparks of his hammer illumine the darkness (449). The blacksmith's workshop appears as a living organism, inhaling and exhaling "the breath of the bellows" and filled with words. The "leathern lungs" of the forge and the reverberations of Danforth's booming voice through the story (his words fill Owen's shop "as with the sound of a bass-viol" [452]) render body, labor, and voice as the triple grounds of the craftsman's physical immediacy.

In Robert Danforth, then, Hawthorne imagines an alternative to the fantasies of incarnated workmanship featured in all three stories of 1844; the blacksmith's voice comes from the strength of his craftsman's body rather than from the projections of embodiment represented by Copley, by Baglioni, and by the legend of the brazen head. Interpreting the stories as a group of works engaged with the utopian stories told about craft—preeminently, for Hawthorne, by the Brook Farmers—both situates Hawthorne's thinking about workmanship in its mid nineteenth-century context and suggests the dual imperatives that I have traced in the final paragraph of *The Scarlet Letter.* On the one hand, Hawthorne is evidently attracted to the transformative, visionary labors he associates with Drowne, with Owen Warland, and with Hester Prynne. Those labors differ from the everyday work that, in Hawthorne's corpus, often appears conventional and embedded in the strictures of time; his tradesmen are often gravestone engravers, watchmakers, or carpenters who build houses freighted with the ancient wrongs of the laboring classes. Their work is prematurely old, like the oaken door of the prison built on "virgin soil" but "already marked with weather stains" and looking "more antique than anything else in the new world" (*The Scarlet Letter*, 39), or like the house in which the "freshly plastered walls" were "infect[ed] . . . early with the scent of an old and melancholy house" (*The House of the Seven Gables*, 9). In an artisanal world of "unimaginative sagacity," wherein engravers conceive of "very little, either of prose or poetry, which had not, at one time or other, been inscribed on slate or marble," craft appears a source of meaning partly to the degree that—like the butterfly, Drowne's carving, or Hester's fanciful letter—it can be reinvigorated, awakened, and transformed.[31]

On the other hand, however, Hawthorne's fiction reveals his acute awareness of how the reinvention of workmanship and the reincarnation of the workman's body were themselves becoming conventions. The popularization of manual labor in Hawthorne's era flowed through an array of literary outlets, including the Lyceum speakers' circuit, texts likes Cellini's, the lecture halls associated with the new Mechanics Associations, and utopian experiments undertaken by bookish people in ventures like Brook Farm and Fruitlands. Hawthorne reacted to these developments, in part, by presenting workmanship's incarnating potential as a specifically vocal or literary projection. Robert Danforth may appear as one of Hawthorne's unimaginative laborers, but the situation of his voice in his corporeal body also distinguishes him from the failed promises of artisanal incarnation that define the stories published in 1844. The conundrum for craft thus revealed in literary terms—that it appears, paradoxically, both in need of "artistic" spiritualization and as a stay against excesses of abstraction or projection—defines the end of *The Scarlet Letter*. The gravestone engraving, I have suggested, not only marks the value reassigned to physical objects through craft (an imperative emblematized by Hester's fanciful embroidering of the letter and by the ambiguities of the gravestone's "legend") but also establishes the durability embedded in traditional languages of artisanal reproducibility (an imperative encoded as the heraldic phrase and as Hawthorne's different approach to imagery he had tested in *Fanshawe*). As an idea circulating in public discourse, craft is celebrated by characters like Copley and translated onto the page by the author—but its purposes, in the sphere of the legendary, are as uncertain for Hawthorne as for the canonizers of Cellini's *Life*. The promises of vitality, fancy, and improvisation that can be achieved by the artisan's inventiveness coexist with the writer's equal obligation to the standards of solidity, durability, and permanence that must be represented by the artisan's devotions.

A WIG OF "MAJESTIC FRIZZLE": CRAFT IN THE CUSTOM HOUSE

In the context of the reading I have proposed here—that Hawthorne's fiction responds to a nineteenth-century culture of craft that was vocally celebrating workmanship—his impulse to spiritualize and to vitalize labor appears shot through with his own misgivings. For Hawthorne recognizes the conventional nature of the impulse. Voices promising, narrating, or even babbling about the transcendence of craft over the merely material—Baglioni's, Copley's, Owen's, the mythic articulations of the brazen head, the legends surrounding Hester Prynne's multiply reinterpreted and ultimately obscure token—echo throughout the fiction. But Hawthorne opposes public accounts of workmanship's transcendence by presenting it as a misinterpretation ("Rappaccini's Daughter," "Drowne's Wooden Image") or an obsession ("The Artist of the Beautiful")—and he experiments with a language of craft, the blacksmith's and the herald's, that by contrast operates to stabilize and cement craft's materiality.

If the gravestone at the end of *The Scarlet Letter* presents one aspect of old workmanship as encountered in the nineteenth century (for it is on that surface that the "curious investigator" may "still discern" and thereby study an artisanal form of the letter), "The Custom-House" offers the novel's other explicit consideration of the letter in the context of Hawthorne's own era. The introductory sketch draws out the complicated status of the scarlet letter as an artisanal object and, more specifically, reveals Hawthorne's preoccupation with the difficulties inherent in the very idea of craft under nineteenth-century pressures. For when the narrator discovers the scarlet letter tucked into an envelope of old documents in a dusty corner, his reaction exposes and explains, more pointedly than anywhere in Hawthorne's corpus, the problematic situation of craft as it became an industrial-era ideal. Consider first how pointedly the narrator's initial reaction to the letter differs from the opening characterization of craft in the novel itself. Boston's "wooden jail," "heavily timbered" prison door, and "congregated sepulchres" appear in the first paragraph of *The Scarlet Letter* as prematurely aged constructions, anticipating *The House of the Seven Gables* by revealing the oppressively long-standing workmanship of the colonial era (39). But the old relics discovered by the narrator in the Custom House impress him as items not to be shunned but to be preserved, saved, and protected. He desires to ensure the longevity of the scarlet letter and its accompanying documents by depositing them with the Essex Historical Society—and the artifacts appear compelling, not oppressive, precisely on the grounds of their physical durability. The envelope, the narrator notices, was made with "more substantial materials than at present." "Carefully done up," its "rigid folds" require not so much unfolding as "unbending" (25). The quality of the scarlet letter is equally evident, even if time and a moth have done their work. It is perfectly symmetrical, three and a quarter inches down each side by the Surveyor's measurement. It reveals "wonderful skill of needlework," which the narrator tries to trace by "picking out the threads" and consulting "ladies conversant with such mysteries" (27). He fails, for the technique, like the better materials of the seventeenth century, has been lost to an era represented by its "political vicissitude," "rusty little schooners," "decaying trade," and general air of fragility (12, 7).

The narrator's first realization, in other words, is that they don't make it like they used to. Craft in "The Custom-House" first appears as a testament to an era of better and more durable goods, an era when—as compared to nineteenth-century manufacture—physical resilience marks the higher quality of goods in traditional handicrafts. The Surveyor himself, devoting his labors to ledger books, feels alienated from "earth and sky," bereft of physical nature and beset by a "wretched numbness" (22). The letter, however, has a famously bodily force, burning the narrator's breast like a "red-hot iron" when he holds it to his chest (27). In the context of the letter's story, of course, its burning aspect marks its history of sin and sensuality. But in the context of the Surveyor's numb traverse through the world of modern commerce, the longevity of the crafts object takes on an aspect unlike the one it suggests when Hawthorne is thinking about the legacy of the witch trials and of Puritanism; if the prison door appears in the novel itself as a sad testament to history's reign even over "virgin soil," that same quality appears in the introduction to the novel as a compelling testament to the imperishable quality of preindustrial things (39). Imperishability is vividly represented by the story told about the exhumation of the narrator's predecessor, Surveyor Pue. His corpse, after eighty years, is entirely decayed. But his wig comes up in "very satisfactory preservation," remaining plump with "majestic frizzle" (26). The narrator recurs to the image of the "immortal wig" twice more in the sketch, first reminding us that it "was buried with him, but did not perish in the grave," and then imagining the ghost of Surveyor Pue urging him to write the novel while "emphatically nodding the head that looked so imposing within its memorable wig" (28–29). The wig appears memorable, as an element of Pue's ghostly return, not by an imaginative projection of the narrator's but because he knows, from the exhumation, that it is indestructible. Taken together, the rigid folds of the envelope, the accuracy of the long-lost techniques of needlework, and the head nodding its still-frizzled wig hint that the narrator's return to fiction may produce novels as long-lasting, as well-crafted, as the things that—in the opening sketch—prompt his literary exertions; the authorial confidence that distinguishes the gravestone engraving in *The Scarlet Letter* from that in *Fanshawe* appears as an explicit statement of "The Custom-House." The writer presents his duty, in translating the notes of Surveyor Pue into *The Scarlet Letter*, as the memorialization of a culture of craft that he experiences as more durable, more substantial, and more bodily than that of his own age.

This way of thinking about the influence of Pue (or, more properly, of Pue's objects) may deepen our understanding of why Hawthorne would set the crucial scene when he discovers the scarlet letter in the large room where "the brick-work and naked rafters have never been covered with paneling and plaster" (24). The room, we are told, remains unfinished because the Custom House was built to accommodate a more vigorous trade than the port of Salem provided. Decayed trade and decayed bodies are the twin principles of the commercial environment that Hawthorne presents. The narrator's body is numb, Pue's simply gone, and those of the officers in the Custom House mostly enervated. In the case of the one sturdy Inspector, his singular obsession with good dinners means that very little else reaches him; all events pass over him "with as little permanent effect as the passing breeze," making the Inspector "so shallow, so delusive, and so impalpable" as to be "an absolute nonentity" (16–17). Framed by the evaporative environment of the Custom House, the story's artisanal burden—predicated on hints about an era of better and more lasting goods—thus appears as one way to save the scarlet letter from the equally partial, incomplete labors of the room in which it is found. If the letter and the story have languished in a room that "remains unfinished to this day," awaiting completion by the "carpenter and the mason," the writer's work is inspired by the durability of the crafts he discovers and that appear to him, through the ghost's adjurations, as the "memorable" aspects of a prior culture experienced in specifically physical terms (24). Bringing the Letter "before the public" (29) and acting "as editor, or very little more" (6), he takes responsibility for one element of what has been left unfinished in the Custom House; drawing a line of equivalence between himself and the carpenter or the mason, the writer gives his predecessor's sketch of Hester's story, left in a corner of the unfinished room, the scope that is "rightfully its due" (29). At the other end of the text, the final paragraph offers the heraldic code as a motto for the "now concluded legend." Taking the "now" to refer all the way back to the genesis of the story, the writer, acting as a craftsman, completes what had been left undone.

Understood in the context of the surveyor's numbingly bureaucratic labor, then, artisanal and authorial crafts accord substantiality, durability, and the satisfactions of finishing something, of telos. Hawthorne presents such values as manifestly threatened, and not only by the conditions of enervation evident in the Custom House: the fact that the stitchery of the scarlet letter cannot be identified reveals how the better material culture of the past has been lost to the nineteenth century. And yet the mystery of the stitch *also*, simultaneously, stands for the nature of creative labor, for Hester Prynne's incomparable genius, and for the "not altogether physical" dimensions of the "mystic symbol" itself (27). Craft's mandate reverses and reverses again depending on whether it is understood from the perspective of the repressive structures of history and the "unimaginative sagacity" of the trades (in which case artisanship's higher potential lies in subjectivity, contingency, and the inimitable aspect of handmade objects) or from the perspective of nineteenth-century trade and manufacture (in which case artisanship signifies objectivity, durability, completion, and the longevity accorded to a prior material culture). Creative and imaginative, craft offers relief from an excessively materialist culture, a trajectory symbolized by the obscure provenance of the scarlet letter; tactile and enduring, craft offers relief from the unreal labor of the Custom House, a trajectory symbolized by the lost stitch of the past and the "more substantial materials than at present."

The ghastly image of a body decayed around a perfectly preserved wig, however, also epitomizes an even deeper quandary: that craft, represented by the practical durability of its objects, runs the risk of reifying labor, of grounding its meaning in its inanimate artifacts. For Hawthorne structures the entire scene of the exhumation around the possibility that the workmanship of the past, while a compelling alternative to the vacuous work of the Custom House, has also become another kind of history whose relics and remnants are invested with an idealized presence and a romanticized tactility. Surveyor Pue's body has rotted behind an object that merely *represents* or mimics corporeal life, the wig; the contents of the coffin in that sense exactly recall the point that Hawthorne makes through the Cellini vase in "Rappaccini's Daughter," the carving in "Drowne's Wooden Image," and the butterfly in "The Artist of the Beautiful," all of which suggest the falseness of using well-made things to enliven bodies or to signify actual biology. More explicitly, the narrator in "The Custom-House" draws out the idealized quality of crafted objects, the theme of the earlier stories, by contextualizing the exhumation as an event he reads about "in a newspaper of recent times, [providing] an account of the digging up of his remains in the little graveyard of St. Peters Church, during the renewal of that edifice" (26). Jonathan Pue's exhumation in fact occurred in 1833, when the original wooden church was taken down and a new stone structure raised; in June of that year, the *Salem Observer* recorded that the corpse's "wig was in a good state of preservation and his worsted sash was not entirely decayed."[32] But if Hawthorne was obviously thinking about the article in the *Observer* when he described the contents of the coffin, the references to a "newspaper of recent times" and to the "renewal" of the church also suggest the prominence of St. Peter's in the Salem news in 1845–46, just as Hawthorne was beginning his tenure at the Custom House; in those years, the prominent Gothic Revival architect Richard Upjohn added a chancel and vestry to the church.[33] In locating the church's "renewal" in recent history, the narrator thus conflates the two restorations. The first, in 1833, when Jonathan Pue was in fact exhumed, would be better described as a razing than a renewal, and in any case occurred sixteen years before the year in which "The Custom-House" is set. The second, in 1845–46, fits better with the language and chronology of the text but did not, in fact, unearth Hawthorne's predecessor.

The interest of these restorations, as conflated into an event of "recent times," concerns the nineteenth-century fad for Gothic renovation and reproduction. As popularized by such architects as Upjohn and Andrew Jackson Downing—both of whom wrote books on rural architecture—Gothic style energized crafts revivalism. Ruskin famously theorizes the correlations of workmanship and the high Gothic in the second volume of *The Stones of Venice* (1853), but the mainstream expression of the style in the United State stressed its suitability for vernacular buildings. Wooden cottages with peaked gables, fretwork, and, often, board-and-batten sheathing defined what has come to be known as Carpenter Gothic, so-called because its details could be managed by the primary builder rather than by specialist carvers. In stone, local churches like St. Peter's reveal a similar predilection. Rather than elaborate carving, simpler details—the few peaked windows, crude crenellations, and square towers—expressed the popularity of the Gothic Revival as it flowed through the countryside and the small town. Architects like Downing and Upjohn played into the nostalgic enthusiasm for vernacular, workmanlike buildings by popularizing a period style suited to the "rural taste of [the] country."[34]

Placing the exhumation of Pue in the context of the revivification of St. Peter's and stressing its currency as a recent event, Hawthorne again hints at the faddishness of the impulse that, I have argued, he takes up as his authorial charge in "The Custom-House": to build well and completely, memorializing an earlier culture of construction represented by the high quality of the scarlet letter and of the wig. The mania for such restoration became so widespread, on both sides of the Atlantic, that William Morris in 1877 formed the Society for the Protection of Ancient Buildings to lobby for architectural decay. Morris held that the era's enthusiasm for "renewals," to use Hawthorne's word, threatened to transform artisans into mere imitators or repairmen (a position into which Hawthorne, concluding the unfinished work of the Custom House, projects himself). For Morris, who located the goals of the craft movement in the elevation of the "lesser arts," an environment of creative originality rather than stylistic mimicry would be better accomplished by protecting old buildings—particularly churches, the archetypal sites of renovation—*from* renovation. What worried Morris, that craft was becoming no more than popular style, also worried T. J. Cobden-Sanderson, a London bookbinder who titled the Arts and Crafts Movement in 1888: Cobden-Sanderson urged his colleagues to exhibit less frequently, arguing that too much publicity would identify the goals of the movement with fine objects rather than with the imaginative liberation of the trades.[35] The correlation between Hawthorne's fiction and these ideas is my major subject in the first section of the next chapter. For now, it is sufficient to say that the problem for handicraft addressed by Morris and Cobden-Sanderson is the problem that Hawthorne tackled in the stories of the 1844, and the problem that informs the context of Pue's exhumation: that the iconicity of crafted objects and the popularity of craft as a style had outstripped the actual appeal of practical, everyday trades. "The Custom-House" idealizes the author's artisanal ability to build for all time, a capacity that the final sentence of the novel asserts and epitomizes. But Hawthorne characteristically doubts the originality of his perspective and purpose, locating his ideas about a better era of craftsmanship in the context of the fad for Carpenter's Gothic. At the same time as Surveyor Pue's remnants represent an era when things were better made, the facts of their discovery—a person decayed around his magnificent wig, a church restoration in a fashionable period style—also intimate, as do the 1844 stories, the fetishization of artisanal things that Hawthorne perceived in efforts at "renewal" through traditional workmanship, its artifacts, and its styles.

I mean to have suggested that the modern contexts of *The Scarlet Letter*, introduced in "The Custom-House" and returning when the reader is invited to study the old gravestone of Hester Prynne and Arthur Dimmesdale, hold craft to a complex and not entirely compatible set of standards. Hester's scarlet letter, the archetypal artifact of Hawthornian Romance, spiritualizes matter and calls attention through its obscurities to the subjectivity of craft that Morris represented as the tradesman's mandate to "come up" to the creative standards of art and imagination; its mysterious provenance distinguishes the letter, as an emblem of labor's capacity to reinvent, both from faddish reproduction and from what Hawthorne saw as the brutish practicality inherent in the trades.[36] But eternally frizzy wigs, still rigidly folded envelopes of uniquely substantial materials, and Hester's antique stitchery also serve as examples of what Walter Benjamin calls the "substantive duration" of handmade things.[37] As alternatives to the vaporous life of the Custom House, these objects excite the author to promise the ghostly form of Surveyor Pue (a correlative of his own ghostly existence) that he too will produce something—*The Scarlet Letter*—as "memorable" and as durable, as fixed and as substantial, as the material culture of the bygone age. Hawthorne's own literary labors, which he describes in "The Custom-House" as a craft of *concluding* what has already been begun, thus suggest not just the familiar practice of Romance—whereby things "seem to lose their actual substance" (30)—but also the reverse case: how creative objects, including the novel as "now concluded" and the scarlet letter as durably encoded as an engraver's language, endure. When Hawthorne looks at craft from the point of view not of Brook Farm but of the Custom House, the false promises that attend narrative projections about workmanship and its incarnating potential are tempered by his desire to find letters as durable as the ones he finds (and, acting as Pue's heir, completes) in the otherwise unfinished upstairs room. The language of labor represents for Hawthorne both a misleading fiction and a medium through which the substantive duration of things can be assured.

CRAFT'S EPITAPHS

The interlacing of reinvention and durability, of what vanishes and what remains, may help us understand why graves or gravestones appear as focal points for Hawthorne's meditations on craft—as they do, in the preceding analysis, in *Fanshawe*, *The Scarlet Letter*, and "The Custom-House." The funerary aspects of Hawthorne's interrogation of workmanship are epitomized by a tale that is his most direct interrogation of the artisan's labor: "Chippings with a Chisel," originally published in 1838 and collected in the second volume of *Twice-Told Tales* (1842). I have already suggested that Hawthorne often correlated fiction and engraving, and that the representation of the gravestone of Hester Prynne draws on a language of workmanship to accord longevity to the scarlet letter (and to *The Scarlet Letter*)—even as the gravestone's indistinct surface epitomizes the "desolidifying" impulse identified by Buell as central to the novel's designs (81). But a marked grave, or an exhumed coffin in which only a perfectly preserved wig remains, also figure as liminal registers of the spirit and the earthly, of mutability and memory. Liminal places, to be sure, define the Hawthornian landscape, physically as well as thematically. But like "The Custom-House," "Chippings with a Chisel" is important because it traces the dialectic of spiritualization and monumentality directly to the situation of craft's texts under the pressures of nineteenth-century commerce.

Those pressures operate over the course of the story to redefine the narrator's original superciliousness about the conventionality of the work produced by a gravestone engraver. At the outset, the narrator, visiting Martha's Vineyard, describes a procession of visitors to the engraver's workshop. A woman arrives to commission a monument for her first lover, killed forty years previously on a whaling voyage; she desires a stone carved with "marine plants, intertwined with twisted sea-shells, such as were probably wavering over the lover's skeleton, or strewn around it in the far depths of the pacific." What she gets is a rose "hanging its head from a broken stem"—the artisan's usual icon of bereavement, one of the "standing emblem[s]" that he carves again and again (411). Another woman comes in with her daughter to arrange a gravestone for the daughter's twin, just deceased. While they are in the workshop, the narrator points out to the engraver after they leave, "at least a dozen simple and natural expressions [fell] from the lips of both mother and daughter. One of these would have formed an inscription equally original and appropriate." What the engraver has sold them, however, is "an ordinary verse of ill-matched rhymes, which had already been inscribed upon innumerable tombstones" (414). The characterization of the engraver by the conventionality of his texts explains Hawthorne's account of his genealogy. A "descendant of the old Puritan family of Wigglesworth" (408), he is obviously related to Michael Wigglesworth, the poet whose *The Day of Doom* (1662) might be described as an extended monument of conventional versifying about death and judgment. Presenting Christ's "strict and straight account / Of all things done under the Sun," the popular poem was "taught our fathers with their Catechisms," wrote Francis Jenks in 1828; "hawked about the country printed on sheets like common ballads," *The Day of Doom* reflects the didactic motifs and familiar sentiments carved by the Mr. Wigglesworth of Hawthorne's invention.[38]

But the story is not set in the seventeenth century of Michael Wigglesworth, and that fact ultimately forces the narrator to reevaluate the "triteness of monumental verses" (414). For the framing of the story concerns modern trade, and in that context, as in "The Custom-House," diachronic continuity, time-proven workmanship, and the character of Mr. Wigglesworth take on a different aspect. Gravestones, the narrator explains in the first paragraph, "have generally been an article of imported merchandise" (407). Even the ubiquitous death's-heads and hourglasses of older funerary, he imagines, "must have been quite beyond the colonial skill of the day, and were probably carved in London, and brought across the ocean" (408). As commodities, then, gravestones typify "the daily novelty, and revolving bustle of the world" rather than security, rest, and monumentality. Even Mr. Wigglesworth circulates to some degree in the realm of modern commerce. He is himself only a visitor to the island and indeed a kind of speculator, hoping to "transmute slate and marble into silver and gold to the amount of at least a thousand dollars" (407). The line of equivalencies and transformations here—from craft to specie to dollars—suggests his implication in an exchange economy, revealing the story's topicality in an age when the relation of gold or silver to dollars defined the national economic debate.

Against the trade in gravestones and the "daily novelty" of modern commerce, Wigglesworth's lack of artisanal imagination turns out to offer stability and to suit the environment to which he takes his trade. Sparsely populated, Martha's Vineyard and Nantucket prove to be the ideal context for the "few months of his sojourn": a resident tombstone engraver would find a "dearth of business," but that same fact—the islands' removal—reflects the "simple and primitive spirit" whereby the dead enjoy a "longer and dearer remembrance" than on the mainland (407). The forty years between the death of the sailor on the whaling voyage and the commission of the monument by his lover suggests the nature of memory on the islands. The narrator ultimately turns that observation to Wigglesworth's duplicative craft: his claim that the comfort of tradition is always preferable to "any new-fangled" devices of bereavement eventually seems to the narrator, observing the interactions between the artisan and his clients, to make the "epitaph anew." Thus, what seems a formulaic artisanal language can also be seen, like the heraldic code in *The Scarlet Letter*, to ensure the eternal relevance and to encode the substantiality of the craft (414). The sketch ends ambiguously: the narrator proclaims his doubts about the desire to monumentalize the earthly life ("our thoughts should soar upward with the butterfly, not linger with the exuviae that confined him") but finally admits that he has only "gained perplexity" on the question of Wigglesworth's ability to comfort the bereaved (418).

The narrator's confusion is founded on the dilemma I have tried to draw out elsewhere in this chapter. Watching the artisan carve his letters, the narrator feels that the engraver's conventional exercise of his skill is an impersonal, coldly materialistic language of artisanship. Wigglesworth's epitaphs, in this view, simply reproduce sentiments in circulation since his ancestor Michael Wigglesworth also aphorized about death. By the end, however, the narrator also feels that such conventionality offers accessibility and diachronic meaning, a point made significant by the vicissitudes of commercial life described in the opening paragraph. This, I have suggested in reading "The Custom-House," is the double bind of craft in the nineteenth-century market. To be different from iterated or merely traditional modes of production (a pressing anxiety in the age of machines), craft must appear subjective and new; that standard explains the narrator's withering attitude toward Wigglesworth's traditionalism, as it also explains Hawthorne's regard for the inimitability of Hester Prynne's stitches. But to represent traditional quality (a virtue also ascribed to workmanship in the nineteenth century), craft must be conventional and reproducible; that standard, struck against a world in which most gravestones circulate in a global market, describes the narrator's regard for Wigglesworth's dependence on the traditional, local, and insular.

Such shifting imperatives characterize Hawthorne's language of workmanship, whether that language is represented by Mr. Wigglesworth's carved letters, Hester Prynne's embroidered one, or *The Scarlet Letter* itself. The major point of this chapter is simply this: that Hawthorne, his own perplexities mirrored by those of the narrator in "Chippings with a Chisel," desires to ground craft and its texts in durability, singularity, and centripetal relations with objects even as he recognizes the forces (opposed to the dead world of the custom house or to the brutish reproduction of traditional practices) that draw craft toward mutability and embed its narrative interest in the sense of possibility it offers. At times, to be sure, Hawthorne can be downright sarcastic about the story of craft that, in the era of Brook Farm and other utopian projects, he clearly saw as misleading. The inability of Cellini, Drowne, or Owen to fashion something expressive or restorative of the true vitality of biological life, I have argued, might be read less as a critique of manual labor's limitations than as a critique of the false promises about craft's incarnating potential peddled in written, read, and oral forms. The triptych of stories published in 1844 establishes one of Hawthorne's subjects as the specifically narrative dimensions of his era's emerging culture of craft. Projecting a more vital culture through the artisan's touch, these echoing and reverberating narratives of workmanship promise embodiment that they cannot deliver—and in that sense, they appear part and parcel of a ghostly, insubstantial culture of modernity that leaves the Custom House surveyor "numb," that characterizes the depersonalizing anonymity of the modern trade in gravestones, and that lies behind Mr. Wigglesworth's speculative, dematerializing impulse to "transmute slate and marble" into paper money.

In other ways, however, Hawthorne tests a language of workmanship that does offer durability and stability. The story of Hester and the scarlet letter reaches the modern era wrapped in rigidly folded envelopes made like nothing is made anymore. The surveyor-author correlates his work of completion and conclusion with the labor of the imagined carpenter and mason who would panel and plaster the attic-room tight. The herald's code serves, in the setting in which Hawthorne presents it—both as a rewriting of *Fanshawe* and a stay against the weather that has all but erased the original engraving—as a text for refreshing or re-engraving the letter. The conventional letters of Mr. Wigglesworth's carved epitaphs come to seem, once the narrator readjusts his perspective, not as falsely conventional but as texts authorized by history and crafted for continuity. None of these instances of literary solidification is unambiguous for a writer who imagined his own labor as building "castles in the air."[39] The gravestone of Hester Prynne and Arthur Dimmesdale may be pictured through a heraldic text that ensures the reproducibility of the engraving against time. But the same text epitomizes the transliterating arc of Romance, expanding the letter into multiple forms *over* time; the gravestone in *The Scarlet Letter*, said to "perplex" the reader, mirrors the "perplexity" of the double standards revealed in Wigglesworth's gravestone texts. Hawthorne, all of this is to say, absorbed and tested the various standards of the print culture of workmanship that his era began to produce—and that later decades would drive into a dizzying array of craft-centered periodicals, lexicons, advertisements, catalogs, how-to books, and style guides.

Consider, as a final instance of Hawthorne's insistence on the nineteenth-century imperatives informing a language of craft, how the last words of *The Scarlet Letter* return the novel to the present tense of "The Custom-House." The gravestone, Hawthorne writes, "bore a device, a herald's wording of which might serve for a motto and brief description of our now concluded legend; so somber is it, and relieved only by one ever-glowing point of light gloomier than the shadow—'On a Field, Sable, the Letter A, Gules.' " It is unclear whether "somber" refers to the gravestone, the device, the legend, or the motto. But all of those possibilities are in one way or another represented by the "wording" that comes after the dash, and the temporal jump—from the device that the tombstone "bore" to the description of how somber the effect "is"—locates the interest of those final words in the era in which the novel was composed rather than in the era in which the novel is set. The grammatical hint here signals the point that I have argued in the preceding pages: that only in the later era—Hawthorne's own—do craft's words, understood as the stonecutter's as well as the herald's, the author's as well as the artisan's, become legible.

CHAPTER 3
THE NATURE OF GOTHIC

Artisanship, Intuition, and the Representation of Expertise

SKILL'S STICKING POINTS

This chapter shifts the focal points of *Talking Shop* in several ways. It considers the work of nineteenth-century artisans and tradespeople as well as the output of writers. It analyzes crafted artifacts as well as texts. Most important, it turns to closer questions about *how* skill might be made legible in the furnishings market, describing specific aesthetic patterns and theories about the translatability of certain styles rather than—my subject in the previous two chapters—the varied imperatives negotiated within a print culture of workmanship.

I return to Hawthorne, in the initial section of this chapter, to locate his interest in the discourses of craft in a new context. Focusing on broad questions of genre, I have argued that Hawthorne's early fiction is driven by the author's meditations on craft as a textual medium. The interpretation of *The House of the Seven Gables* that opens my concerns here—and that introduces the dynamics of craft's marketability traced in the rest of this book—has to do more narrowly with the emergence of a specific style, the Gothic, as an initial cultural form through which handicrafts skills were thought to be most describable. Taken together, the two preceding chapters might be said to explore tactics that were essentially compensatory: the authors I have examined hinted that craft's narratives, despite representing labor in an immaterial medium, might nonetheless constitute a viable sphere for revivifying practical labor, reinvigorating traditional workmanship, and defending a relation with real things. This chapter and the next instead explore tactics that were explicitly proactive: the figures I examine transformed the very definition of skill to reflect the terms of the market's demand for craft as a recognizable style and a subject animated by its depiction.

Skill, to repeat a point that structures much of *Talking Shop*, appears poorly translatable or transferable in the Platonic tradition describing its virtuousness as its telos. Vitruvius's *De Architectura* is typical: Vitruvius lodges the merit of craft in the artisan's ability to realize an intention established before the work begins. The practice of making *(fabrica)* is the "continued and expert practice of skill by the hands" according to the mandates of the design *(propositus)*; the principles of the design, in turn, should be clearly visible in the final product.[1] Vitruvius inextricably ties outcomes to their initiating purposes by representing the two concepts as grammatical inverses of one another. Form appears as *quod significat*, that which signifies, and purpose as *quod significatur*, that which is signified (3). Intent is thus bound to result, plan to product: the two concepts are complementary sides of the same process, indeed of the same word. Skill, in this model, is the essential agent of craft, for it ensures the continuity of beginnings and ends. Peter Dormer, one of craft's most important recent theorists, depends on just this aspect of skill when confessing his own failure to meet the standard of "honest work." That failure is accidental: trying to mold a clay sculpture of a man and a cat, Dormer ends up sculpting a woman whose long overcoat provides the structural stability he could not achieve in the projected model. Shifting goals in the middle of making something, of course, is commonplace. But it is also, Dormer claims, antithetical to the purest and most honest application of crafts knowledge. In Dormer's essentially Vitruvian model, craft loses definition at the limits of skill. Artisans "work strenuously to clarify their goals and seek out rules . . . that will keep them to the sticking point."[2]

The Gothic idioms of nineteenth-century efforts to revive workmanship, however, suggest a less stable relationship between craft and skill, of artisanship and its sticking points, than these accounts of workmanship's virtues. In craft as in its other aesthetic outlets, the Gothic Revival—the focal point for the formal crafts movement between 1840 and 1890—emphasized qualities of sensibility, unexpected occurrences, and subjectivity against standards of certainty and predictability. To trace ways in which the nineteenth and early twentieth centuries defined skill through the Gothic is to follow threads that the Platonic and Vitruvian heritages tend to obscure. Those threads interweave the virtues of skill not with narrow concentration but with the broader patterns of craft's emergence as a way of feeling, a sensibility, and therefore—most significant for my purposes—a vital and exciting subject that could be effectively translated into the public sphere. The literary accounts of workmanship analyzed in chapters 1 and 2 make visible the pressures under which craft operated as it became a cultural style, a represented virtue oriented to something more complicated and more nebulous than the physical command of the maker over the medium. The correlative of this pattern was a notion of skill, propounded by advocates for reformed artisanship, that shifted the locus of craft's meaning away from the primarily agentive nature of expertise and toward the artisanal sensibility epitomized by Cellini and theorized by the Gothic Revivalists who are my subject in the following pages.

In considering how artisans and their advocates relied on definitions of handicraft other than the Vitruvian, I hope to resist the idea that the interests of artisans were sold short in the industrial nineteenth century. Instead, those interests were changing, for reasons already discussed through Hawthorne's fiction; craft's heritage of telos looked much less attractive in the historical context of factories and, ultimately, of assembly lines than it did in the context of Plato's ideal commonwealth. Craftsmanship's most vocal advocates, in other words, were implicated in—not categorically opposed to—the emergence of craft as an affective style as much as a material practice, a represented sensibility as much as a learned or actually practical ability to execute designs. Because I see the emphasis on artisanal sensibility within crafts advocacy as part and parcel of the popularization and translation of craft in the popular market, my examples range widely in this chapter and depart, in some cases, from the discussion of craft as text per se. First reading *The House of the Seven Gables* (1851) in the context of A. W. N. Pugin's manifesto for the Gothic Revival, *Contrasts; or, A Parallel between the Noble Edifices of the Middle Ages, and Corresponding Buildings of the Present Day* (1836), I move on in the second section to a question that seems to have an easy answer: why did craft advocates in the latter half of the nineteenth century ignore the extraordinary technical accomplishments of the eighteenth century in workmanship of various sorts? Finding their inspiration in Norman cathedrals rather than Louis XVI secrétaires, in bulky medieval goblets rather than in fine ceramics, craft revivalists would seem, on the face of it, to be reacting against the private and elite aspects of the extraordinary domestic furnishings sold in the eighteenth-century market.

But advocates for the crafts also preferred medieval forms for reasons other than populism: these forms, they believed, suggested meeting points of physical media and the artisan's intuition, subjectivity, and instinct. The cases I consider include Ruskin's chapter "The Nature of Gothic," T. J. Cobden-Sanderson's "Arts and Crafts Movement," and William Morris's reinterpretation of a story from the thirteenth-century *Golden Legend* in an important piece of furniture—the St. George Cabinet—on which he collaborated with the architect Philip Webb. These instances help us understand the textual, representational vectors of workmanship in several senses. First, they all present the meaning of craft as a discussable idea and as a relevant "legend" inherited from the medieval age. Second, they tag workmanship as having a particular style, whether called "Gothic" or, the later name predicated on the same ideas, "Arts and Crafts." Third, and most important, the examples in this chapter reflect how the crafts movement accommodated ideas about skill to the subjective qualities through which artisanship became a popular discourse, a narrative of more than technical interest that could—like Cellini's account of his lifestyle—hold a reader's interest. The broadest claim of *Talking Shop* is that a vigorous print culture of craft developed in the context of nineteenth-century industrial production: industry created a market for accounts of human handiwork as more compelling than the physical, machinelike iteration of tasks, and thus embedded craft in a network of changing imperatives and new definitional standards. How Morris reframed old legends in the St. George Cabinet reveals as much about these imperatives, of craft under the pressures of nineteenth-century commerce, as how Hawthorne reframed legends for the same purposes in *The Scarlet Letter.* The chapter concludes by extending the Gothic tradition of artisanal advocacy to contemporary crafts, and by briefly considering a single piece of workmanship as depicted in a novel, *Brideshead Revisited* (1945), written nearly a century after Ruskin's "The Nature of Gothic." Evelyn Waugh's depiction of a medieval-themed chapel "in the arts-and-crafts style of the last decade of the nineteenth century" reveals his acute perception of the pattern this chapter historicizes: how lasting associations of skill with sensibility, of labor with legend, emerged under the aegis of a style that continues to define our sense of good craftsmanship today.[3]

THE "GROTESQUENESS OF A GOTHIC FANCY": THOMAS MAULE'S BRUTAL DEXTERITY

Complaining about the thoughtless renovation of Gothic structures that led Morris to found the Society for the Protection of Ancient Buildings, A. W. N. Pugin offers the example of the Vicar's Close, a fourteenth-century street containing the residences of the vicars associated with the Wells Cathedral in Somersetshire. For Pugin, the "modern degeneracy" of the "married worldly clergy" can be read in their "horrible mutilations of the ancient ecclesiastical residences attached to cathedrals," and one of the vicar's residences in Wells provides the most extreme case: "a baker's shop-front has been inserted in the end gable, adjoining the close gate."[4] In Hawthorne's *The House of the Seven Gables*, the Gothic building is an old aristocratic mansion rather than a fourteenth-century vicarage, but the "mortification" of the commercial, to use Hawthorne's word, is premised on much the same problem and expressed in much the same language. "A shop-door," Hawthorne writes, has been inserted "in the front gable, under the impending brow of the second story, and contiguous to the street" (28).

The instance of the shop under the gable in the Vicar's Close also prompted outrage from Thomas Larkins Walker, an architectural student of Pugin's father, although his language is not so near to Hawthorne's. Walker had seen the Vicar's Close on a sketching trip with both Pugins, and described its condition emphatically: "a *modern shop front*," Walker records, "has been inserted by one of the senior of the Vicar's Choral, who, being a baker in the town, I presume will carry on his trade here" (emphasis in original).[5] Hawthorne left no certain record of having read these sources, or of having encountered the Vicar's Close in another context—although Pugin's prominence in the 1840s makes it possible, at least, that his description of the baker's shop inspired the storefront Hawthorne imagined in *The House of the Seven Gables*. The real interest of the comparison, in any case, has to do with the thematic similarity between the two commercialized gables. Consider, first, Pugin's account. For Pugin, steeply pitched roofs reflected the natural architecture of faith, drawing one's eye and soul to God. The shop's appearance "under [a] beautiful little oriel window," a tall Gothic detail that projects from the wall, interrupts the building's vertical elevation—a point that Pugin makes architecturally by refusing to sketch the whole elevation (he depicts only the oriel window) and spiritually by insisting that shop-keeping is a fundamentally "incompatible occupation" with serving the church. Pugin asks his readers to imagine the idea of a man of God "hurry[ing] over the service" because he has to get back to his customers (*Contrasts*, 25).[6]

But the baker's shop is most outrageous, for Pugin, because it emblematizes his major theme across his career, the nature of renovation in the nineteenth century. Pugin railed against copying and imitation not because he rejected revivalism per se (indeed, Puginian Gothic was one of the Victorian era's most important revival styles) but to the degree that updating and repairing ecclesiastical buildings appeared a "mere trade," a primarily material and commercial activity rather than one imbued with spiritual feeling.[7] The insertion of the baker's shop into the fourteenth-century building may mark the vicar's capitulation to secularism, but it also symbolizes the larger threat to workmanship and to buildings themselves as no more than a *tradesman's* livelihood; the problem, in the context of Pugin's outrage at builders who do not feel the uplift that should flow from working on churches and their outbuildings, is as much that a carpenter would insert a shopfront as that a vicar would staff it. Pugin is often identified with "the authenticity of materials and method," in the same way that the Arts and Crafts Movement is often identified with the revivification of skill.[8] But Pugin, anticipating what I will describe as the major principle of the Arts and Crafts Movement, also stressed that something can be "accurate and well-worked," that it can be materially perfect while remaining dishonest as to faith, intention, and spiritual purpose (*Contrasts*, 43). Form follows not function or design but faith: the craftsman's soaring devotion, as Pugin saw it, naturally expressed itself as the affective exuberance of the pointed Gothic. The bakery reveals and epitomizes the commercialization of the Gothic that for Pugin was a matter of the feeling—or, rather, the lack of feeling—with which something was built.

If verticality and uplift were compromised for Pugin by the earthly purposes of the bakery, the House of the Seven Gables is also "divided horizontally" by the two halves of the shop door that Hawthorne describes; that door itself appears "under the impending brow" of the overhanging second story (28). Gothic verticality, we might say, spreads out into the horizontal layers to which Hawthorne draws the reader's eye, a pattern that Hawthorne encoded with surprising regularity as an "impending brow." Across his corpus, Hawthorne described a number of persons—but no other objects—by this characteristic, and in all cases seemed to have meant an equivocal or complex relation to the higher faculties by it. The phrase appears most memorably in the first description of Arthur Dimmesdale, whose "purity of thought" and "high native gifts" of intellect seem to be signified by his "white, lofty, and impending brow"; Dimmesdale, of course, turns out to be less pure of thought, more earthly, than his parishioners suppose (*The Scarlet Letter*, 54). Abraham Lincoln's "thick black eyebrows and impending brow" characterize a man Hawthorne experienced "as coarse . . . as you would meet anywhere," and yet "redeemed" and "illuminated" by his "homely sagacity."[9] The "impending brow" of Jonathan Cilley, the firebrand Democrat whose notorious death in a duel was prompted by a quarrel on the floor of Congress, serves like Lincoln's forehead as the seat of an everyman's unique intelligence, marking a "strong and shrewd sense" that was "but a higher degree of the popular intellect."[10] Nineteenth-century phrenologists ascribed the reasoning powers to the lower part of the forehead and the reflective powers to the upper, developing a theory of refinement around what one medical journal called a "two-storied brow."[11] The brow in *The House of the Seven Gables* is more literally two-storied than the rest, but the examples I have cited suggest that Hawthorne seems to have used the horizontal image of the impending forehead when describing figures who possessed both a "higher degree" of mind and a decided earthliness. In *The Marble Faun*, he draws out the relation of this figure to workmanship—as he does in *The House of the Seven Gables*—by depicting a sculptor with a "slightly impending brow." The interest of the sculptor, a minor character in the novel, has to do with the originality of his vision. Endowed with a "beautiful fancy, and possessing at his fingers' ends the capability of doing beautiful things," the sculptor is "gifted with a more delicate power than any other man alive." But what might be his "dream-work" turns out to be "frost-work," for it all appears "a vapory exhalation out of the Grecian mythology"; the sculptor carves imitative Roman gods and goddesses defined by their "artificial warmth" and by a nudity so sensual that "they stood forth to the eyes of the profane in the guise of naked women." Suggesting a higher ideality even in his smutty reproductions, the sculptor (a "quiet, simple, elderly personage" respected in the "aesthetic company" of Rome) prompts Hawthorne's typical equivocation about the purposes of skill. His "business or efficacy, in our present world," Hawthorne writes, "would be exceedingly difficult to define" (134–35).

That issue, the business of workmanship in the present world, appeared to Hawthorne as it did to Pugin—namely, along a scale running from the mere trade of accurately imitating past forms to the ideality of creative feeling. As a novel as well as a structure, *The House of the Seven Gables* transforms Pugin's vertical polemic into Hawthorne's horizontal perplexity; the impending brow of the house itself signifies the structure's centrality to the major question about craft's purposes—whether they were oriented to spiritual elevation or to earthly exertions—that Hawthorne negotiated throughout his career. The construction of the House of the Seven Gables, to begin with, represents what is probably the most brutally unfeeling act of craftsmanship in Hawthorne's corpus. For the building of the house involves the desire to make a living exactly in spite of the builder's expected ties of feeling and identity. "The reader might deem it singular," the novel states, that the carpenter of the House of the Seven Gables would be the "son of the very man, from whose dead gripe the property of the soil had been wrested" (10). The dispute between the aristocratic Pyncheons and the laboring Maules, dispossessed of the real estate on which the house is built, is generally read as a commentary on matters of class, property, and the ethics of ownership. But from another point of view, Hawthorne uses the dispute to interrogate the relation of craft to feeling, a driving concern of theories of workmanship in an age of reproduction, mechanical mimicry, and stylistic revivalism. The Gothic locus of these questions, epitomized by Pugin's insistence that pointed architecture must engage the builder's soul, appears as the house itself: Thomas Maule builds a heavily ornamented structure of "seven gables [that] pointed sharply towards the sky," a home "conceived in the grotesqueness of a Gothic fancy" (11). Pugin would concur that the house is grotesque, not just because the ornamental figures are tawdry (we are told that they are stamped in the plaster), but, more important, because of the emotional distance that characterizes Thomas Maule's labor. For Maule builds the home for his father's archrival and his family's dispossessor. The erection of the

House of the Seven Gables cannot but draw our skepticism, even if, Hawthorne tells us, it was not "out of keeping with the general coarseness and matter-of-fact character of the age, that the son should be willing to earn an honest penny—or rather, a weighty amount of sterling pounds—from the purse of his father's deadly enemy" (10–11).

The Gothic conventionality of *The House of the Seven Gables*, that is, does not just revolve around the curse that the Maules bring on the Pyncheons or the labyrinthine floorplan of the structure, with each gable housing its own apartment and the design calculated, as Gillian Brown argues, to secure retreats from the marketplace and to obfuscate the labor of housework that sustains the domestic idealization of the home.[12] The Gothic conventionality of the novel also inheres in the issues of craft *as* commerce that the house raises, and more particularly in the commercial sensibility of a laborer who suppresses the expected feeling (in this case, his identity as a Maule) to the expertise of his hands. Thomas Maule "performed his work so faithfully, that the timber frame-work, fastened by his hands, still holds together," the shingled roof remaining "thoroughly water tight" (10, 190). Thinking about the grotesqueness of such mastery, in the contexts I have described, we might conclude that Hawthorne's statement of the story's moral has as much to do with the Maules as with the Pyncheons; in the preface, Hawthorne avers that the novel describes "the folly of tumbling down an avalanche of ill-gotten gold, or real estate, on the heads of an unfortunate posterity, thereby to maim and crush them, until the accumulated mass should shall be scattered abroad in its original atoms" (2). To be sure, this legacy refers most obviously to Colonel Pyncheon's original acts of dispossessing Matthew Maule, the first settler of the land, and commissioning the House of the Seven Gables. The Colonel's act proves horrible for generations of the family. "Maule's curse," characterized by the "skeleton hand" that strangles the worst of the Colonel's descendents and leaves the "print of a bloody hand" on their ruffs, seems readily interpretable as the revenge of a family characterized by their hands (all the Maules work "at handicrafts") on the line of aristocrats descending from the Colonel (16). But the moralizing sentence, naming "ill-gotten gold" as well as "real estate," also suggests the carpenter who did in fact take his reward in money from the deal: Thomas Maule is actually and directly responsible for the oppressive longevity of the house, framed of "oaken timber . . . calculated to endure many generations" (9). The moral, in other words, not only involves the horror of the structure for the Pyncheons but also, I think, the skepticism with which we are meant to read Thomas Maule's work. We might say that the Gothic curse stems both from the insult to Lockean rights of labor to property (rights denied Matthew Maule when Colonel Pyncheon seizes his land) and from what is nearly the reverse case: the Puginian anxiety of workmanship's commodification as *no more* than labor.

I do not mean to imply that Thomas Maule is entirely indifferent to his father's fate or that his anger is not to some degree transmitted through the house. Indeed, in building so well he leaves the Pyncheons a mortifying legacy that they cannot easily overcome; the curse of the Maules is intractable for the Pyncheons because the house, and thus the embarrassing circumstances of its construction, are so durable. But Thomas Maule is willing to profit from the dispute and is made a representative of the "matter-of-fact" sensibility that Hawthorne routinely questioned. Hawthorne's superciliousness about the son of Matthew Maule taking the commission joins this Gothic building to the Gothic structures interpreted according to the same antinomy, of brutish exertions of expertise on the one hand and human feelings on the other, by Pugin. What I do mean to suggest, then, is that the pressures of greed and materialism in the novel, as represented by the events surrounding the original dispute, comprehend the problem of skill: its commercialization as an objective way of working, a marketable and eventually faddish practice in the era of Gothic architecture's popularization. Interpreting the novel along these lines helps explain how Holgrave, in the main plot of the novel, offers a redemptive alternative to the past—not just because he, secretly a Maule, falls in love with Phoebe, a Pyncheon, but also because his handicrafts labors reinvent the single-minded application of trade skill characterizing Thomas Maule. To be sure, Holgrave, like his ancestor, will take whatever living he can get: at twenty-two, he has been a teacher, salesman, editor, peddler, civil servant, Fourier socialist, and lecturer. But unlike the master carpenter, as the variety of his occupations suggests, Holgrave specializes in no trade—a point made rather excruciatingly vivid when we read that Holgrave practiced dentistry "in an episodical way" for factory workers (176). The labor he performs within the novel itself, most significantly, serves not to fasten and fix for all time, but to transform and refigure: Holgrave writes stories and makes daguerreotypes, working artistically in a "shifting world" by reframing tradition around its "wild, chimney-corner legend[s]"—as Holgrave describes his story of Alice Pyncheon—rather than around its monuments (184, 197). Thomas Maule reifies the past in a timber frame. Holgrave pierces through appearances via photographs in picture frames, telling Phoebe that his photographs have to do not with the "merest surface" but with the "secret character" of his subjects (91). His portrait of

Jaffrey Pyncheon in fact reveals the malevolence beneath the Judge's performance of kindliness, standing for Holgrave's "lack of reverence" for what appears "fixed" in the public eye (177).

Bent toward inner reality rather than material surfaces, toward private character rather than public front, Holgrave's desultory prior occupations and present labors—daguerreotyping and writing legends—mirror Hawthorne's characterization of his own workmanship in the preface. There is, Hawthorne insists, no clear public truth or certain lesson to Romance—a fact perhaps encoded by what I have described as the applicability of the story's moral about "ill-gotten" gains to the Maules as well as to the story's more obvious villains, the Pyncheons. However "skillfully wrought out," Hawthorne tells us, didacticism in fiction suggests purposeful authorial expertise pursued "relentlessly." Didactic fiction appears in this sense like Thomas Maule's labor: designs that become clearer "at every step . . . crowning the final development of a work of fiction" turn novels into exercises of telos. Hawthorne's craft, variously figured in the four paragraphs of the preface as weaving, building, cooking, making, and mixing, instead offers "fancy-pictures" (anticipating Holgrave's daguerreotypes) and "legendary mist" (anticipating how Holgrave describes his legend of Alice Pyncheon) (2–3). Chapter 13 of *The House of the Seven Gables*, a complete transcription of Holgrave's legend, indeed renders Holgrave and Hawthorne indistinguishable; the reader is asked to see this chapter as if authored by the character in the story.

Holgrave's artisanship thus diverges from his handicrafts patrimony to the degree that it appears like Hawthorne's work—or at least like Hawthorne's typically coy representation of his work as having little to do with purposeful specialization, cultivated expertise, or the motivation to monumentalize facts. But that very connection, between Holgrave's renunciation of a brutally materialist artisanal heritage and Hawthorne's professed literary endeavor to transmute the actual into the imaginary, also hints at the limits of the young Maule's ability to actually distance himself from the legacy of the carpenter. I argued in the previous chapter that Hawthornian workmanship—more precisely, the language of workmanship—reflected standards that were not entirely compatible. On the one hand, Hawthorne often fantasized about the spiritualization of the merely material practice of the trades. But on the other hand, a host of other ways of thinking about workmanship (as a utopian fiction, as an aspect of Hawthorne's own desire to ensure his literary legacy, and as an antidote to the vaporous experience of working in the Custom House) led Hawthorne to experiment with a language of craft that inscribed artisanal durability and practical, everyday longevity. The form of the Scarlet Letter as a tombstone engraving, to recall one example, offered both the satisfaction of erasing a punitive past (to the degree that the engraving is faded and nearly illegible) and the promise of eternal reproducibility (to the degree that the herald's code represents instructions for remaking the engraving on another surface). In *The House of the Seven Gables*, Holgrave, the representative of a line of artisans, also offers tradition and continuity as much as transformation through his labors. Consider the legend of Alice Pyncheon, one of the items he produces in the course of the narrative. When Holgrave ceases reading his manuscript, he finds his audience, Phoebe, in the same trance as the one described as the work of a Maule over Alice Pyncheon in the legend. The discovery makes the fictional tale not a reframing of history but an account of it, in a double sense: it describes both the past (because the mesmerism acted on Alice now looks like a plausible fact, not a legendary invention) and the present (because listening to the story actually puts Phoebe in the mesmeric trance). Holgrave returns to this aspect of his legend at the end of the novel, when he produces the long-lost deed to the Pyncheon claim to lands in Maine from a secret compartment in the House of the Seven Gables: "This is the very parchment," he proclaims, "the attempt to recover which cost the beautiful Alice Pyncheon her life and her happiness.' " "Alluding to his legend," Hawthorne reminds us, Holgrave draws the lesson also apparent in his story's mesmeric action on Phoebe: fact and fiction, real things and legendary ones, become inseparable when the "very parchment" of what is properly a story appears in Holgrave's hand (314).

Alan Trachtenberg makes a similar point about Holgrave's other craft of the moment, daguerreotypy. Holgrave's photographs are a "dodgy" medium, a way of revealing the secret character of Judge Pyncheon; I have described this aspect of Holgrave's work, oriented to the unseen, as an alternative to the worldly, all-too-practical labors of fixing and fastening associated with Thomas Maule. But dauguerreotypy also appears as a repository of the real to the degree that it captures and holds "what flits away," to quote Trachtenberg.[13] This evidentiary aspect of the medium becomes especially clear when Holgrave takes a second photograph of the Judge, after he has been killed in the ghastly manner prescribed by Maule's curse. "Such as there represented," Holgrave says when showing this daguerreotype to Phoebe, "he sits in the next room" (302). Conceptualizing this image "as a point of evidence that may be useful to Clifford" in clearing his name from presumed connections with the Pyncheon deaths, and declaring its "memorial valuable to myself," Holgrave's work of photographing, like his work of writing, registers his kinship with Thomas Maule; the crafts he practices in this novel return to the kind of endurance that Holgrave initially abjures as the legacy of the house and of the "moss-grown and rotten

Past" (302–3, 179). In the context of the Maules' handicrafts patrimony, the notoriously happy ending of the text—in which Holgrave gives up his wanderlust, settling down with Phoebe and celebrating "permanence" as the best principle of "domestic architecture"—looks less like a hasty resolution than like the extension of the artisanal principle of durability that the original construction of the house introduced (314–15).

Holgrave, to be sure, does not exert his skills primarily for profit. Nor is there any sense of the coldheartedness of Thomas Maule's labor for his father's "sworn enemy." But Holgrave's trajectory does reveal the ambiguities about the nature of skill that Hawthorne, opening the novel with the subject of Gothic workmanship and its relation to commerce, encoded in the house itself. Drawing the eye to the lateral plane of the house's "impending brow," an effect furthered by the description of the upper and lower halves of the shop door, Hawthorne plays the "seven acutely peaked gables" against an earthly horizon (5). Thomas Maule's labor makes that horizon look brutish; he builds his arched windows and inserts their "diamond-shaped panes" because he will be paid to do so. But Holgrave makes the earthly horizon look bright. His crafts, as they develop, are literally imitative and, in the end, surprisingly practical; they ultimately prove to reveal not inner secrets but real facts, and to clearly represent and reproduce history rather than to transform it. Pugin, sketching the building containing the baker's storefront in the Vicar's Close, denied the viability of that storefront by drawing the building only above the shop door; his truck is with vertical elevation, understood metaphorically as well as literally. Hawthorne instead redoubles the effect of the door's upper and lower halves, placing the visual effect of its horizontality underneath another horizontal line, that of the second story's penumbra. Most important, Hawthorne sets the implications of the building's horizontality, for the idealization of Gothic workmanship as both visual and affective elevation, in more ambiguous terrain. Projections of a greater ideality for labor—projections to which Hawthorne, across his career, was uniquely attuned—turn out to be as fantastical, in *The House of the Seven Gables*, as Thomas Maule's mere trade is unfeeling.

THE LOST GENERATION OF THOMAS CHIPPENDALE: THE BRITISH ARTS AND CRAFTS MOVEMENT

Characteristically, then, Hawthorne interrogates the values imputed to craft and skill under the pressures of their nineteenth-century idealization. In the fiction written immediately after his return from Brook Farm, I suggested in chapter 2, he casts a skeptical eye on utopian narratives about the vitalizing aspects of manual work. Seven years later, in *The House of the Seven Gables*, he adapts Pugin's example of the shop door inserted in the end gable to raise all kinds of questions about the relations of craft, commerce, feeling, and skill; Hawthorne's presentation of the Maules—Thomas and Holgrave—focuses on the boundaries of higher sensibilities and practical skills in the trades. That the aesthetic terrain of those questions should be the pointed Gothic looks forward to the development of the crafts movement as well as backward to the specific ideas about that style put forth by Pugin in the 1830s and 1840s. For as the formal craft movement crystallized in the second half of the nineteenth century, Pugin's perspective on the artisan's proper sources of motivation (emotional susceptibility, realized through Gothic forms, rather than the skills of a "mere trade") appeared again and again in a burgeoning theoretical literature on workmanship. Holgrave's negotiation of the lines between craft's immaterial and its practical aspects, its imaginative and its physical dimensions, thus anticipates issues at the forefront of craft discourse in later decades. Indeed, representations of craft between 1850 and 1900, my subject in the remainder of this chapter, often raised these issues as matters of style: how, the craft movement asked, could the affective nature of true workmanship be recognized in furnishings and objects that were also practical, durable, traditional, and well-made? How, to use the terms most central to *Talking Shop*, could artisanal feeling be made translatable and legible in such pieces? What were the terms of craft's appearance in the public sphere and—as the crafts movement adapted Pugin's ecclesiastical enterprise to residential architecture and furnishings—in the consumer marketplace?

It may be useful to begin with what crafts revivalism, as it defined the nature of skill in aesthetic terms, was not. It was not an eighteenth-century style. In furniture-making, the great artisans of the Enlightenment—Andre-Charles Boulle, Thomas Chippendale, John Goddard, George Hepplewhite, Duncan Phyfe—meant little to the handicrafts revivalists who emerged after 1850. Boulle's marquetry and veneering for Louis XIV or Goddard's "undercut" ball-and-claw foot (in which only the tips of the talons seem to touch the ball) are signal accomplishments in an era of furniture-making characterized, in the work of its best-remembered practitioners, by great technical difficulty. Delicate carving, fretwork, veneer, and inlay require advanced skills. The archetypal double curve of eighteenth-century furniture, epitomized in Queen Anne cabriole legs and bow-front desks, demanded that artisans deal with complex surfaces and difficult joints. Similar innovations defined furniture finishes, as varnishing and buffing became specialized disciplines in their own right; eighteenth-century French guilds began to distinguish the skills of builders (*menuisiers*) from those of veneerists and finishers (*ébenistes*).

Advocates of skilled labor in the next century, however, looked right through these tradesmen to a much earlier era. From the pre-Raphaelite fantasies of Morris & Co. to the heavily rectilinear furnishings of Gustav Stickley's Craftsman style, the artisanal movement variously represented itself through the medieval. A silver cup designed by C. R. Ashbee, the translator of Cellini's *Treatises*, is typical (fig. 7). The cup is pointedly about craft and crafts history itself: it was commissioned by Harris Heal at the end of his term as Master of the Worshipful Company of Painter-Stainers, one of the guild-like organizations of London tradesmen whose roots extend back to the fourteenth century. Ashbee's design invokes Gothic architecture in its slender verticality, pointed finial, and naturalistic ornamentation; the surface of the bowl presents a frieze of embossed tulips, and its particularly heavy texturing—achieved through the final planishing of the metal but looking almost brushed—may make reference to the trade organization of painters that Heal had led. Other Arts and Crafts objects offered plainer but equally self-conscious styles of medievalism, both in the United Kingdom and the United States. Figure 8 shows a characteristic piece by Gustav Stickley, on which the strap hinges, massive oak construction, and copper hardware mirror the styling used in late nineteenth- and early twentieth-century furnishings by such British architects, designers, and craftspeople as C. F. A. Voysey and Mary Seton Watts. From William Morris's early cottage furniture to Stickley's heavily rectilinear designs and Charles Rennie Mackintosh's modernist reinterpretations of high-backed chairs from the middle ages, the crafts movement between 1850 and 1920 took shape around other examples than the pieces of Chippendale's era. While Ashbee's vigorous Gothic detailing and Stickley's solid joinery obviously depend on high levels of skill, both also turn back the clocks of craft's *aesthetic* interest to an age prior to the one that represented, across the trades and in the marketplace, one of the high water marks of fine workmanship.

The reasons for disregarding the eighteenth century appear obvious; at least, they appear obvious when one thinks by way of now-familiar ideas about craft pioneered by the handicrafts revivalists themselves. For craft, as a self-conscious critique of modern culture, seems more populist than the delicate, elite styles that represented the zenith of eighteenth-century form. Artisanlike independence seemed to inhere in the bolder and (as it continues to look, since the crafts revival) more characteristically handcrafted style of the middle ages; Ashbee's cup for Harris Heal may be highly detailed and in fact expensive, but its references are to an age of chalices, Gothic audacity, and hammered metal rather than to an age of snuffboxes, gilt etageres, and fragile fretwork. To keep skill from devolving into a sign of gentility, leisure, and cost, in this way of

FIGURE 7. C. R. Ashbee (designer) and W. Poyser (maker), Painter and Stainer's Cup, 1900–1901. Silver and semiprecious stones. (© V&A Images; courtesy the C. R. Ashbee Estate)

FIGURE 8. Gustav Stickley, Sideboard No. 817. (*Catalogue of Craftsman Furniture*, 1909; courtesy the Winterthur Library, Printed Book and Periodical Collection)

thinking, the crafts revival eschewed the details favored by Boulle or Chippendale. In 1898, the year Gustav Stickley met C. R. Ashbee and returned to America fired with ideas for his own crafts enterprise, Thorstein Veblen articulated the anxiety on which crafts medievalism was apparently founded: artisanship, Veblen asserted, was in danger of becoming a handmaiden of conspicuous consumption if it depended on extremely laborious, time-consuming, and expensive techniques.[14] The central example of the invidious "canons of taste" in Veblen's landmark *Theory of the Leisure Class* is in fact a crafts item—a hand-wrought silver spoon.

And yet the medievalism of Morris in his middle and late career, of the pre-Raphaelites, and of Ashbee was precious in its own right, and their designs were hardly cheap. In *The Theory of the Leisure Class*, Veblen criticizes Morris and Ruskin exactly for their exaltation of time-consuming methods of handicraft, at least when compared to what machines might do. Veblen charged that the self-consciousness of Gothic detailing (carved foliation, for instance) was a prime example of the "conspicuous waste" of handicraft labor that made things "serviceable"—in his ironic pun—not for use but for social distinction (126). (The silver spoon, which Veblen also calls a "homely" example, is in that sense a very clever image: in one object, Veblen invokes the cliché about silver-spoon privilege, puns on his larger point about "canons of taste," and denigrates the preciousness of handicrafts culture.) As an alternative, the furniture Veblen made for himself, basic constructions using packing crates, would hardly have constituted a style capable of supporting tradesmen; craft seems no better off when self-consciously crude than as a set of skills so painstaking that only the wealthy can afford the handmade.[15] But the irony identified by Veblen complicates the assumption that the crafts movement skipped over the eighteenth century just because its works were too precious. Morris and his colleagues served as wealthy a clientele as the eighteenth-century cabinetmakers they pointedly overlooked. In turn, the guildsmen Morris and Ashbee praised—especially Benvenuto Cellini—were as beholden to the patronage of popes and princes as Boulle, for instance, was to Louis XIV.

Anxieties about Chippendale's genteel highboys or Boulle's royal patrons thus only tell a part of the story, for they reflect a problem of audience endemic to the handicrafts revival itself. The perversity of skipping over the eighteenth century is that nostalgia for skilled labor failed to notice the artisans who might have been its own best representatives. But ball-and-claw feet and double curves and codified standards for veneering also brought a predicament more complicated than their expense. Here again, Veblen articulated the problem—although he waited until 1914, when in *The Instinct of Workmanship* he went beyond the specter of craft as an agent of conspicuous consumption that he had introduced in *Theory of the Leisure Class*. I would like to turn in some detail to that lesser-known work of Veblen's, which shifts the center of the discussion from conspicuously wasteful labor to the relations of craft, industry, and skill—and, with respect to my larger concerns in this chapter, casts light on the Gothic aesthetics of those relations in the last century and a half. *The Instinct of Workmanship* opens with a familiar definition of the crafts impulse, or, rather, it poses a familiar definition of the crafts impulse in the language of early twentieth-century psychology. Echoing ideas most frequently associated with William James, Veblen declares at the outset that all "instinctive action"—parenting, acquisition, emulation, workmanship—is teleological, impelling the subject toward some well-conceived end.[16] Unlike tropism, the reflexive response of organisms to stimuli, the instincts discussed by Veblen and James are drives, adaptive and resourceful efforts to bring about certain material results. In this sense, according to Veblen, the instinct of workmanship is something like the governing instinct—for it is the instinct of telos itself, the instinct of getting things done and finished in the most efficient way possible, the instinct of achievement and production founded on "economy," "efficiency," and the adequate "management of resources" (31). A "temperate urgency," operating "under circumstances of moderate exigence" and avoiding "passionate excess," the instinct of workmanship streamlines labor and advances practical accomplishment (34).

Founded in "functional content," "serviceability," and a mistrust of wasted energy, the instinct of workmanship fits traditional definitions of craft as teleology and purpose. The instinct of workmanship also looks like it might promote a spare style of the rustic (31).[17] When Veblen came to make his own furniture, he took to the work with a decided taste for the utilitarian; hammering together his crates and hanging his burlap doors, Veblen would seem to have worked with decidedly "moderate exigence" and "temperate" ambition. The only other evidence we have of how Veblen might have aestheticized the instinct of workmanship is a counterexample; Veblen claimed he was trying to avoid that "exaltation of the defective . . . of which John Ruskin and William Morris were such eager spokesmen."[18]

Yet the major argument developed in *The Instinct of Workmanship* offers a more complicated account of the crafts instinct and a different aesthetic implication. The words Veblen uses to describe the instinct of workmanship—"economy," "efficiency," the "management of resources"—are corporate as well as artisanal idioms. That circumstance is intentional and figures the book's aim: to account for the "contamination," distortion, and inversion of the instinct of workmanship as it became a driving engine of modern industrial production.[19] The exact mechanisms of such distortion take the rest of the book to describe, but one stands out for my purposes. In a late chapter, Veblen describes what he sees as the "growth of handicraft" in postfeudal Europe; the "era of handicrafts," marked by increased production, the growth of skills, and better goods, replaces the "frankly predatory and servile" economy of feudalism with a prosperous economy of artisans, merchants, and consumers (231–32). But—this is the central irony for Veblen—the era of handicrafts also expressed the instinct for efficient workmanship on a grand social and economic scale. The systemization of handicrafts training, the appearance of labor-saving devices, and the specialization of artisans worked to streamline workmanship into canonical processes and methods. Rather than vitalizing the individual artisan's instinctive, Jamesian pragmatism (his natural ability to figure out the best way to get a job done), craft was rationalized, regularized, and channeled through system and procedure. This distinction is what Veblen means when he says that the principles of the era were "drawn not simply in terms of workmanship but specifically in terms of craftsmanship" (263). Craftsmanship, in Veblen's essay, refers to the physics of forces ("impact, pressure, displacement, . . . coordinated movements, and a shifting of equilibrium") involved in making something (264). Veblen holds that the regularization of these bodily forces in particular—their increasing efficiency and precision, whether born of better tools or better methods—represents the deflection of the instinct of workmanship away from the autonomy of the individual and toward the automatic processes of industrial labor.

Skill, in short, is to blame. The more reproducible the action, the more likely it is to be taken over by a machine or to fall victim to corporate efficiency. This perspective has not lodged itself in the western tradition with anything like the explicitness of the reverse case: that skill is an ideal standard of crafts meaning. "Neo-Luddite" jeremiads in our own day complain about an era of skilled labor lost.[20] "Money supplants skill," Bill McKibben says categorically, going on to lament that "the great push" of western history is toward consumable goods and "always *away* from individual skill and engagement" (emphasis in original).[21] But the problem of the real in the modern age, if we move with Veblen away from the specter of conspicuous consumption, as much involves the *reinvention* of the meaning of skill itself. In looking through the eighteenth century to the medieval era, crafts advocates specifically sought to revivify a quality of mind. They passed over the mere expertise of the hand; they looked, to borrow Veblen's terminology, to the subjective instinct of workmanship rather than the bodily accomplishments of craftsmanship. One of the most striking aspects of the sixteen-year run of Gustav Stickley's magazine *The Craftsman*, the major American periodical of the handicrafts revival, is how articles billed as "practical lessons" in cabinetmaking or metalwork tend to downplay specific technical instruction, often focusing instead on design and the finishing of wood or metal to bring out its best luster. Worried that systematic crafts pedagogy would lead "workers to machine-like perfection," *The Craftsman* represented Veblen's logic as a minimum of didacticism even in its instructional series.[22] To be sure, craft is not learned through magazines. But *The Craftsman*'s audience of basement hobbyists could have used something more specific than breezy comments about how rectilinear pieces were "very simple and easy to put together," and something more concrete than the magazine's stress on the generic "spirit" of raw materials; this spirit, of white oak or wool or copper, was held to vitalize the individual craftsman to figure out the techniques of craftsmanship from the material itself.[23] Thus, the instructions for the hobbyist blacksmith, in one feature article, explain not how to shape the metal but how to smoke it in a fireplace and then buff it out with an oil-soaked emery cloth to reveal the bluish-gray spirit of iron and the copper essences of copper.[24] A few articles do offer aspiring artisans a review of the tools needed to get started, or (especially in articles about needlework and a short-lived series called "Lessons in Metalwork") brief excursions into more practical matters. But as to the actual shaping of the material, the amateur, more often than not, is reminded of the necessity to "feel the grain of the wood" or to consult the metal for its own lessons.[25] Founded on an idea about instruction as "suggestive" rather than systematic, *The Craftsman* sidestepped the dangers of predicating handicraft on the consistent, trained application of the hand itself.[26]

The theoretical populism of the crafts movement also influenced its recoil from advanced or systemized technique; thinking not of traditional apprenticeship systems but of a cultural revolution, *The Craftsman* stressed the accessibility of craft, available to everybody's instinct rather than only to highly trained tradesmen. But even when addressing professionals, crafts partisans could be just as flip about canonical training or technique as when addressing amateurs and hobbyists. This was especially evident in Britain, where the handicrafts movement was oriented more to working tradespeople than in America, and where *The Craftsman*'s preference for a suggestive crafts pedagogy was anticipated by C. R. Ashbee's staffing of his Guild of Handicraft: Ashbee hired unskilled laborers on the remarkable grounds that their proper instincts would not be sullied by excesses of knowledge. Discovered by Ashbee pushing carts or sweeping stoops in London's East End, these new artisans excited him, Ashbee's biographer writes, on the basis of "their inexperience as craftsmen; untainted by contact with the metalworking trades, they were the material out of which the Guild traditions of skill and style [would] be built up."[27]

Such attitudes were grounded in the foundational document of the crafts revival, John Ruskin's chapter "The Nature of Gothic" in *The Stones of Venice*. Ashbee was a student of Ruskin's at Cambridge and gave courses on Ruskin's writings to the unskilled workers whom he took as the craft movement's best promise. Morris, writing the introduction for the Kelmscott Press edition of *The Nature of Gothic* as a stand-alone work, recalled the chapter as a "new road out of the folly and degradation of civilization."[28] Stickley named Ruskin, alongside Emerson, as one of his two major influences; the second volume of *The Craftsman* was dedicated to Ruskin, as was half of the first volume of another American outlet for Arts and Crafts ideals, Elbert Hubbard's *Little Journeys to the Homes of the Great*. In Ruskin's theory, the elaboration of Gothic carving is a condition and a mark of the worker's liberation. Freed from the Grecian labor of producing symmetrical structures and unrelieved surfaces, the craftsmen of the cathedrals at Strasbourg or Rouen expressed their personalities via profuse and irregular detailing. Consistency and telos were not, for Ruskin, the standards of skilled labor. The best artisans, he fantasized, care "not a whit" for getting their "curves . . . true" or keeping their "edges perfectly sharp"; instead, they "invent . . . a new design for every glass" and "never mould . . . a handle or a lip without a new fancy in it."[29] "Very accurate workmanship" is deemed a "bad sign" that suggests the builder's inability to pass through the sensuous and into the richer medium of imaginative expression. Praising those who have "something like disdain" for their craft (they are able to "see *past* the work they are doing" [emphasis in original]), Ruskin takes imperfection of style and execution as the litmus test of authenticity (229). The hard stone of northern Gothic climes is conducive to reformed artisanship because it "compel[s] the workman to seek for vigor of effect, rather than refinement or accuracy of form" (204).

When Ruskin enjoins artisans to avoid "edges perfectly sharp," he means on the one hand the edges of the wood or stone or whatever other medium the artisan works—or, rather, can't work, for the attractiveness of German, Danish, English, and northern French stone is that it resists attempts to break it square or chisel it plumb. On the other hand, in describing edges that are not just uneven but imperfectly "sharp," Ruskin invokes the edges of the workman's chisels, gouges, and planes. The doubly dull edge of Ruskinian workmanship, of medium and of tools, joins the resilience of materials to the worker's liberation from obsessive concern about his technical labor. The genuine, in this model, is at once a product of the medium's inherent form and of the artisan's subjective freedom from tyrannical, materialist ways of thinking. The irregular—for Ruskin, elaborate Gothic carving—flows alike from the immanence of nature and the imaginative freedom of the worker who cannot perfectly work it.

One might reasonably be concerned, in "The Nature of Gothic," for the hands of Ruskin's artisans: exerting a great amount of force to push a relatively dull chisel through resilient material is not very conducive to keeping all one's fingers. But that physical peril bespeaks some more theoretical problems for practical workmanship under Arts and Crafts ideals. The Gothic Revival—in literature and art as well as in architecture and craft—stressed sensibility and reactivity; abjuring the clarity of Enlightenment systems of thinking, the Gothic novelist's attraction to labyrinthine settings as a way of prying into the psychological reactions of characters mirrors the crafts movement's interest in the affective responsiveness of artisans to their material. Oriented to subjectivity and psyche, the crafts revival minimized the teleological satisfactions of a job simply well done. Defending craft, the Arts and Crafts Movement could be awfully hard on the practical or vocational motives of tradespeople—whose labor, after all, has to be practical and reproducible enough to put food on the table. The bias encoded in Ruskin's notion of the Gothic can also be read in the name "Arts and Crafts" itself, first applied to the already-established British crafts revival in 1888 by T. J. Cobden-Sanderson. With Ashbee and others, Cobden-Sanderson, a bookbinder, founded an exhibition society that showed handcrafted furniture, ceramics, glass, and textiles. For Cobden-Sanderson, the "and" in the name he gave to this group, the "Arts and Crafts Society," was unidirectional: the goal was to bring art—defined as an experience of visionary creativity—to the work of tradesmen rather than to accord that work, in itself, its own authenticity. For a practicing tradesman and leader of the handicraft revival, Cobden-Sanderson had remarkably little interest in talking about objects themselves. Insisting that the movement was "in the main of ideas," Cobden-Sanderson felt bored by his society's exhibitions: they were "but repetitions, with variations only of detail, of the first, and need no description."[30]

To be fair, this may not have been meant as archly as it sounds. Cobden-Sanderson's refusal to describe craft, essentially a refusal to review his own exhibitions in print, indeed suggests the anxiety that *Talking Shop* as a whole hopes to frame: the rise of artisanship as a subject for so many words. Periodicals devoted to the crafts aesthetic as well as to decorative history more generally represented a Victorian penchant for talking about interiors and for translating every detail of workmanship. Cobden-Sanderson's disinclination to talk about things thus mirrors Henry James's attitude in *The Spoils of Poynton*, my subject in chapter 5: James pillories Mrs. Brigstock's translation of the handicrafts furnishings at Poynton into the lexicons of bourgeois taste. But just as James's position turns out to be more complicated than satire, because the novel itself transcribes the antiques into text, Cobden-Sanderson's position also suggests something more complicated than his recoil from popular periodicals. Indeed, an anxiety about the seductive aspect of things in general, as much as his anxiety about their translation into print, appears to have motivated Cobden-Sanderson's recoil from talking too much about his colleagues' work. If Karl Marx worried that the products of factories would seem more compelling or more real than the human labor that produced them, Cobden-Sanderson curiously relocated this idea to the custom workshop and to traditional practices of workmanship. Artisans, he wrote, should abjure work done "from the outside"—that is, with an eye to the physical results—in favor of channeling the free flow of the active imagination, the mystical wellspring that distinguished the creative process from technical know-how and crude materialism. The appeal of very fine craftsmanship, on display in the exhibitions

Cobden-Sanderson denigrated, might seduce the public into identifying the aims of the Arts and Crafts Movement with perfect joints rather than the abstract idea of self-realization through reflective labor (14). The "art" in "Arts and Crafts" thus originated in a fear of the fetish quality of objects, the risk that even craft could transform the process of labor into its products. In an 1878 lecture later titled "The Lesser Arts"—an unironic title—Morris had harangued his audience, mostly tradesmen, with the idea that they had the obligation to "come up" to the visionary standards belonging to the "great arts" of architecture, painting, sculpture, and poetry.[31] Cobden-Sanderson echoed the point: the trades were striving to "speak afresh" under the influence of the arts, and the union projected in the title "Arts and Crafts" would only be achieved when physical "actuality" was "redeemed" by "ideas" and "imagination" (14).

The grounds of Cobden-Sanderson's discomfiture about crafts exhibitions, moreover, are reflected in the kinds of pieces actually turned out by the English Arts and Crafts Movement. A common design paradigm for British crafts furniture treats the wood as a canvas for painting or complex inlaid design; the most famous example is a cabinet designed by Philip Webb and painted by Morris with scenes of Saint George (fig. 9), a piece I will consider in detail shortly. Collaborations between decorators and cabinetmakers were common, and subjects in stained glass, tile, or gesso characterize many other pieces. Designers left little doubt that they considered this sturdy but elaborately decorated furniture closer to the supreme ideal of artistic expression than the plainer medieval forms that had sparked the movement in the 1850s. Shown at the first exhibition of the Arts and Crafts in 1888, for instance, a piano designed by Edward Burne-Jones (fig. 10) offered a surface for intricate patterns—executed in gold and silver gesso by Kate Faulkner, a wallpaper designer for Morris & Co.—intended to complement the surface décor of the client's house. More important than the decorative flexibility they offered, however, painting, carving, and rich detailing stood for the play of vision as it responded to the medium and the emerging structure of the piece. Morris, while aiming to work for the masses, called these exquisite accomplishments his "state" pieces and freely admitted that he thought of them as the triumph of the "art of furniture."[32] At Morris & Co., a joint venture of craftsmen and pre-Raphaelite painters, the art of furniture was a literal as well as a theoretical conjunction. In many of the best Arts and Crafts pieces, the furniture-making craft, as a vehicle for the pictorial, played host to the higher form of imaginative work practiced by painters and sculptors.

As icons of a theoretically populist crafts revival, the obvious problem inherent in the "state" pieces is that they demanded substantial investments of time,

FIGURE 9. Philip Webb (designer), William Morris (painter), and Morris, Marshall, Faulkner and Co. (makers), cabinet showing scenes of St. George, 1861–1862. Painted and gilded mahogany, pine, and oak, with copper mounts. (Photo © Victoria and Albert Museum, London)

of technique, and, ultimately, of capital. The notorious paradox of the British Arts and Crafts Movement is that the state pieces appeared to sell out the vision of democratic style to the very wealthy; the central "disparity" of Morris's life, one of his biographers has written, is that he denounced capitalism while selling his work to an "increasingly grand clientele" and while "pandering to the tastes of the haute-bourgeoisie."[33] But if the state furniture is essentially paradoxical, it is so on different terms than its conspicuity or cost; presuming an incompatibility between craft and consumption obfuscates ways in which the definition of the handmade was itself transforming. Rather, the state furniture represents a tension internal to the very notion of a handicrafts critique. Rarity signified sensibility rather than mere skill, affective use of the imagination rather than the relatively brutish practice of the hands; rarity, that is, was inseparable from the very notion of workmanship that the crafts movement was trying to advance. In the minds of the handicrafts revivalists, the exquisiteness of English Arts and Crafts pieces made them viable and recognizable critiques in the first place. As Veblen realized between writing *The Theory of the Leisure Class* and *The Instinct of Workmanship*, handicrafts authenticity in the machine age

FIGURE 10. Edward Burne-Jones (designer), Kate Faulkner (decorator), and Broadwood and Sons (makers), piano, 1883. Oak, with gold and silver-gilt gesso. (Photo © Victoria and Albert Museum, London)

was shaped by attitudes about the paucity of mere skill more than it was shaped by a binary of craft and conspicuous consumption. Judged by traditional standards of workmanlike telos, a machine may be the ideal craftsman. Levering handicraft away from the hand, workmanship away from the machine-like consistency of iterated results, the crafts revival found itself in the complicated position of selling the image of craft as something richer, more intricate, and—therefore—more recognizable as one-of-a-kind artisanship.

The St. George Cabinet addresses this aspect of the British crafts revival—that craft, oriented to the semiotics of sensibility, channeled its energies through necessarily costly pieces—as a matter of its design. The point of the St. George Cabinet, I would like to propose, is to authenticate medievalism by rendering it not a reproduction style but a creative, original mode of workmanship. The cabinet indeed materializes the vertical hierarchy of art and craft presumed by Cobden-Sanderson. The cabinet's lower half is all natural wood and practically, massively built. That impression, however, gives way along the center line to an upper half that is entirely painted, preserving little of the thick, exposed joinery or the natural wood from which it arises. The arched buttresses of the base accentuate the unfolding, emerging effect of the piece's vertical movement. The "greater art" of painting, to borrow Morris's terms, thus literally arises from the "lesser art" of woodwork; the piece narrates the visionary uplift which, in Arts and Crafts philosophy, makes craft more than craftsmanship. The painting itself, moreover, transforms the medieval tradition that it seems to resuscitate—the St. George story. The story of St. George and the dragon was best known to the Victorians through William Caxton's *Golden Legend* (1482), a translation of Jacobus de Voragine's *Legenda Aurea* (c. 1260–75). Morris himself published a Kelmscott Press edition of Caxton's translation in 1892. In that telling, the story of St. George is a cautionary tale. A pagan town in Libya is being held hostage by a dragon, whose appetite for sheep, thrown to him every day by the townspeople, soon becomes an appetite for the people themselves. The town agrees to cast lots to determine who will be sacrificed, and in time the lottery, not discriminating between citizens "gentle or poor," falls to the King's daughter.[34] The King tries to trade all his riches to any family who will provide a substitute, but no one comes forward. Then St. George arrives and injures the dragon, which is led into town, a "meek beast," by the daughter (128). St. George finally imparts the coup de grace to the dragon and takes to the road to do more saintly deeds, refusing the King's offer of "as much money as there might be numbered" (129) and having nothing more to do with the damsel—who in fact drops out of the story before St. George administers the final blow.

The general outline of this story is told, from left to right, in Morris's five panels. But the narrative of ascetic Christianity is gone. In Caxton, the King's inability to buy his daughter's life suggests the futility of worldly desire; St. George's refusal to accept a reward and the disappearance of the princess from the narrative draws the lesson. For Morris, the story ends not with St. George departing but with St. George, facing back in toward the center of the piece in triumphant procession, returning. Rather than arranging for the daughter to lead the dragon into town—the picture of the meek made strong—St. George kills the dragon on the spot (the sword remaining in the beast in the fourth panel) and leads back the daughter in a scene that is clearly amatory if not exactly (or yet) matrimonial; in this version, St. George, his head inclined toward the daughter and her hand in his, is not so averse to whatever rewards might flow from his prowess. The princess herself is the archetype of pre-Raphaelite desirability: she is clearly modeled on Jane Burden, whose figure appears throughout the work of Morris, Edward Burne-Jones, and especially Dante Gabriel Rossetti. The St. George Cabinet is in this sense autobiographical, for Morris married Jane Burden in 1859—although the woman (like the rest of the story) is herself made much richer, transformed from the actual daughter of an Oxford footman into a gold-clad princess.[35]

In the most basic sense, Morris's treatment of the St. George story recapitulates the transformation of the piece from its lower to its upper halves: the traditional framework of the story is imaginatively rewritten into a personal account. More particularly, the way in which it is rewritten suggests the larger point I have tried to make about the handicrafts revival. The upending of simplicity—a simplicity manifest in the piece both as the utilitarian base and as the conventional account of virtue in the St. George myth—is less a paradox than a principle of the design. Rather than selling out the properly populist idioms of craft, the piece rewrites the aesthetic, material, and narrative asceticism it invokes. On both the horizontal axis (the painted panels) and the vertical one (the transition between the lesser and the greater arts), it testifies to the values that make it a testament to the elevating basis of Arts and Crafts workmanship in the first place. The design itself, in short, anticipates and inverts the ironies attributed to it.

CODA: THE ARTS AND CRAFTS LEGACY

The basic logic informing the St. George Cabinet, the naming of the Arts and Crafts Movement, and "The Nature of Gothic" is both alien and familiar to popular notions of craft in the last century and a half—for while the explicitly medieval idioms of the craft movement have faded, its idealization of the unstandardized and uneconomical remains. Consider first the familiarity of the perspective, to use Veblen's terms, that precise craftsmanship (a reproducible bodily practice) is a threat to workmanship (an instinct for adaptive, resourceful crafting). Raku-fired pottery, burlwood jewelry boxes, and all manner of one-of-a-kind materials define handicraft in galleries and craft fairs in a way that, say, a carpenter's accurate and speedy hanging of rafters does not; the latter appears as construction, the former as craft. Irregular surfaces, asymmetrical rims, and boldly expressive materials reflect the exuberant nature of the Gothic, as defined by Ruskin; handmade objects are identifiable and valuable for their uniqueness, an attitude that has to do both with the incommensurability of the material and the incommensurability of the person who works it. An article in a recent issue of *Craft Arts International* has the following to say about Todd Hoyer, a contemporary woodworker who is the subject of a retrospective feature: "That Hoyer view[s] pieces [of raw wood] in terms of their individuality is representative of the manner in which he has long approached the medium of wood as a means for exploring his own individuality."[36]

By the "individuality" of wood, the writer of the article means its idiosyncrasy. Rare, irregularly figured woods are a clear mark of artisanal woodworking today. Figure 11 shows a very simple trifold screen by Richard Judd made one-of-a-kind (and included in the exhibition "Defining Craft" at the American Craft Museum in New York) not by its simple construction but by its unique patterns of grain. The woods are mahogany, sapele, moabi, makore, and ebony—and the artisan's eye for nature's irregularity, more than the Vitruvian ability to bend the medium to a complex design, constitutes the workmanship of the piece. Such unique boards as those used by Judd may be highly figured in normal growth or contain the often beautiful marks of mold (a phenomenon called "spalt" in maple and cherry), disease (exemplified by what woodworkers call "birdseye" figure), or deformation (burls and burs). As Michelle Holzapfel puts it, her naturalistic bowls and lathe-turned objects often flow from irregularities suggestive of "the tree's own testimony of rain and drought, growth and injury."[37] Such language suggests Walter Benjamin's: "the testimony to the history which [an] object has experienced" is its "aura" of authenticity.[38] But the complement of that kind of authenticity in modern crafts thinking is the subject who must respond and react to such irregular pieces. Natural forms, Holzapfel says, are the occasion for "personal narrative," for the emergence of the "unconscious," for a wooden vessel that is a "metaphor of the self" (25). The piece about Hoyer goes on, after making the statement quoted earlier, to distinguish between tedious woodturning ("highly polished work that reflect[s] the natural beauty of the wood") and Hoyer's use of "rot, insect damage, bark inclusions, and cracking" as the staging grounds for introspective subjectivity. Irregularities in the material force the artisan to a level of creative activity surpassing perfect, predictable, or teleological execution. Hoyer, we learn, crafts according to mood; his labor represents not executable design but spontaneous acts of responding to an inconsistent medium as it spins on his woodturning lathe (30–31).

The artisan's self-expression is thus predicated on the expressiveness of his medium. James Krenov, probably America's most influential woodworking teacher, urges his students to seek out difficult-to-work species like pearwood and to sidestep too much uniformity by drying the lumber by air rather than in the controlled environment of a kiln; such material, "elusive . . . and only partly predictable in its ways," emphasizes the imaginative contingencies of handwork by prying apart associations of craft and telos.[39] David Pye, professor of

FIGURE 11. Richard Judd, Folding Screen, 2001. Birch plywood, mahogany, sapele, moabi, makore, and ebony veneer. (By permission of Richard Judd; photograph by William Lemke)

furniture design at London's Royal College of Art and an important theorist of craft in the mid-twentieth century, describes genuine artisanry as a "workmanship of risk"—at any moment the hand shaping a clay pot or wielding a chisel can slip, breaking through the side of the clay or punching through an ornately carved filigree.[40] Pye's artisans, of course, do not actively court disaster. But the obverse of the piece's occasional ruination is the greater tragedy: the mechanically controllable "workmanship of certainty" that removes the human dimension from the object.

However familiar in the lineage extending from Ruskin to craft fairs today, such notions are also dramatically alien to enduring definitions of handicraft. For they are predicated on the failure rather than the transcendence of skilled labor, at least in the Vitruvian sense that identifies skill with consistency and unvaried enactment. It is much more comfortable to draw a distinction between crafts skill and machines than to follow Veblen from the master craftsmen of the "era of handicrafts" to the routinized nature of industrial production. But Veblen's logic is exactly what is demanded by the aesthetics of uncertainty; *The Instinct of Workmanship* suggests that an excess of consistency turns humans into machines. Uncertain results in that sense mark a conundrum. The rise of irregularity as a defining mark of the handcrafted is founded on an equation of perfect, regular workmanship with industrial processes—but that same equation begins to erode the putative distinction between industry and "skilled labor" (in the basic sense of skill as practical consistency) on which the value of craft is also based. The crafts, in other words, embody ideas both about irregular, contingent workmanship and about the unwavering "traditional handcrafted quality" available in artisanal objects. The artisanal movement is often held to be a revivification of skilled labor. But skilled labor, in modern culture, is not something one can simply and unproblematically restore or reinvigorate. There is no easy return, as Veblen suggests, from modernity to a primordial instinct of good workmanship. The very meaning of skilled human labor is transformed and destabilized by the industrial context of the crafts movement.

The fate of master artisans of the Enlightenment like Chippendale and Boulle, then, was sealed by the equivocal relation of skill to handicrafts in an age when the dividing lines of skill and mass production were not clear; our own era's aesthetic sensibilities serve as reminder of how something more than mere technique, a mechanizable capacity, has come to define handicraft. Victorian furniture, moreover, suggested even more specific parallels between eighteenth-century artisanship and the mass market. The prototypical bedroom suite in figure 12, sold by Sears in 1897, uses rococo carving and seashell motifs—at the center of the headboards—to represent eighteenth-century

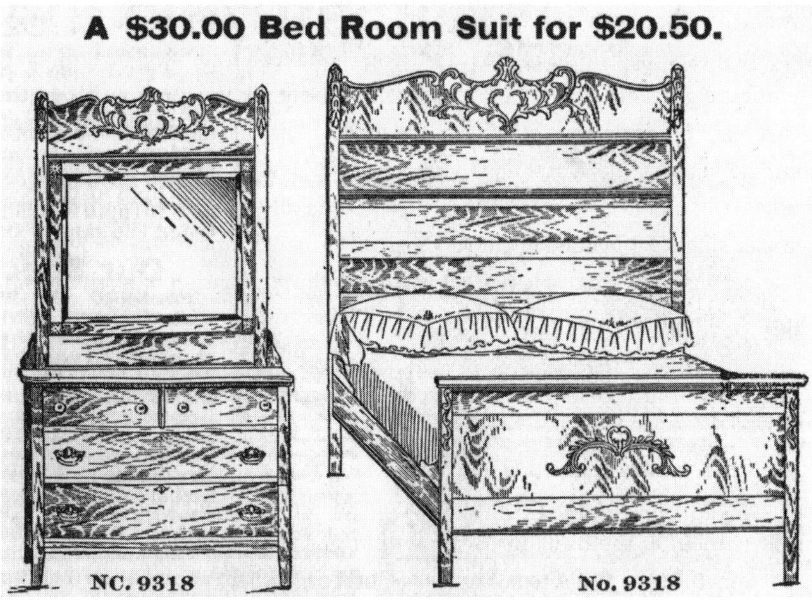

FIGURE 12. Sears, Roebuck, and Co., bedroom suite, No. 9318, c. 1897. (Sears, Roebuck, *Catalog* [1897]: 655)

fancywork; in this and many other examples, the forms through which an eighteenth-century furniture maker would display his skills become generic features of nineteenth-century manufacture. Consider, in the same sense, another Victorian equation of eighteenth-century style and mass commerce: the history of the word "veneer." A veneer is a thinly sliced piece of wood—as little as 1⁄64 of an inch thick—that is glued on top of a substrate; the traditional reason for doing this is to create remarkable patterns of color and grain. The technique, of which Boulle was the master, is one of the great crafts innovations of the Enlightenment. It was invented in the early eighteenth century when the development of special saws made it possible to slice such thin pieces. The English word, according to the OED, was first printed as a noun in 1702 and as a verb, describing the action of fixing the veneer to the substrate, in 1728.

The use of the word "veneer" to refer to dissimulation, to "a merely external or specious appearance," does not appear until 1847, nearly one hundred and fifty years after the term itself. This development thus occurs in the context of industrial manufacture. By the middle of the nineteenth century, veneers of straight-grained, average wood were being glued over cheap substrates to simulate solid stock. "Veneer" came to connote a technique of imitation, a skill performed so well, with respect to the invisibility of glue lines and the matching of grain, that the result was indistinguishable from real, solid wood. The century and a half of delay between the original and the secondary meanings of the word suggests the central point I am trying to make: a traditional technique of the finest eighteenth-century craftsmanship evolved, in the nineteenth century, into a technology and a language of the ersatz. The master artisan's ability to combine veneers seamlessly, without any gaps, was transformed from a remarkable handicrafts achievement (the special skill of the *ébeniste*) into a marketplace sham. Embedded in our very lexicon of inauthenticity—in the notion of a "veneer" as opposed to the real thing—is not the attenuation of workmanship but its excess of skill.

The notion of artisanship as a subjective rather than just a technical practice thus flowed through a wide range of visual and textual outlets. Resistance to craft as expertise is embedded in everyday language relating workmanship and authenticity; in the theoretical statements of the Arts and Crafts Movement (itself named on the basis of its abjuration of merely practical skills); in the terms of workmanship's renascence as Gothic or otherwise irregular and improvisational in form; and—looking back to instances discussed in this as well as in previous chapters—in the questions about the limits of mere skill raised across Hawthorne's corpus as well as in the canonization of Cellini's untechnical *Life* as the paradigmatic nineteenth-century account of the artisanal sensibility. The first argument of *Talking Shop* is that workmanship emerged as a popular cultural style, a viably represented experience, on the basis of its association with ways of feeling rather than just ways of working; as lifestyle rather than labor, it landed compellingly on the page. The second argument of *Talking Shop* concerns the ways in which these emerging dimensions of craft were held up to the mirror of classic standards of workmanship, sometimes (as in the case of Cellini's text) for the purpose of soothing the translation of craft into new idioms and in other cases (as in Hawthorne's fiction of the 1840s) for the purpose of revealing the idealizations and projections on which reframed definitions of workmanship depended. The frictions and questions attending the emergence of workmanship as a cultural style, and in particular as the British Arts and Crafts style, are experienced by the main character in Evelyn Waugh's *Brideshead Revisited* (1945), whose experience of craft revivalism revolves around the dynamics of objectivity and subjectivity I have outlined. The novel was written well outside the period primarily discussed in my chapters, but Charles Ryder's conceptualization—or rather his reconceptualization—of the meaning of building through an Arts and Crafts structure epitomizes what the movement tried to teach as well as the legacy it left.

The novel is framed by the barracking of Charles's World War II company at

Brideshead, the family seat where in the 1920s he spent extraordinary days with his Oxford companion Sebastian Flyte. That framing device is all one needs to know of the plot to appreciate the suffusing of the novel with the language of revisiting and returning, as, for instance, when Charles, in the 1920s, sees the chapel at Brideshead for the first time:

> The whole interior had been gutted, elaborately refurnished and redecorated in the arts-and-crafts style of the last decade of the nineteenth century. Angels in printed cotton smocks, rambler-roses, flower-spangled meadows, frisking lambs, texts in Celtic script, saints in armor, covered the walls in an intricate pattern of clear, bright colors. There was a triptych of pale oak, carved so as to give it the peculiar property of seeming to have been molded in plasticine. The sanctuary lamp and all the metal furniture were of bronze, hand-beaten to the patina of a pock-marked skin; the altar steps had a carpet of grass-green, strewn with white and gold daisies. (38–39)

The space is a transparent representation of the chapel at Madresfield Court, the home of Waugh's friend Hugh Lygon. In the real chapel (fig. 13), the rambler roses climb the painted trellis just above the wainscoting on the front and side walls. The angels in smocks and the Celtic script appear on the wall to the right of the altar. The bronze furnishings are obvious, and the winged figure in armor flies a standard of the angels.

But the passage, read against the image, is not complimentary. It is cut through with skepticism about the imitativeness of the chapel, starting with the description of a space "gutted," "refurnished," and "redecorated" in a fashionable style. The medieval triptych is manifestly not old, seemingly "molded in plasticine." The white and gold daisies strewn on the steps are not real, for Brideshead is shut up for the season when Charles and Sebastian visit; rather than lying on a blanket of grass, the daisies are woven into a carpet of "grass-green." The metals, "hand-beaten to the patina of a pock-marked skin," suggest a different relation to the handicrafts past than the vivid healthiness promoted by the Arts and Crafts Movement. For Charles, himself an artist whose ambitions are to do something new, the chapel is an image of the retrograde pretensions of late nineteenth-century medievalism.

The imitativeness of the chapel helps explain an initial oddity in its presentation. Sebastian first describes it, while he and Charles are walking there, as a "monument of art nouveau" (38); moments later, once they arrive, Charles identifies the chapel as in the "arts-and-crafts style." The two styles are in some ways similar. Art Nouveau typically refers to the floriform designs and the soft pastel interiors preferred, for instance, by Samuel Bing, George Logan, Charles

FIGURE 13. Chapel, Madresfield Court, Worcestershire, constructed c. 1902. (Courtesy the Trustees of the Madresfield Estate)

Rennie Mackintosh, and Louis Comfort Tiffany. Like the Arts and Crafts Movement, Art Nouveau sought to harmonize architecture and interior design, used medieval idioms, and espoused one-of-a-kind workmanship. The two styles also had some of the same outlets. Gustav Stickley's early inlays, for instance, are archetypes of Art Nouveau design.

But Art Nouveau surfaces are characteristically lighter, more abstract, and more curved than those of the Arts and Crafts Movement. Art Nouveau designers were also much less explicitly moralistic about décor, tending to ally with Aestheticism's emphasis on art for art's sake—a fact suggesting why Sebastian, the aesthete, may name the chapel as Art Nouveau while Charles, the academician, cites the more cerebral Arts and Crafts style descending from Ruskin and Morris. Charles's identification is more conventional and, technically, probably more accurate: the dominant medievalism and the general heaviness of the chapel, realized in expanses of unfinished wood and "angels in printed cotton smocks" (a detail suggesting Morris's notorious preference for wearing a workman's blue smock), define the Arts and Crafts rather than the Art Nouveau interior. What Sebastian's description captures that Charles's name does not, however, is the irony of the chapel. A "monument to art nouveau" sounds like an oxymoron in its fusion of the monumental and the new. Sebastian's playful description anticipates what Charles is about to discover and to reveal in the paragraph about the chapel: that the space, its medievalism "plasticine," is a representation of a faddish décor that is itself founded on the revitalization of a prior style. A monument commemorates; a "monument to art nouveau" pointedly jokes about the relation of the past and the contemporary, the original and the copy.

Sebastian's phrase and Charles's longer description thus identify the same effect in the chapel: a confusion of the authentically old and the new. Yet the distinction between the stylistic tags they offer is important because Charles, revisiting the chapel in 1944, changes his mind. At the very end of the book, he describes "art-nouveau paint . . . as bright and fresh as ever" and an "art-nouveau lamp [that] burned once more before the altar" (350). In the final paragraphs of the novel, which ends with Charles's return to the chapel, words like "new," "newly," "anew," and (now) "nouveau" appear prominently—and they connote something sustaining, not the ironic revisiting that first defines the chapel. The final paragraphs of the novel describe Charles's return to the chapel with a sense of historical continuity. Where the first visit prompts him to imagine Brideshead's builders, over time, seeking to "unify its growth" by such retrograde periodicity as the faux medievalism of the chapel (38), the last visit returns to the builders with a different attitude. The builders

> made a new house with the stones of the old castle; year by year, generation after generation, they enriched and extended it. . . . Something quite remote from anything the builders intended has come out of their work . . . : a small red flame—a beaten-copper lamp of deplorable design, relit before the beaten-copper doors of a tabernacle; the flame which the old knights saw from their tombs, which they saw put out; that flame burns again for other soldiers, far from home, farther, in heart, than Acre or Jerusalem. It could not have been lit but for the builders and the tragedians, and there I found it this morning, burning anew among the old stones. (351)

Charles—or really, at this moment, Waugh, whose questions about faith are the novel's major subject—is talking about Catholicism. He is talking about the Crusades, about faith regained and rekindled, about spiritual depth and spiritual renewal brought on by the "human traged[ies]" (351): the loss of innocence, the passing of youth, the breaking up of the Marchmain family,

Sebastian's alcoholic collapse. But, in returning to the idioms of oldness and newness that defined the first appearance of the chapel, he is also talking about décor. Beaten copper, formerly the pock-marked surface of a relentless past, remains a "deplorable design"—but the beaten-copper lamp is also the vessel of historical continuity experienced as a comfort, a felt connection, a past that unfolds diachronically rather than just starkly imitating. The paint is "fresh," everything is "new"—yet less this time as an irony than as a tradition. Everything was "as fresh and bright *as ever*," and not just because it is a recent, faux recreation; the place grows to "ripeness." That which "burns anew among old stones" looks not like the light of a pock-marked reproduction lamp in a plasticine chapel but like the same flame seen by the old knights.

Charles, in short, rethinks the meaning of building. The expressiveness of the chapel is "remote from anything the builders intended"—its meaning is oriented not just to the objects themselves, their realness or their fakery or their material origins, but to the genuineness of the historical experience they prompt. The end of *Brideshead Revisited* is characteristically modern in its sense of the way history flows through and gives meaning to the individual; the flame is like the light at the end of Daisy Buchanan's dock, drawing us back inexorably to the past.[41] More generally, *Brideshead Revisited* deals with the impossibility, tragic and affecting alike, of not revisiting: Sebastian tries to leave his family's false piety behind but is destroyed by the effort; his sister Julia may love Charles but cannot cast off the idea that a marriage between a Christian and a non-Christian is a sin. For my purposes, the chapel is important for presenting the inevitability of revisiting as a mode of decorative and aesthetic authenticity. Asked by Sebastian's brother what he thinks of the chapel, Charles, halfway through the novel, calls it a "remarkable example of its period"; it is a revival piece that he doesn't "like very much" (92). In the final paragraphs, this attitude toward period styles disappears. Rather than seeing an ironic fakery in the Arts and Crafts style, rather than imagining what the builders "intended" and executed (a traditional model of crafts as physical result, exemplified by Plato and Vitruvius), Charles divests the meaning of the Arts and Crafts and of the chapel from material objects and their provenance.

In stressing the sensibility of a building rather than its objective authenticity, Charles Ryder comes closer to the meaning of the handicrafts movement—as it flowed through Gothic and medieval styles like the chapel—in the first place. The real problem with imitation, according to Pugin, is not physical reproduction in itself but the attenuation of a connection between the builder's feelings and his projects—a Gothic recreation is only absurd when it is raised by an architect and craftsmen who do not feel the piety and devotion on which Gothic vaults and points were based. In *Brideshead Revisited*, Charles approaches the Arts and Crafts spirit most nearly (and comes to appreciate the chapel) by learning to dissociate the effect of authenticity from the builder's material intentions or the actual provenance of the thing. Arts and Crafts figures managed the paradox of nineteenth-century medievalist and handicrafts pretensions—that they too promoted period styles—by shifting the nature of workmanship away from execution. There are, to be sure, important differences between the way in which Morris, say, and Pugin carried out this shift: Morris and his colleagues stressed the individualized experience of art while Pugin and his heirs pushed the diachronic experience of religious feeling. But an emphasis on sensibility is what, in the mind of the handicrafts revivalists, made them more than just revivalists. That principle is essential to industrial-era thinking about handicrafts, as it descends from Ruskin and Morris and the medievalist crafts movement; in the machine age, skill and craftsmanship, the builder's Vitruvian intentions, focus as much a problem of authenticity as a solution. Labor's authenticity coheres not around enactment or telos but around the affective experiences the crafts prompt. The crucial legacy of the handicrafts revival, for my purposes, was to adapt workmanship to new forms of representation by defining its interest and its viability on grounds other than the merely material relation between maker and object.

To be sure, the iconicity of the handicrafts as a sensibility, an effect of authenticity, will always raise eyebrows, from Charles Ryder's—when he first sees Brideshead—to those of the critics who stress the contradictory imperatives of representation and reality, expensive effects and populist principles, in the crafts movement. We may viably wonder at the ways in which handicraft has become less a mark of rusticity or practicality than a consumable aesthetic, just as nineteenth-century readers recoiled from the vigorous promotion of Cellini's thrilling escapades as an example of the craftsman's lifestyle. But these developments did not occur outside the workshop. They are not a hoax perpetrated on artisanship's interests by consumer culture. Instead, they are fundamental to the situation of skill under modern conditions. Minimizing physical origins and pulling back from technique, handicrafts culture anticipated the vanishing points of skilled labor and made craft available to a variety of representational practices; to testify to something that cannot be machined, craft had to develop a sense of style predicated on more than just the actual details of something's making. As the "Arts and Crafts" ideal presumed—and as Morris's furniture testifies—practicality and affect, handicraft and its image, the object and its representation, are less the dividing lines of authenticity and fakery than the twinned principles of workmanship in the modern age.

CHAPTER 4

IN THE AMERICAN GRAIN

Gustav Stickley and the Artisanal Type

THE CRAFTSMAN IMPRIMATUR

The adaptations of craft and image described in the previous chapter originated in the promotion of workmanship, from the 1830s onward, that was identifiably subjective; the iconicity of labor in the consumer market—the association of certain styles, rather than certain skills, with the handmade—can be read as the result of the British crafts revival's attempt to differentiate the meaning of artisanship from material, and thus potentially mechanizable, practices. When the crafts movement migrated to the United States in the late nineteenth century, its predication on the legibility of style seemed to take a further turn into the iconic modalities of consumer culture. The enormous banner on the side of Gustav Stickley's thirteen-story Craftsman Building, on Thirty-Eighth Street and Fifth Avenue in Manhattan, bespoke the fashionable appeal of the Arts and Crafts style in the United States; placing Stickley's enterprise among the marquees for Bloomingdale's and Bonwit Teller, the banner represented the apex of craft's popularity as a consumer style. Between 1901, when Stickley began selling his line of medieval crafts designs, and 1915, when he filed for bankruptcy, his furnishings and writings brought the craft revival to a much wider audience than the mostly well-to-do connoisseurs supporting his British counterparts. The idioms of representation and reproduction that, I have suggested, Charles Ryder comes to accept within the foundational logic of the British craft aesthetic in *Brideshead Revisited* were explicit in the vision that Stickley brought to the mass market.

The following pages interpret the relations of word and image in Stickley's Craftsman project, by which I mean that my primary subject involves the tactics that made Craftsman furnishings recognizable in a consumer world of named styles and advertisement copy. As pointedly as any example in *Talking Shop*, Stickley's project reveals the strenuous effort required to popularize handicraft as a brand name ("Craftsman") that was distinct from period styles ("Chippendale," "Colonial," "Louis XVI"), and to popularize the meaning and visual effect of Craftsman furnishings through the large body of propagandistic writings published in Stickley's magazine *The Craftsman.* Stickley is such a good example of the era's adaptability, moreover, because he initially resisted the textual modality on which he would come to depend. The contention that "work itself resists representation," to recall Michael Denning's terms, informed Stickley's early philosophy—for he began, in 1901, by drawing the attention of his audience *away* from efforts to translate workmanship. The name he chose for the new enterprise pointed out not his debt to his British forebears (whose encouragement, when he visited England in the 1890s, prompted him to sell his stake in a period-furniture manufactory and to set out in a new aesthetic direction) but his opposition to what he saw as the excessively theoretical basis of their project. Leaving out the first term of the Arts and Crafts dyad, the one that was most important to its founders, Stickley inaugurated the Craftsman company by praising the British craft movement, and William Morris in particular, but felt that he had reached his conclusions "from a direction opposite to that great benefactor of society."[1] Identifying Morris as "first a thinker and afterward a craftsman," Stickley located his own origins in his practical experience with tools and his vocational understanding of material. Where Morris started with ideas and words, Stickley described a lifetime of work on farms and in shops, claiming to have advanced from the "fact" to the "principle underlying the fact" (42). Where the British crafts revivalists defined art as "intuition" and craft as "knowledge," to quote Cobden-Sanderson's terms, the second issue of *The Craftsman*—a tribute to Ruskin—invoked this language only to reverse the Ruskinian ascendancy of the former over the latter.[2] Fearful that "intuition often supplied the place of genuine knowledge" in Ruskin, Irene Sargeant, a professor of art history at Syracuse who edited the early numbers of the magazine and wrote many of its articles, instead stressed the minor Ruskinian claim that "every artist should be a workman"; the more salient point of "The Nature of Gothic" and the British crafts movement in general, I have suggested, is the reverse.[3] In his designs, Stickley rejected most of the Gothic elements that Ruskin took as confirmation of the unalienated nature of labor. The accretion of ornament and the lack of symmetry that testified to subjective workmanship in *The Stones of Venice* did not appear in the simple and symmetrical Craftsman pieces (fig. 14). Ruskin saw the soaring effort of the workman's imagination in the "elastic tension" of a Gothic building, but Craftsman furniture was much closer to the Greek ideal—wherein each piece sits "passively incumbent on another"—that Ruskin found so dull.[4]

Stickley thus defined his enterprise by stressing its material over its expository or artistic origins; he opposed the real experience of the artisan to the

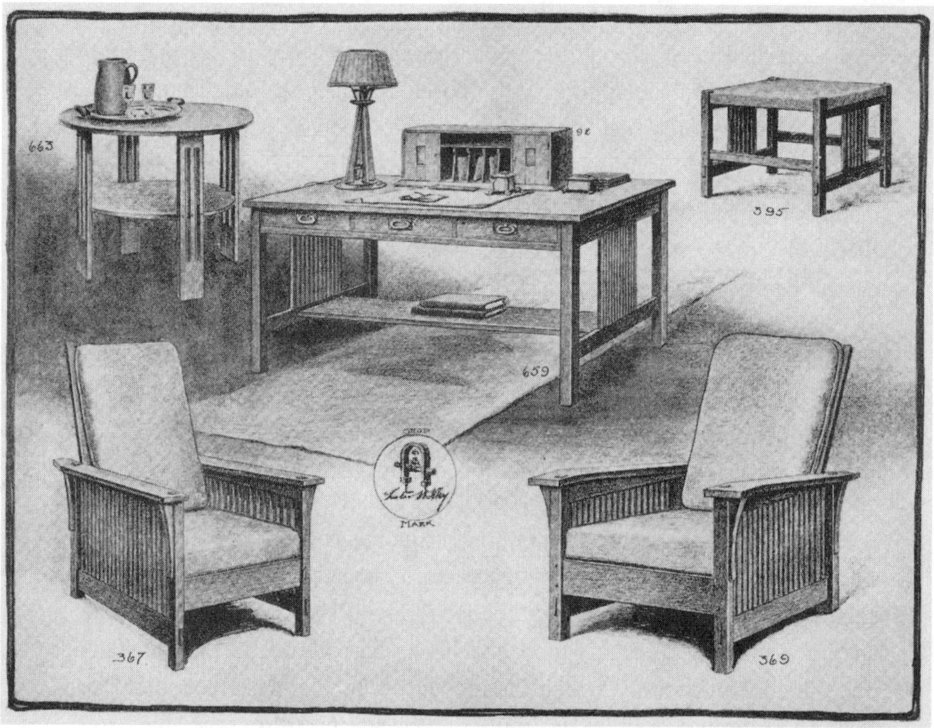

FIGURE 14. Gustav Stickley, Craftsman "spindle" furniture, c. 1909. (Stickley, *Craftsman Homes* [New York: Craftsman, 1909]; courtesy the Winterthur Library, Printed Book and Periodical Collection)

symbolic content of British Arts and Crafts pieces, to descriptions of workmanship by theorists, and to the "hypnotic influence of words" that he identified in the advertising industry.[5] But if Stickley offered a new vision of the Arts and Crafts Movement, highlighting his closer relation to reality than to representation, this very resistance also lodged in a name that he aggressively marketed, defined, and promoted. The near-simultaneous founding of *The Craftsman* magazine and the Craftsman Furniture Company (as well as the extension of the enterprise to include a publishing company) marks the inextricability of words and things, printing and manufacturing concerns, in Stickley's business; in practice, Stickley presumed that purchasers would want to read about the theoretical foundations of Craftsman furniture and, in reverse, that reading about objects would lead the magazine's subscribers to buy them. Even as Stickley broke from the British movement by emphasizing material practice over visionary content, the scale of the enterprise named "Craftsman"—which, at its height, included the furnishings company, publishing operation, and building as well as a restaurant, farm, interior design consultancy, and retail outlets from coast to coast—reinforced the orientation of craft to stylistic recognizability implicit in the British movement's notion of craft as art. The wide currency of Stickley's name in fact had much to do with the enterprise's ultimate collapse, for Stickley's own brothers capitalized on their suddenly famous surname and streamlined production to undercut Gustav's prices while copying his designs; the "Stickley" Company currently flourishing is the actual remnant of the enterprise headed by Leopold and John George Stickley. Mass-market retailers like Sears Roebuck in turn knocked off versions of the Craftsman style even more cheaply than Stickley's brothers. The final irony came in 1927, when Sears named a line of tools with the "Craftsman" moniker it retains today.

Stickley's struggle to distinguish his furnishings from those of his brothers —an effort conducted largely in the introductions to his catalogs and by the invention of a series of trademarks meant to distinguish his work from "imitators . . . who bear the same name as myself"—epitomizes the theme of this chapter and indeed of this book.[6] For the connections at the center of *Talking Shop*, between craft and language, labor and its representation, may have been no more pressing than for a man who, seeking to restore craft's grounding in its physical media, also worked mightily to establish and then to defend the links between his name and his work. For good reasons, given the scale of Stickley's Craftsman enterprise, his efforts, like those of Morris & Co., have been read skeptically; the size of Stickley's handicrafts empire, as it developed, appears disproportionate to the ideas about traditional, small-shop workmanship that he celebrated.[7] The following pages, however, approach Stickley from the opposite direction, considering less how the Craftsman enterprise outstripped the traditional scale of the workshop than how Stickley's foundational theories in fact correlated handicrafts authenticity and the artisan's ability to name, describe, or otherwise represent his labor to a wide public—a pattern that, from the beginning, presumed a market of consumers who were also readers or who thought about décor via the taxonomic lexicons modeled, for instance, by Owen Jones's *The Grammar of Ornament*. Describing the craftsman as a "translator," an idea he drew from Ralph Waldo Emerson's view of the poet, Stickley predicated crafts "honesty" and the artisan's right regard for the imperatives of the material on ideas about how wood speaks to the woodworker, how craft speaks to the nation, and how the promise of the crafts movement lodged in its ability to translate matter into meaning. Locating his inspiration in a "course of reading, largely in Ruskin and Emerson, which I pursued in my youth," Stickley loaded *The Craftsman* with literary criticism, fiction, poetry, and essays.[8] Accounting for his origins as a furniture maker in his life of reading seems to reverse Stickley's claim that he began not with theory but with wood. Yet the two origin myths, variously indulged over the course of Stickley's career, suggest his larger, often implicit project of accommodating labor and literature, material and its translation. As the contest with Leopold and John George Stickley suggests, certain pitfalls attended the idea of translating artisanship into a name, and at various points in the magazine's history, Stickley worried that *The Craftsman* had become too literary—declaring, for instance, that "the study of handicrafts as an end in itself" had been sacrificed to the indulgence of handicrafts as a reader's subject.[9] On those occasions, Stickley tried to steer the enterprise back to the grounds of practicality, usually by inaugurating series of how-to articles on crafts techniques.

These series, however, were either short-lived or more about design than method, and the magazine inevitably returned to a format that minimized the skills of enactment—thus mirroring the British crafts movements—and celebrated craft as a describable aesthetic and an ideal vitalized by narratives about it. Such narratives clearly branded and commodified the Craftsman idea. But those same accommodations, of objects and narrative or craft and its lexicons, also fulfilled what Stickley saw as the democratic promise of translating artisanship into the popular tongue, cohering no less than a national artisanal sensibility around his projection of the people's "demand [for] the real thing."[10] The sequence of translations that Stickley projected began with the wood itself, my subject in the first third of this chapter. I will suggest that the strategies by which Stickley accentuated the generic qualities of his preferred material, quartersawn American white oak, tapped into both Emersonian notions about the translatability of nature (a facility Emerson accorded to the poet, and Stickley to the craftsman) and Victorian predilections for the broad typologies promoted by a culture of decorative magazines, design encyclopedias, and taxonomized styles.

The rest of the chapter considers, first, how fiction published in *The Craftsman* reflected the imperatives of linking craft's promise to its representational capacity, and second, how Stickley drew on all of these ideas at the end of his career to defend the period pieces—Chippendale, Jacobean, and Colonial Revival—that he was forced to produce as the Craftsman company began rapidly losing money, ultimately filing for bankruptcy in 1915 and dissolving completely by 1917. These late reproduction pieces, many of them in maple or elm, appeared to sell short the promise of Stickley's original handicrafts style, capping his absorption by the mass market as a capitulation to period style; the "Chinese Chippendale" pieces shown in figure 15 have carved surfaces, fanciful brackets between the legs and the aprons, upholstery in Chinese motifs, and

THIS GROUP OF CHINESE CHIPPENDALE FURNITURE GIVES BUT A FAINT IMPRESSION OF THE BEAUTY OF A ROOM FURNISHED WITH THIS NEW AND DISTINGUISHED ADAPTATION IN MODERN FURNISHING: THE WOODWORK IS BROWN CUBAN MAHOGANY WITH THE USUAL CARVING IN SLIGHT RELIEF, AND THE UPHOLSTERY IS IN HEAVY MODERN BROCADE OF CHINESE BLUE, SILVER AND GRAY: A NOVEL USEFUL PIECE OF FURNITURE IS THE LAMP OR FLOWER STAND AT THE HEAD OF THE SOFA.

FIGURE 15. Gustav Stickley, "Chinese Chippendale" furnishings, c. 1914.
(*The Craftsman* 27, no. 1 [October 1914]: 73)

sinuous lines. Derivative and uneasily situated in the line of Craftsman design, they have prompted little interest among collectors, antiques dealers, and scholars. But from the start, the Craftsman ideal of authenticity had a mass-market aspect that, in ways I will explore in the final section of this chapter, limits the presumed gap between the early work and the late work. In adapting crafts labor to the world of decorative taxonomy, and orienting objects to a narrated meaning, Stickley laid the groundwork at the beginning of his career for an involved later argument, conducted in the pages of *The Craftsman*, about authenticity and originality as virtues embodied in the affective, typological experience of a home. Even when (indeed, sometimes because) the individual objects were reproduction period pieces, the home could appear connected to an idealized crafts past on account of its coherent suggestion of traditional style. In the early years of his enterprise, Stickley stressed how to best finish oak to typify its grain, orienting his notion of craft less to the construction of a piece than to the kind of identifiability associated with the lexical universe of Victorian interior design—and less to the physical making of a thing than to the effect of coherence by which the "crafted" was coming to be understood. He adapted these notions, in the specific ways described at the end of this chapter, when forced to explain how his mass-market Colonial Revival imitations could be nonetheless authentic and suitable for the Stickley imprimatur.

AMMONIA FUMING, QUARTER SAWING, AND CRAFTSMAN OAK

For Stickley, the "beauty of color and grain" of white oak, its "peculiar quality of woodiness," defined the "basis of the whole Craftsman idea of interior decoration."[11] This was a moral as much as an aesthetic argument: Stickley asserted that the straight, even grain of Craftsman oak would produce a corresponding ethical straightness in those who lived with it, an uprightness that was all hard principles and no fuzzy edges. Coming back again and again in *The Craftsman* and his catalogs to the "influence of material form on mental mood," or to the "inevitable . . . influences which pass from the eye to the brain," Stickley told his readers that the robust grain and rectilinear form of his white oak furnishings would make them better people. At base, this was an idea born in corporate America.[12] "Professional people," whether they bought their furniture from Stickley or made it on the weekends, required an atmosphere of "stability and symmetry" to balance the uncertainty of the marketplace (53–54). Yoking the ideologies of secure domesticity, craft, and the free market, Stickley insisted that Craftsman furnishings were prophylactic, a guarantee that the "state of flux" endemic to a speculative economy would be guided by stern ethics and sober habits of mind (54).

White oak's "peculiar quality of woodiness" (and its peculiar quality of moral suasion), however, was even more peculiarly produced. "The beauty of color and grain" named by Stickley had little to do with the artisanal labors of staining and finishing, with hand-rubbing a finish to accentuate the natural surface. Craftsman finishing, on the contrary, was seriously caustic. Stickley fumed his oak with highly concentrated ammonia vapors; the 26 percent solution (household ammonia is 4 percent) burns skin and eyes and sears the lungs if inhaled. Today, one wears a respirator and other protective gear when reproducing the Craftsman finish. Stickley's artisans squeezed their eyes shut and held their breath while placing the ammonia in pie plates and lowering tarred-canvas fuming tents over each piece by rope and pulley, scrambling out of the shops for the night. Addressing homeowners who wished to fume their interior trim, and therefore could not use fuming tents, Stickley had only dry advice: "It is hardly necessary to say that the person to whom the pouring of the ammonia is entrusted will get out of the room as quickly as possible after the fumes are released."[13]

Overnight, the work of finishing would be completed. The concentrated tannins in oak—the reason wine is aged in oak barrels—react to ammonia fumes, darkening the wood evenly and without obscuring the figure of the grain. Because stain or other applied colorants do not collect in the pores, a phenomenon I will address in more detail shortly, fumed wood looks rather more natural than less; the color and grain pattern, as Stickley always insisted, looks immanent, inherent in the wood rather than applied. The chemical process in that sense was not merely a commercial expedient, for the point of Stickley's method was to suggest the taxonomic, generic sturdiness of white oak, to ground the "woodiness" of Craftsman furniture in a perfectly even color and pattern. Consider figures 16 (a drawing of an everyday piece of oak) and 17 (a drawing of oak as Stickley preferred it to appear). The intricate grain of the first image is one of the aesthetic challenges of working with oak and its siblings. Oak, elm, ash, and chestnut belong to the family of ring-porous woods, meaning that only the earlywood—the first growth of the tree each spring—contains the network of vessels for distributing sap. When the tree is conventionally milled (fig. 18), the cut of all but the center boards exposes varying amounts of the open-pored earlywood (represented in the exploded portion of the figure by gray shading) and close-pored latewood. Conventionally sawn boards, sometimes called plainsawn, present varyingly oblique angles between the cut and the annual rings. This will be most obvious in figure 18 by considering the second board from the top or the bottom of the tree; the angle of cut is such that very long sections of earlywood will be exposed,

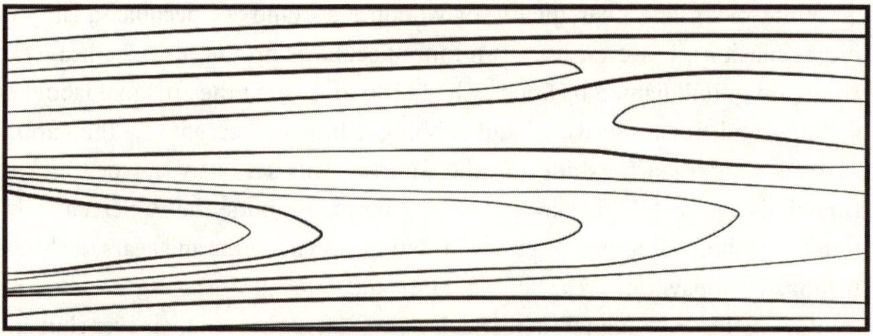

FIGURE 16. Plainsawn white oak. (Graphic by Warren Lawless)

FIGURE 17. Quartersawn white oak. (Graphic by Warren Lawless)

especially in the portion of the board nearest the middle. The result of all this variation between the saw blade and the annual rings is the familiarly wild, uneven grain of oak, a pattern like that in figure 16. These large, exposed sections of open-pored earlywood collect applied pigments like oil-based stains and aniline dyes. The residue of stain and dye appears in the earlywood channels as the dark, garish tracery of already irregular grain.[14]

In addition to preventing the buildup of stain in oak's irregular earlywood by fuming, Stickley used boards that were sawn differently. Figure 19 shows a quartersawn tree, in which the interval between earlywood and latewood is standardized across the width of every board because the cut and the growth rings intersect not obliquely but perpendicularly. Looking at the edges of each board in the figure demonstrates that the grain will be regular and straight, as in figure 17. (Only the center board is the same in both methods, which means that there is some quartersawn lumber in every plainsawn tree.) A quartersawn tree wastes wood because some of the boards are too narrow to be used; indeed, the sawyer would not bother to mill the outer boards in each quadrant of figure 19 because they would only be a few inches wide. But the grain is wonderfully strong and straight, very easy to work, and (also for reasons related to the more

FIGURE 18. Plainsawn tree shown in section. (Graphic by Warren Lawless)

regular distribution of the porous earlywood) highly stable against changes in humidity.

As Stickley put it, the task of fuming was to "release" or "reveal" this perfect, straight grain by "drawing out" its subtleties where stain would penetrate, saturate, and trace irregularity.[15] The idealized coherence offered by quartersawing and ammonia-fuming—through which the "robust" qualities of evenness and verticality, "stability and permanence," were realized—became the central logic of Craftsman design and the starting point of its organic aesthetics.[16] Prominent vertical lines, extreme stability, and stylized immanence are features of Stickley's furniture as well as of his treatment of material. Craftsman

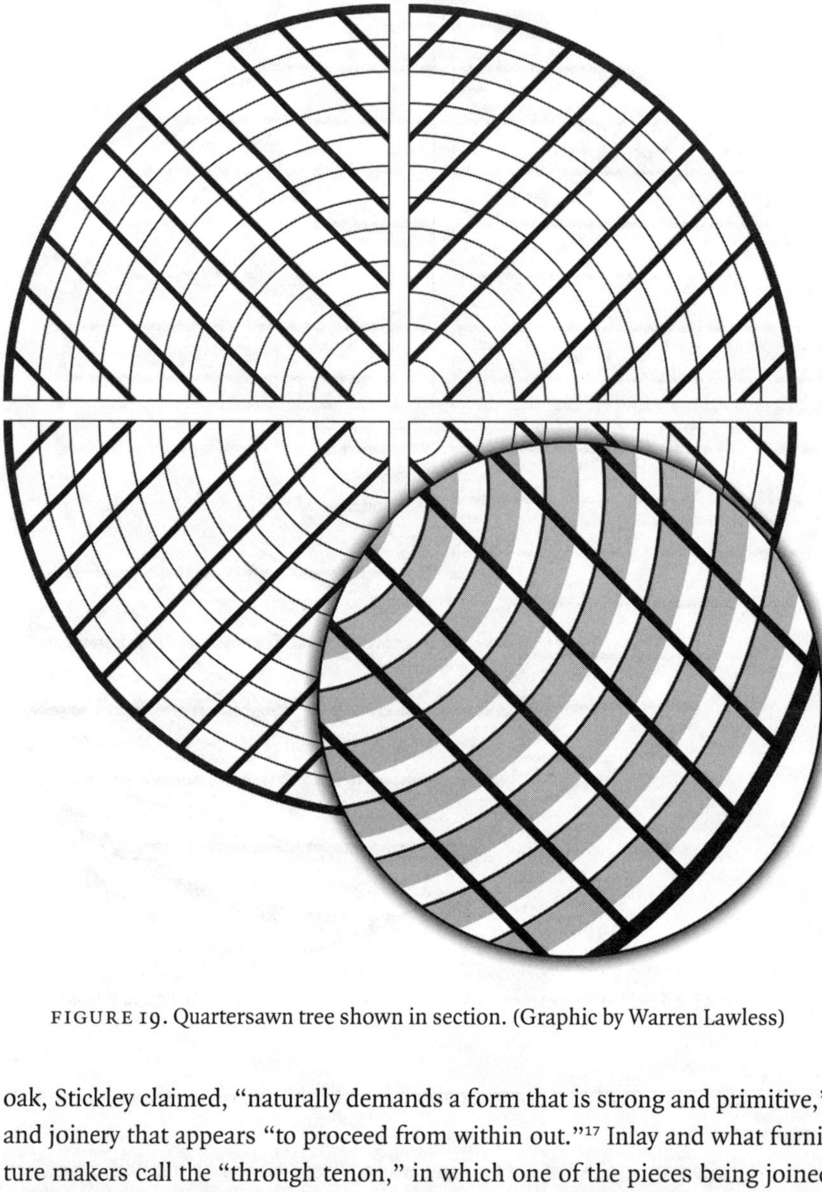

FIGURE 19. Quartersawn tree shown in section. (Graphic by Warren Lawless)

oak, Stickley claimed, "naturally demands a form that is strong and primitive," and joinery that appears "to proceed from within out."[17] Inlay and what furniture makers call the "through tenon," in which one of the pieces being joined projects clear through the other, represent two examples of how the sturdiness and transparency accorded to fumed (rather than stained) quartersawn oak generated a design predicated on immanence, emergence, and the abjuration of ornament applied to the surface. Through tenons are visible in figure 14 where the lower aprons of the two chairs and the footstool (pieces 367, 369, and 395 in the image) pass through the front legs, and where those legs, on the chairs, pass through the armrests. Releasing the wood as a generic type of straightness and regularity, as Stickley formulated his project, fuming and quartersawing gave shape to the design rather than the other way around. "The harmony that exists between the form and construction of the furniture and the wood of which it is made," Stickley wrote, "is complete and satisfying."[18]

The Vitruvian correlation of craft and telos, predicated on the artisan's ability to bend material to the design, thus appeared to fade behind an idealized notion of craft as an organic correlation of form and medium. That organic correlation, however, is a tautology: inverting Vitruvius, Stickley predicated design on the immanence of the wood, but he also managed and crafted that wood to match the designs it putatively inspired. The immanence of oak, in other words, is both an origin and—via ammonia-fuming and quartersawing—a goal of Stickley's process; the circularity of Stickley's organicism linked nature to type, yoking an idea about beginning with materials to the production of the generic essence of the same materials. Craftsman organicism also attempted to create what Stickley saw as a type of person, for the generically coherent oak Stickley elicited was the basis not just for design but for better, more natural living. The founding sociological principles of the Craftsman company held that certain kinds of rectilinear objects, acting on "mental mood," were a salve for the tensions and strains of modernity; the founding aesthetic principles held that these designs were inherent in native materials from the beginning. A chain of deterministic relations thus began with American white oak—Stickley preferred trees harvested from Indiana or the Southwest—and worked its way through design and construction to influence social ethics; circling back, the sense of uprightness attributed to Craftsman furnishings and its purchasers shaped the handling of the wood to best realize its ideal qualities of verticality and constancy in the first place. Addressing his furnishings to the psychic health of "men and women of business," Stickley betrayed the consumerist basis of handicrafts utopianism in the nineteenth and early twentieth centuries, a point that many of Stickley's commentators have treated with withering irony. The point I am trying to make, however, is that Stickley's notion of immanence, implicit in his handling of oak, comprehended some of the urgencies of modern production from the beginning. The inherence of material, the basis for organic design, was elicited, stylized, and rendered generically stable at the same time as it was, for Stickley, basic and essential. White oak advanced a notion of the authentic that, because it was taxonomic, could also be efficiently, consistently, and (in the case of fuming) chemically made.

These ideas did involve some trickery. Tracing squares (with edges at least twice as long as the represented boards are thick) onto the image of the quartersawn tree in figure 19 will expose a problem for Stickley's purposes: in most

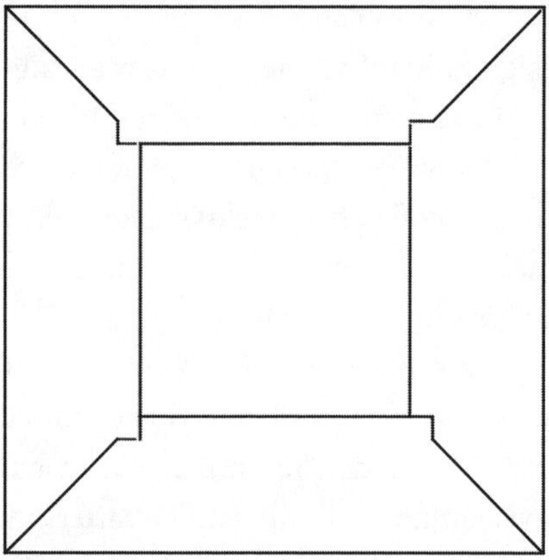

FIGURE 20. Quadrilinear post construction shown in section. (Graphic by the author)

cases, two faces of that square will be conventionally sawn, even when the log as a whole is quartersawn. If one takes a square core of the tree, the orientation of the grain lands in the direction of quartersawn grain on one axis and in the direction of plainsawn grain in the other. While an involved method of cutting does exist that can split the difference (in "riftsawn" trees the sawyer moves the log around in an attempt to get angles of 45 degrees between the cut and the grain, thus presenting decently straight figure on all four sides), most lumber has plainsawn grain on two faces—opposite to one another—and quartersawn grain on the adjacent faces. A round piece perhaps best illustrates the problem. Imagining a circle cored out of the figure (or looking at any chair, table leg, or baseball bat turned from a ring-porous wood) reveals that the grain alternates in each quadrant of the cylinder from wide, irregular grain to straighter grain as the angle between the cut edge and the tree's annual rings changes. For this reason, the logo on a baseball bat is an important aid; it enables the hitter to orient the bat in the same way each time, so that the quadrant containing the tighter quartersawn grain contacts the ball.

Excepting riftsawn boards, a chair or table leg in a ring-porous species that displays straight grain on all four sides—as did most of Stickley's—thus has to be constructed in one of two ways. The builder can arrange individual boards (generally about ¾ inches thick) with quartersawn faces around a hollow or a solid core, beveling the long edges of the four pieces to join with one another. This technique, depicted in section in figure 20 and producing a post that looks solid while offering four faces of quartersawn grain, was patented by Stickley's brothers and is usually referred to as "quadrilinear" construction. Alternately, the builder can veneer thin pieces of quartersawn material on the plainsawn edges of a square post—which is exactly how Stickley handled most of his legs. Figure 21 presents an intriguing detail of a Stickley daybed on which the veneer at the bottom of the leg was either damaged and removed or never installed. Whatever the history, the photograph makes Stickley's stratagem clear. The top of the post is veneered with quartersawn oak to a point about four inches above the cushion, where someone evidently softened the transition to the unveneered section below by beveling the edge of the veneer. Where the veneer is missing, one can see the edges of three boards glued together to constitute the post. (Although the face on the right side does not show the straightest possible quartersawn grain—because the degree of perpendicularity of each board to the growth rings does vary somewhat in any quartersawn tree—that face and the one opposite it, on the other side of the leg, are in fact the quartersawn top surfaces of the boards glued together to make the leg.) Like the quadrilinear design, this method of construction—applying veneer to the two faces of a leg that in solid construction, are not quartersawn—gives the illusion of relatively straight grain around all four sides. In furnishings with large legs, like this daybed, the faces of very irregular grain of a truly solid post would be sufficient to distract from the overall Craftsman effect. In these situations, Stickley abandoned the ideal of solid-wood immanence, of wood that emanates from the inside out, in favor of a glued-on representation of the grain he favored.

When it comes to the authenticity of grain and pattern, then, Stickley's veneered posts are a white lie about white oak. But even veneering, in the context of Craftsman notions of organic design, was an attempt to preserve what Stickley took as the generic straightness and stability of oak; the expedience of veneering flowed, in his mind, from a notion of immanent design predicated on an essential character purer and truer to oak's type than the large leg's two necessarily irregular surfaces. In adapting his notion of immanence to an idea about the typical and reproducible, Stickley was not perpetrating a hoax. Rather, he tapped into emerging modalities by which turn-of-the-century Americans consumed authenticity. Ammonia-fumed, quartersawn white oak presumed relays between nature, production, and the individual person; an elicited version of a natural essence, it promised, in turn, to remake people in its image. The remarkable instrumentality accorded to wood in this model looks overblown when read in the context of Stickley's aggressive salesmanship, for Craftsman furnishings bear nothing less than the promise of cultural salvation. But the instrumentality of wood looks more familiar in the context of what Mark Seltzer and others have described as nineteenth-century American beliefs in "the natural person" and "nature's nation . . . *as* typical, standard, and reproducible" (emphasis in original).[19] Orienting his work to iconic elicitations

FIGURE 21. Gustav Stickley, knock-down daybed (detail), 1907. Oak. (Photograph by David Rudd; courtesy Dalton's American Decorative Arts, Syracuse, NY)

of strength, purity, and type, Stickley offers a handicrafts version of the outlets Seltzer identifies with the concentrated industrial "making," at once authentic and imitative, of a more natural and putatively American condition. Those outlets—including, for Seltzer, bodybuilding, physical exercise, composite photography, and late nineteenth-century fiction by Frank Norris and others—stress the programmatic realization of a generic essence and movement toward the authenticity of category.

Stickley's emphasis on Craftsman oak as a "strong and primitive type," a "robust, manly sort of wood," also marks how the era often gendered such relays of nature, production, and the individual.[20] Seltzer tracks programmatic disciplines for "making the man" through Teddy Roosevelt, the Boy Scouts, and naturalist attitudes about the primeval conflicts between man and nature (149–72). As Wendy Kaplan has shown, Stickley's enterprise tied into Rooseveltian ethics via his plan for the Craftsman Farms School for Boys, a never-realized institution that proposed to develop traits of vigor and strength through strenuous programs of manual labor; one of the repeat contributors to *The Craftsman* was Raymond Riordan, whose articles chronicled his experiences as the founder of a residential school where boys did everything from running the heating plant to sowing and harvesting crops for their own meals.[21] The "manly" type of Craftsman oak appealed to such notions of becoming natural while, in its handling of grain and color, emblematizing some of the idioms of regularization and rationalization that historians have traced to Victorian masculinity itself. Oak's stylized robustness offered a generically producible example of a masculine type while also suggesting that such type was the result of discipline and the concentration of certain qualities. The "action of 'fuming' and other chemical processes," Stickley wrote, "might be compared to the experiences and trials of an individual."[22] The tempering force of difficult circumstances acted on wood as it did on men, making both more natural while also making them more typical.

In discussing ways to firm up the grain and draw out the character, in other words, *The Craftsman* adapted Rooseveltian values of achievement and activity. Describing himself as an "American man who has loved and worked with oak for a lifetime," Stickley stressed "enthusiasm," "steady courage," and "energy" as the virtues that enabled him to "expand [the] qualities and heighten [the] value" of native woods.[23] As an exercise in unity, the activities of focusing, purifying, and—to use Stickley's word—expanding the immanent qualities of white oak seem to run counter to the decorative miscellany that constituted mainstream interior décor in Victorian America. The crafts revival in general and the Craftsman enterprise in particular are well known for "cleaning up . . .

cluttered Victorian buildings," drawing on local and vernacular traditions, and thinning the layered effect of heavy tapestries, cozy corners, and walls teeming with patterns, pictures, and photographs.[24] But Stickley's ideas about oak tapped into the evidentiary elements of Victorian decorative historicism as much as they resisted its eclectic idioms. The profusion of things characterizing the late nineteenth-century interior flowed from the natural sciences, and from the emerging discourses of anthropology and ethnography, to the degree that furnishings appeared as instances and examples of "natural structure"; Debra Schafter, a historian of ornament, explains how Victorian discourses of decorative taste assessed floriform details, for example, through botanical taxonomies and described the history of architectural styles as a record of evolutionary paradigms associated both with the natural world and with the march of culture.[25] As industrial manufacture rapidly expanded the kinds and numbers of furnishings available to consumers, decorative historiography organized and abetted the glut of things along lines of order, analogy, and taxonomy.

Most important for my purposes, decorative historiography also organized furnishings along the lines of language. Owen Jones may have stretched a point in calling his visual encyclopedia of pattern the *Grammar of Ornament*. "One must search hard," Schafter writes, to find concrete correlations between recognizably grammatical structures and the designs depicted by Jones.[26] For John Summerson, the *Grammar* is better described as a "polyglot phrase-book."[27] But precisely to the degree that Jones construed relations between objects and language visually and generically—emphasizing naming rather than true syntax—his title suggests how new magazines like *House Beautiful* and new reference books like Charles Blanc's *Grammaire des arts décoratif* (1886) generated a vigorously taxonomic print culture. Original and reproduction furnishings alike appeared as nameable and discussable "specimens" of a host of styles: titles like Henry Shaw's *Specimens of Ancient Furniture* (1836) and Arthur Marshall's *Specimens of Antique Carved Furniture Measured and Drawn* (1888) bespoke a wider habit of describing, for instance, "foreign specimens" reproduced by American manufacturers, or "relics, specimens, objects of art [and] curiosities" that would serve to "make talk" on subjects other than "politics, dress, fashions, and scandal."[28] Many of these specimens represented the imitative period styles that *The Craftsman* excoriated. But Stickley also appealed to the decorative spirit from which period styles emerged. Fuming and quartersawing provided Victorian consumers—used to thinking about décor, nature, and the real thing in broadly typological and lexical terms—with the stereotyped, stylized, and ultimately reproducible essence of oak. When cut and finished as he prescribed,

"Hercules of the Forest," Stickley's name for the white oak tree, epitomized the convergence of elicitation, immanence, and representation on which his audience depended to understand the kind of naturalized authenticity he peddled.

Indeed, Stickley's first statement of his decorative vision, the oaken "Eastwood" designs with which he launched the Craftsman style, tapped a material and a name that the end of the nineteenth century *already* understood in generic terms. In the period between 1870 and 1920, oak jumped from a minor furniture wood (only used in early Colonial furniture or, in the eighteenth-century, for invisible details like drawer slides) to the major species of American woodworking. This had something to do with forestry: overharvest of the fine-grained, diffuse-porous woods favored in the eighteenth century turned the attention of sawyers to oak and chestnut.[29] But the popularity of oak was also launched by the British writer, architect, and designer Charles Locke Eastlake, who named oak as the best wood for those wanting something more solid than the imitation styles of the day. Eastlake described the sort of furnishings he favored—objects in the style of a "packing case," according to one commentator (fig. 22)—as symbols of "straight-forward manufacture" and "legitimate" provenance in a world that craved "Etruscan necklaces . . . Persian rugs, Greek vases, and Roman lamps."[30]

Stickley did not name the Eastwood furniture (fig. 23) after Eastlake himself; the line takes its name from the Syracuse suburb where Stickley's shops were originally located. But Stickley cannot have been indifferent to the associations between his massively rectilinear pieces and Eastlake's: the stylistic similarities of Eastlake and Eastwood furnishings made the happenstance of Stickley's geographical location—appearing even more serendipitous by the "wood" in "Eastwood"—suit his purposes perfectly. For in hinting at Eastlake, Eastwood furnishings tapped into the correlation between oak and the "straight-forward" stressed by the British designer. Eastlake did not quartersaw his wood to make the grain straighter; the jagged, irregular grain of plainsawn oak and the Gothic detailing of his designs constituted a style more in keeping with the terms of the English handicrafts revival. But Eastlake's aesthetic was as much subject as Stickley's to the paradox of its own iconicity. In the United States, where Eastlake's *Hints on Household Taste* (1868) went through six printings, his furnishings became so popular that he excoriated American retailers for copying his style and transforming his beliefs into an imitable, conspicuously fashionable aesthetic. Mass-market retailers offered Eastlake-inspired pieces in "solid oak," finishes in "golden oak," and furniture suites in "genuine oak"; the "brown decades," as Lewis Mumford called the end of the nineteenth century, were brown in part because the era's heavy, somber interiors—a brown element cited

FIGURE 22. Arthur William Blomfield, Design for chiffonier, c. 1872. (Eastlake, *Hints on Household Taste*, 1st American ed., Boston: J. R. Osgood & Co., 1872, p. 187)

FIGURE 23. Gustav Stickley, "Eastwood" armchair, No. 347, c. 1912. Oak. (Photograph by Ray Stubblebine; used with permission of the Craftsman Farms Foundation, Inc., Parsippany, NJ)

by Mumford—were oak.[31] One figure who would have liked such an interior is Edith Wharton's Newland Archer. In *The Age of Innocence*, set in the 1870s, Newland wants Eastlake furnishings for his library because they seem authentic and original; he fantasizes about "Eastlake bookcases" and " 'sincere' armchairs and tables."[32] But the problem at the center of the novel is that Newland's desire for the authentic is an impossible fantasy; his dream of a "real life," better than the "sham" one he lives in New York society, looks terribly naïve to Madame Olenska, with whom Newland would escape the stifling fakery of polite existence (243). Newland's romantic and social problem—that authenticity is a fantasy—is recapitulated in his ideal home. Oaken Eastlake furnishings, knocked off by the dozens, were at the center of the "hieroglyphic world" Newland deplores, a world wherein "the real thing was . . . only represented by a set of arbitrary signs" (44).

For Stickley, the real thing and its sign were axiomatically, not arbitrarily, related. The sturdiness of oak was the paradigmatic starting point of an organic aesthetic addressed both to the aesthetics of design and the ethics of living. But that sturdiness was also, in the ways I have suggested, where workmanship arrived. Stickley elicited the grain he took as essential and relied on an established market for decorative objects as specimens, for oak as a medium of resistance to period styles, and for "tempering" as a way to arrive at the more natural. For such a square aesthetic, there is a lot of circularity in all this. The inherence that would make more rugged people was also made by them. The origins of Craftsman design were also their finish: because fumed color only penetrates a sixteenth of an inch and would be cut through by sawing or sanding, one cannot fume the materials and then build the piece. The piece has to be built and then fumed, drawing out the nature of the quartersawn wood that is also the source of the style.

But the tautology of Craftsman design also cuts through hierarchies of value that have been attributed to the nineteenth-century marketplace in general and to Stickley's efforts in particular; Stickley related beginnings and ends, design and finish, symbol and fact, discovery and production, trees and chemicals, the authentic and the imitative. Relocating the British movement's emphasis on singular artistry to the generic type of white oak, Stickley's project had similar implications for technique. Actual craft skills, I have already suggested, seldom appear in *The Craftsman;* the series on "Practical Lessons in Cabinetmaking," for instance, gives far more information on design, proportion, and material—elements of craft's iconicity—than on cutting wood or fitting joints. Stickley's how-to articles in some cases begin and end with the only skill, fuming quartersawn oak, that he felt really mattered; the "construction shows for itself" in the simple, rugged forms naturally demanded by the qualities of the wood.[33] Stickley believed that the woodworker was to "reveal and continue the mysterious operations begun in secret, when the wood was yet a living tree."[34] Those animistic operations were predicated not on the woodworker's ability to "reveal and continue" a *particular* tree, responding to its idiosyncrasies, but on his willingness to expose the "mysterious operations" that all white oaks, every tree, would have in common. The Craftsman vision, educing the essences it took as origins, began with what the craftsman already knew about the nature that would putatively inspire his design.

It is in that sense that Stickley, in an early essay called "Structure and Ornament," adopted Ralph Waldo Emerson's dictum about the poet as the "sayer, the namer," he who is the "translator of nature into thought," timeless facts into human creations.[35] Emerson's formula of organic poetry rests on the way in which thought takes off from material: the specially constituted individual ("the man without impediment") makes a "new thought, a new experience" from the "conversation [he has] had with nature" (223–24). Emerson here sounds like Ruskin, the other author named as an inspiration by Stickley. The immanence of physical facts—for Ruskin, the unworkable stone of northern Europe—prompts originality of thought. The fragile stone of Venice, demanding "fine discipline of the hand" not to break, threatens the adaptability, the "impetuosity," of the mind.[36]

Stickley, however, ran the formula in both directions. Rather than describing, with Ruskin, the elevation of nature into art or, with Emerson, the organic activity that "translates nature into thought," Stickley wrote that craftsmen are the "instruments, the translators of thought" back into nature; the craftsman is the figure who begins with an idea and ends with a fact at the same time as he takes facts—the essential nature of white oak—as the basis of everything from design to ethics.[37] When Stickley describes craftsmen as the translators of thought, in the larger context of "Structure and Ornament," he means that craftsmen could supply a fundamental "need" among Americans for the "real thing." The artisan's mandate appears as the effort to fulfill the organic basis of American identity ("to the American the real thing is something he needs and understands") in furnishings that materialized natural facts. What Stickley did *not* mean in describing artisans as "translators of thought" is what, out of context, it seems he might: that artisans translated their own creative and singular thoughts into physical forms, enacting unique visions of the mind in material. That model would abandon the organicism of the Craftsman vision. Instead, the "thought" represented a concept about the "real thing" that organic design would fulfill. Craftsman white oak directly reflected the stakes of the process. Its grain was an elicited basis for an immanent aesthetic, a thought about oak before it was a discovery in oak or a physical reality. Straightened and regularized, it enacted the presumed American need for the authentic as an idea, a generic coherence from which the natural immanence of Craftsman furniture emerged.

THE CRAFT OF FICTION, 1905–1907

Stickley's craftsman became a "translator," in the tradition of the Emersonian poet who relates nature and words, by operating as an agent of typicality. Thus, I have suggested, the craftsman also appeared as an agent of the grammar of ornament; Craftsman oak fit into an emerging system for classifying decorative objects on the basis of their generic features. The anxieties associated with that system appear from the beginning. Owen Jones himself worried that *The Grammar of Ornament* would abet the industrial reproduction of period styles, and insisted that readers should consult the volume only as an inspiration; by encouraging readers to draw freely from examples across historical eras, recombining details in original works, Jones resisted his own summing-up of design within a conventional encyclopedia of style.[38] Stickley sidestepped some of the anxiety prompted by the project of translating craft and décor by running his model bidirectionally. Orienting workmanship to the recognizable, imitable, and nameable style called "Craftsman," he also made that very typicality the basis for a restored relation with primacy, authenticity, and physical material.

Of course, Stickley's typological handling of white oak links the craftsman's process to the nineteenth-century invention of a *lexicon* for furniture, not to the literary representations of labor—especially in fiction—that have prompted other, more recent critical anxieties about the shortfalls of representing work in words. But *The Craftsman* enterprise did begin to regularly publish short stories in late 1905 and 1906; hitched to a project that romanticized craft and that praised oak for its generically reproducible qualities, the literary output of the Craftsman enterprise would seem particularly vulnerable to the idealizing abstractions excoriated by critics of fiction about labor. Predictably, many of the stories in *The Craftsman* did offer didactic parables and trite, easily distilled morals praising the virtues of work. The innovation, however, also raised the stakes and complicated the terms of the Craftsman enterprise as a literary endeavor. From the beginning, *The Craftsman* had published excerpts of nonfiction, generally panegyrics to working people, by Morris, Ruskin, Thomas Carlyle, Edward Carpenter, Charlotte Perkins Gilman, Henry David Thoreau, and Leo Tolstoy. Its pages also included critical essays about such writers as William Cullen Bryant, Maxim Gorky, O. Henry, Henrik Ibsen, Jack London, Henry Wadsworth Longfellow, Robert Louis Stevenson, and Walt Whitman. But the original *fiction* in the magazine raised deeper questions about the relationship between craft and its represented, projected, invented, idealized, or moralized significance. The dematerialization of labor has become the preoccupation of literary criticism about work and narrative; that preoccupation was anticipated as a practical problem when *The Craftsman*—the literary organ of a project said to originate in "facts" rather than "ideas" and to translate matter into recognizable and immanent forms—began to print moral stories about work in general alongside essays on particular or practical topics in craftsmanship, sociology, architecture, and aesthetics.

I want to suggest, however, that the early fiction in *The Craftsman* did not wholly capitulate to the thematizing of craft as conventional moral parable. Just as Stickley's handling of white oak comprehended the imperatives both of typicality and of originality, of categorical recognizability and of natural immanence, *The Craftsman* asked its readers to frame correlations between craft as a virtue presented in fiction and craft as a physical, embodied activity. Cautioning readers against seeing manual labor too abstractly, *The Craftsman* subtly resisted the threat that its new direction would abet the transformation of craft into a secondhand image: even as the magazine's pages began to fill with parable-like stories about the generic virtues of craft, its editors included fictional contributions explicitly critical of too much sermonizing. The shape of the magazine as a whole asked readers to see workmanship on a continuum. If craft could be ennobling, *The Craftsman* also prompted its audience not to let their ideals stray too far from craft's physical locations and its practical skills; the parameters of that new subject were introduced in ways that recalled the three-dimensionality of the expertise translated onto the page.

This process is most clearly seen in the editorial shaping of the magazine by Mary Fanton Roberts, George Wharton James, and Muriel Irwin MacDonald between 1905 and 1907. But the stakes of allying a craft enterprise to fiction were articulated by Stickley himself in the interim between the first piece of fiction published in the magazine, an anonymous contribution to the French *Magasin Pittoresque* translated for *The Craftsman* as "The Fatal Hand," and the publication of the first original story, Harriet Joor's "A Lover of the Beautiful," in 1905. Between "The Fatal Hand" and "A Lover of the Beautiful," Stickley published an essay called "The Flood of Fiction," asking readers to consider the potential contribution of the crafts movement to narrative literature. Dramatically stating that the short story "as it is now produced in enormous quantities and at rapid rates, is a real peril to the country," Stickley lambasted the derivation of early twentieth-century fiction from tales of romance, adventure, and international playboys—a genre represented for Stickley by Anthony Hope's popular novel *The Prisoner of Zenda* (1894). Calling for a "renewed originality in fictional literature," Stickley projected the crafts movement as its agent; the literary hopes of the nation, he suggested, might be predicated on the "originality . . . of the handicraft movement of today which decries—and justly—the machine and the copy."[39] Stickley's hopes were not borne out by the often formulaic stories that eventually began to appear in *The Craftsman*. But the bid to ally craft and fiction governed the editorial decisions of the magazine as it began to include narrative representations of an activity ideally belonging to bodies and material.

Consider, first, how the virtuous influence Stickley attributed to his furniture—and particularly to its straightened, regularized grain—was reflected in the virtuous influence attributed to iterative labor in early stories in *The Craftsman*. The plot lines of the works appearing in the magazine between 1905 and 1907, the era in which Stickley and the magazine's editors framed the place of fiction in the Craftsman project, are not just formulaic; more pointedly, they appear to minimize the appeal of craft as an original act, instead featuring the moral dividends that flow from the practice of craft as an activity oriented to conventions, types, and reproducible forms. Thus, for instance, Helen Fitzgerald Sanders's "The Gift of Angelo" describes an old sculptor whose life making copies—his shop is full of "plaster of Paris casts of classical statues and prim figures of the saints"—suddenly appears prosaic and uninspired when it is discovered that his son Angelo has virtuoso talents on the violin.[40] Angelo goes abroad so that his gift can be "trained to the point of perfection," but mainly develops an inflated aesthetic ego (182). When he returns to San Francisco, his loving father's workshop appears "mean and small" by comparison to Old World models, and Angelo excoriates his imitative statues as untrue to the right proportions of the real thing (184). Angelo's skill and the pursuit of perfection ultimately appear as dehumanizing values in the story, leaving the diminutively named father, Angelotti, and his humble craft—he works late at night to earn as much as his son requires to live in Europe—as the icons of constancy and integrity. Angelo's virtuosity falls short of the virtue displayed by the man whose life is turned to derivative labors.

For a magazine that decried the fictional and the decorative "copy," to use Stickley's language, it is striking how many of the stories in its pages follow the pattern of "The Gift of Angelo": skeptical about singular achievement, they derive a conventional moral lesson from figures who, like Angelo, are dehumanized by their expertise and their pursuit of the highest standard of their craft. Two more examples may suffice to set the pattern, which interests me primarily to the degree that the magazine's editorship, as it introduced fiction into its pages, raised questions about the distillable lessons and the attenuation of perfectible skill in the very stories it featured. Perhaps the most moralistic of the moral tales about craft were those by an otherwise-unknown author named Burton Richards. "The Brother of the Cross" describes a stonemason who believes himself to be working in the name of "supreme love" on a magnificent female figure carved from a "flawless piece of stone."[41] Absorbed by his labor, performed on a hillside where his stone is set under the shadow of a stone cross, he ignores the passersby who require various kinds of aid of him; when he finally finishes, he discovers that his coldheartedness has left the sculptural form equally devoid of human tenderness even as, day by day, his vision seemed to grow "fairer under his hand" (97). The irony of the mason's working so uncharitably under the shadow of the cross appears as an even more explicitly Christian parable in "The Master Workman," a story about a workshop visited overnight by the invisible and unseen figure of the master workman, who selects which pieces he prefers from those left out for his judgment. The artisans are divided on the question of whether "the Master notes only a perfect work" or whether he "shows His face to them who only strive if so be they earnest and faithful."[42] By the end of the story, the question is answered for the reader. An old man tells a young apprentice the story of how he once saw the master, who appears as "a nearness of something sweet and pure and holy," when he abandoned a perfect work—a piece with "an exquisite curve that made me weep for the very chasteness of its beauty"—to fashion a "rudely hewn" bowl to offer to some beggars (851–52). The lesson of the old man's story is reinforced when the apprentice to whom he is speaking accidentally ruins a delicate cup that is a "marvel of skill" (853). That night, the old man sneaks into the workshop and, after some debate with himself, replaces the broken cup on the boy's bench with the finest piece of his own—a carving he had hoped to leave on his bench for the master's approbation. Such generosity, of course, is the occasion for the master's second coming to the elderly artisan; the story ends with him standing "face to face with the Master Workman" (853). Objects of great skill—the piece with the "exquisite curve" in the old man's tale, the cup broken by the boy, and the carving the old man gives up—are systematically sacrificed to the compassion that appears as the truer standard of workmanship.

The interest of "The Gift of Angelo," "The Brother of the Cross," and "The Master Workman" lies in the imperatives of craft that they suggest. First, the stories—typifying an entire line of contributions to *The Craftsman*—dramatize the suspicion about skill that, I have suggested, grounded the craft revival's sense of its difference from the routine labor of machines. Second, the stories represent how the Craftsman project turned suspicion about skill in a different direction than did the British Arts and Crafts Movement. Stickley's project lodged its account of the workman's intuition and human feeling in typicality rather than singularity, and in imitable forms—the regularized grain of white oak, the plaster casts of Angelotti, the crude beggar's bowl made by the old artisan—rather than in complicated and incommensurable ones; conventional notions of the Craftsman project as an effort to revivify authenticity through original works do not account for its foundational emphasis on reproducibility and typology.[43] Third, and most important for my purposes, *The Craftsman* was hardly univocal about the appeal of the plots that, in stories like "The Gift of

Angelo," it featured. For the imperative to typify craft's virtues by stressing craft's orientation to typical objects is put to the test by some of the most prominent stories published in the magazine, as well as by the inclusion of other stories that complicate or even oppose the morals advanced by Burton Richards and Helen Fitzgerald Sanders. To be sure, one does not normally judge a literary magazine by the level of conceptual agreement among its contributions. But *The Craftsman* was not an ordinary literary magazine. It was a piece of a larger project, a mission in reformed workmanship that aimed to "gain the . . . co-operation of a wide public," as the first sentence of the first issue put it—and its fiction, Stickley claimed, would be part and parcel of the effort. Against that standard, of a relatively coherent voice, some of the more pointed equivocations within and between the initial stories mark the various imperatives flowing through the Craftsman movement as it struggled to work out the place of creative fiction in its celebration of handiwork, of material, and of a restored relation with the real thing.

A few pieces are direct challenges to the fictional paradigm that stressed the virtues of humble, iterative work. Given its title, Carolyn Sherwin Bailey's "The Regeneration of Benvenuto" seems as if it would reinforce the moral of stories like Frank H. Sweet's "The Bridge Keeper" and "The Plowman"—pieces in which an outcast of one sort or another is redeemed by performing some unpretentious labor with workmanlike care. In Sweet's stories, every kind of labor appears a craft: an out-of-work man earns a job as a bridge keeper by attending the wind and tide vigilantly, timing the opening of the span for passing ships with "as fine a bit of calculation" as the owner has ever seen; a ne'er-do-well boy gains redemption, surprising even himself with the pride he takes in plowing.[44] But "The Regeneration of Benvenuto" offers a different account of craft's transformative qualities, while perhaps hinting at an association between its title character and the paradigmatic artisanal figure of Benvenuto Cellini. The story describes a charity society visiting an experimental kindergarten wherein arts and crafts are used to ennoble the "children of the slums"; "Give his little hands something to do," one of the visitors aphorizes, "and his little heart will follow."[45] The most recalcitrant boy, Benvenuto, refuses to join the basketry class and hurls a chisel at the carpentry teacher (540)—and turns out to represent the only authentic thing in a story when he leaps through a window ("To be let loose in the sunshine of New York, and on Grand Street!" [543]) and runs to a tenement home saturated with the "refreshing odor of frying garlic" and spilling over with "spaghetti, yards of it" (544). Benvenuto appears in the final line as the "unregenerate," but that description only applies according to the definitions of the visitors, satirized as paternalistic and out of touch in the story as a whole.

The reader thus experiences Benvenuto's salvation not through labor but by his return to his genuine, if disadvantaged, life; the narrative forces us to reinterpret the epithet in the final line—"unregenerate"—through the actually regenerated joie de vivre of the boy. In the same sense that Bailey's title, "The Regeneration of Benvenuto," prompts readers to redefine the original terms, predicating "regeneration" on the "unregenerate," the story as a whole begs its reader to perform a similarly critical operation on the literary paradigm defining many of the early stories in *The Craftsman.* The appealing character of Benvenuto challenges the moral universality of labor, as advanced in stories delimiting the appeal of specialized skills and idealizing work not as accrued or focused knowledge but as a generic virtue. Bailey's choice of the name "Benvenuto," hinting at the unapologetically roguish behavior of the figure who was nonetheless the exemplar of craft accomplishment in the era, draws the lesson implied by the reassignment of the meaning of "regeneration" and by the reassignment of the moral values implicit in the other texts—the stories in *The Craftsman*—that Bailey challenges.

Carolyn Bailey was not the only contributor to pry the language of craft away from narratives of typicality and type. The title of Paul Harboe's "The Taming of the Bear" suggests the same pattern of redemption as "The Regeneration of Benvenuto." But Harboe's title, like Bailey's, is ironic, for the "bear," a "big, strong, [and] burly" shipwright, turns out to be unredeemed by the moralizing domesticity of his wife and mother-in-law, who make a home that "fairly sang with all its beauty"—but wherein "the song somehow did not seem to come from the heart," turning as it does on stilted efforts at bourgeois sociality and conventional interior décor.[46] Stultified by the polite guests at the house, including "a wealthy lumber dealer, a railroad president, and a certain prominent manufacturer" (36), the shipwright finds "human values" and his own "vital needs" in his hale-and-hearty working-class companions at the grog shops (35). The vitality of craft, as represented by the shipwright and his friends, lodges outside the middle-class narratives of moral suasion and personal transformation advanced by stories like "The Gift of Angelo." The shipwright's name, Page, may be a kind of pun, suggesting the ways in which "The Taming of the Bear" overturns the conventional moral trajectories brought to the more literal page in *The Craftsman;* certainly the story's title invokes the genre of redemption stories that "The Taming of the Bear" in fact goes on to abjure.

"The Regeneration of Benvenuto" and "The Taming of the Bear" thus operate ironically, challenging the moral abstraction of craft by situating the real drama in the streets and in the grog shops where workers congregate. The stories ask readers to note the terms of their literary intervention, hinting at the correlation of Benvenuto's character with Cellini's unsuitability for parable and liberating "Page" from the stultifying framing narrative of the artisan's redemption. Some of the most interesting early fiction in *The Craftsman*, moreover, takes up the relationship between craft and language not as an ironic judgment of generic conventions but as a question at stake in the plot itself. The Jamesian drama of Katherine Metcalf Root's "The Angel in the Stone" compares a widow's marriage to her deceased husband, the "greatest sculptor of the day," with her new marriage to a sculptor who turns out conventional pieces in stone for the façades of New York buildings.[47] The story's center involves the different conversational patterns of the two marriages. With Victor Ward, the deceased husband, Madeline says what she feels about his work; she is his best critic. But when the commercial sculptor, Richard Maxwell, asks her for an opinion on an unimaginative figure for the building of the Morton Trust Company, "for the first time in her life . . . she took refuge in words" (526). She goes on equivocating, encouraging Maxwell about the quality of the piece despite her knowledge that he "would never do better" (529). "She had lied," the story dramatically concludes (529). "The unaccustomed shield of words" becomes habitual under the pressures of a secondhand art that aspires to nothing new (527).

The association of imitative workmanship and inauthentic language in "The Angel in the Stone" places critical questions about craft, narrative, and labor within the diegetic frame of the story. Derivative or iterative labors, the agents of a generic notion of craft's moral virtues in many other stories in *The Craftsman*, generate platitudes and untruths—an observation that the reader, asked by Root to consider the interplay of "words" and craft, seems invited to extend from the relationship of Madeline and Maxwell to the relationship of narrative and typology within the larger Craftsman project. Understood collectively as well as individually, the early stories published in *The Craftsman* draw the reader to a critical consideration of the very operation—translating the meaning of manual labor for a general audience—on which they are predicated. If Sanders's Angelotti represents the quotidian labor that made craft a universal lesson, pulling it away from its most professionally skilled or singular forms, Root's Maxwell (also churning out derivative sculptures) represents the contraction of craft into a superficial language. Angelotti and Maxwell, that is, stand for *The Craftsman*'s two positions on the literary dimensions of labor: Angelotti's constancy bears out the moral lessons peddled as unpretentious and humble workmanship in many of the magazine's stories, while Maxwell's constancy bears out the risk that such thinking translates workmanship's originality into banal communications. *The Craftsman* put to its audience an open question about craft's literary representation.

That open question, indeed, was introduced in the very first piece of original fiction published in the magazine—a piece that alludes quite clearly to Nathaniel Hawthorne's framing of the same issues. Like Hawthorne's "The Artist of the Beautiful," "A Lover of the Beautiful" features a protagonist—in fact named Nathaniel—who discovers an artisanal talent that is extraordinary, dangerously absorbing, and potentially dehumanizing. At the beginning of the story, the monk Nathaniel leaves off his work in the monastery's bakery to begin illuminating manuscripts; over three months, "his touch grew ever more skillful."[48] But, like the fanatical Owen Warland in Hawthorne's story, Nathaniel's humanity and his spirituality contract as he becomes more and more obsessed with his craft. Over time, the "morning gladness no longer sang in his heart" (76); he denies succor to the sick in order to stay at his work and finally confesses to the abbot that his obsession with skill has ruined his capacity for feeling. He no longer sees the face of Christ before him, and vows sobbingly that "I—can paint—no more,—until it come again!" (79). Nathaniel returns to baking, and the story appears in that regard a conventionally cautionary tale about contentment with humble labors. It ends with the face of Christ finally appearing to the man who is devout again.

But whether this means Nathaniel will return to illuminating manuscripts is left unresolved. "The hunger in his heart for the work he had renounced could never be stilled," although that same hunger appears demonic, like a "strangling clutch upon the throat" and like a force that "fired his blood like wine" as he tries to stay focused on the "humble work" of baking (79). The story was written by Harriet Joor, a New Orleans ceramist whose art pottery reflects Nathaniel's decorative energies rather than his quotidian trade—and the story ends ambiguously, prompting us to wonder if Nathaniel can in fact return to the manuscripts with a more temperate attitude. In the final scene, the vision of the "Christ-face" appears one morning "from the doorway" of the bakery Nathaniel is about to enter (80); leaving Nathaniel at the "threshold of the bakehouse" without telling us if he enters or if the face represents the sign that he can now return to the studio, Joor leaves the reader at the threshold of a question about his future trade. That unresolved question is centered in a quite literal way on the relation of craft and letters—involving as it does the illumination of manuscripts—and the story as a whole figures the issues surrounding the literary representation of labor in *The Craftsman:* excesses of skill appear subject, as in "The Master Workman" or "The Brother of the Cross," to a moralizing lesson in Christian humility, but that same narrative ends with the possibility that Nathaniel can now return to rendering manuscripts as testaments to his exquisite skill. Reading the story in that way—as involving a tension between moralizing letters and skillfully illuminated and imaginatively elaborated ones—makes it unsurprising that Nathaniel's first vision of illuminated manuscripts should appear as follows: "Leaf and flower and floating cloud are forming themselves into patterns before my eyes! Last night, as the sun set, the boughs of the cherry trees wrought a beautiful pattern against the ruddy sky; and this morning, as I sliced the carrots, the curling leaves seem to wreathe themselves around a scarlet letter upon a golden ground" (75).

The invocation of Hawthorne's scarlet letter hints at the shame that will visit Nathaniel as he strays from the path of humility; his fantastical letters becomes the moralizing ones of the story itself. But the allusion also recalls an icon as much redemptive as ignominious, a crafted object that is salvific because it is wrought so imaginatively and with such "wonderful skill"; the letter embellished by Hester Prynne, moreover, mirrors the imaginative embellishments also achieved through letters by the initially stultified *writer* who narrates "The Custom-House" (27). The early allusion to the scarlet letter thus anticipates the ambivalence with which "A Lover of the Beautiful," not revealing whether Nathaniel returns to the manuscripts, concludes. Read as a token of shame projecting later developments, the scarlet letter seen by Nathaniel marks what develops as his excessive sensuality in the skillful pursuit of beauty. But read as an instance of the natural forms that fire his imagination and as a type of the letters to which he might return, the scarlet letter appears in its aspect as the premier American icon of great skill turned to imaginative, humane, and visionary purpose. The nature of craft's relation to literature is tested by this scarlet letter: the story appears to support the moralizing abstractions about the virtues of "humble work" and the dangers of obsession attending worldly skills, but—unlike stories like "The Gift of Angelo" and "The Brother of the Cross"—it also invites us to wonder about the possibility that Nathaniel will again take up his tools and begin producing manuscripts of unparalleled creativity and original beauty. As in *The Craftsman* itself between 1905 and 1907, the reader is left to determine the boundaries, if any, between craft as moral humility and craft as manual skill and material ingenuity. The question about the fate of Nathaniel's manuscripts in "A Lover of the Beautiful" is also the question that the magazine, negotiating the place of fiction in the Craftsman vision, put to its readers.

THE EVOLUTION OF THE CRAFTSMAN STYLE

The previous sections each describe a different manifestation of craft's translation into popular idioms. From the outset, Stickley forged correlations between white oak, Craftsman furnishings, and a typological model of décor understood as the "grammar of ornament"; several years into the company's development, *The Craftsman* magazine expanded the company's efforts to translate craft for the public by introducing fiction to its pages. These patterns each constitute only a single aspect of a project that depended on all kinds of textual media, from advertisements to essays to the blurbs about craft and authenticity that appeared at the outset of Craftsman catalogs and on some of the stickers affixed to Craftsman furnishings. But the examples of craft's translation I have considered also reveal with particular clarity how the Craftsman enterprise defined its mission of resuscitating artisanship on a scale that ran from singular expertise to moral generality; from the uniqueness of the medium (and the artisan's relation with it) to its categorical aspect; and from the immanence of nature to its industrial elicitation. This spectrum challenges the prevailing interpretations of Stickley's career, which tend to stress either his efforts to bring about a restored relation to the real or his capitulation to an ersatz commercial market. My interest in studying the craft movement as a textual phenomenon, a system of translation, instead parallels the interest of Mark Seltzer in studying literary and photographic representations of the body around 1900: as elements of the meaning of craft, I mean to configure correlations between typicality and originality, between legible categories and specific things, and between representation and actual practice.

These values shaded into one another for Stickley and for the editors of his magazine, but they also blurred for consumers of the American Arts and Crafts style—or rather, for those consumers as their needs and interests were imagined and projected, sometimes peculiarly, by figures who popularized the aesthetic in America. Consider the first real public manifesto of the American craft movement, written by a professor of English at the University of Chicago and a contributor to *The Craftsman*. Oscar Lovell Triggs's *Chapters in the History of the Arts and Crafts Movement* (c. 1902) named Andrew Carnegie's commercial energies as the instrument of a revivification of the handicrafts. To some degree, the identification of the industrial tycoon as the agent of craft and artisanship mirrored Carnegie's representation of himself. In 1886, Carnegie had made a case for the compatibility of Jeffersonian republicanism and the expansion of the industrial state; his book *Triumphant Democracy; or, Fifty Years' March of the Republic* recurs to an outmoded comparison of British monarchical decadence and capacious American democracy in order to describe the physical geography of the United

States, its magnificent rural landscape, as large enough to balance all interests. *Triumphant Democracy* insists that a country rimmed by mountains (the Appalachians in the east and the Sierras in the west) but with a low, watery interior would be cohered by centripetal social and commercial force. The country appears to Carnegie like a bowl in which democratic strength stems from the vast lowlands pulling everything together.

Carnegie, to be sure, would like to see those lowlands dotted with oil derricks and manufactories; he claims that what distinguishes modernity from the early eras of settlement, when undeveloped country stretched west of Plymouth and Jamestown, is the commercial actualization of the heartland's integrating geography via canals, turnpikes, railways, and roads. *Triumphant Democracy* resuscitates Jeffersonian equations of republicanism with the land—and an older genre of monarchy-republican comparisons—in order to make the claim that such geography is potential only; Carnegie turns back the cultural and literary clock so he can reflect the origins that America might reach. That sensibility reflects Stickley's, as I have described it, and it also explains the case that Triggs would make for Carnegie as an agent of the crafts movement. For Triggs, industrial tycoons in general, and Carnegie in particular, would widen the corps of skilled craftsmen by unearthing new raw materials and training laborers in an expanded set of trades. Smoothing over the reality that oil production and steelwork would be driven by the pace of the assembly line rather than the pleasures of the shop, Triggs located the promise of the crafts in the advance of industrial and commercial energy, and he named the instinct of tycoons to "stand at strategic points, where materials are most accessible and laborers most numerous."[49] In Triggs's vision, craft extracts and refines raw material, tying people to natural essences on the grounds that those essences required realization; in this, coal and petroleum look not entirely unlike Craftsman white oak. The cause of the worker would be advanced, Triggs felt, as new natural resources were drawn from the land, as new jobs were created, and as the nation rushed onward toward the revivification of the crafts.[50]

Triggs's synthesis of craft and large-scale industry is one of the stranger statements of the handicrafts movement. Stickley's idealism was more cautious, but it was founded on a similar adaptation of a romantic ideal of immanence to industrial idioms of progress and production. Moreover, the relays of the real and the represented that defined Stickley's ideas about oak, and that shaped the inclusion of fiction in *The Craftsman*, developed into attitudes about consumer desire as the Craftsman company turned more and more fully to the mainstream furnishings market. The remainder of this chapter considers how Stickley tapped the correlations established early in his career to justify the expanding scale of his company and the conventional period styles that he was ultimately forced to produce as the now-oversized company's finances began disintegrating. Here is Stickley, in 1909, describing why customers would be attracted to the simple Craftsman style:

> [In early America] it became apparent than we were evolving a type of people distinct from all others,—a type essentially American. And the distinguishing characteristic of this type is the power to assimilate so swiftly the kind of culture which leads to the making of permanent standards of life and art. . . . Such Americans have fundamental intelligence and the power of discrimination, and the direct thinking that results from these qualities inevitably produces a certain openness of mind that responds very quickly to anything which seems to have a real and permanent value. . . . As we grow older, we show an unmistakable tendency to get away from shams and to demand the real thing.[51]

The passage is about America's exceptional connection to the "real and permanent," yet the onward pressure of time is inexorable. An essential need for the "real thing" is fulfilled diachronically. Americans possess not permanence per se, but the "power to assimilate so swiftly the kind of culture which leads to the making of permanence standards of life and art." Those "permanent standards" are buried in an extraordinary string of conditions: first, one needs the capacity for swift assimilation; then, a generic "kind of culture" that "leads" to permanence not directly but "to the making" of that which is beyond time.

Thus, even as the passage trades in the language of timeless, essential authenticity, it allows for progress as its method. The authentic—and the authentically American—is a function of becoming: from the stream of possibilities that life presents, Americans identify the "real and permanent," and leap "swiftly" on its appearance. What interests me most particularly in this passage is the agent of such motion. Stickley is really describing a mode of perception, a consumer disposition, an "openness of mind" capable of differentiating things that "seem" to have permanence and those that do not. Such a description concedes the limits of immanence as a physical discovery, for the idea that things announce their own transcendent reality does not hold up to a theory of subjective "discrimination" among things that might only "seem" real and permanent.

The title of the essay, "The Evolution of an American Style," reveals one of its essential contexts. In positing selection and discrimination—oriented to the visual environment of consumer culture—as the agents of stylistic evolution, Stickley invokes Darwinian concepts. There is some absurdity to the essay's evolutionary logic. Natural selection, the flow of time that leads toward an organism perfectly adapted to its environment, appears a matter of good shopping: the agents of America's development are the well-adapted citizens, themselves "evolving," who so "swiftly" pick out the objects—Craftsman objects—that are part of the evolution of an "American style" toward the real thing. If exaggerated, however, the essay's figures of selection and evolution, discrimination and progress, anchored Stickley's claims about Craftsman authenticity as he was forced, late in his career, to remake his line of furnishings. In early 1913, the Craftsman store in Boston announced a dramatic drop in sales, and account books for the next three years show a steady decline in company assets.[52] A combination of factors was at work, including the too-rapid development of the company in 1912 and 1913, the expense of the Manhattan building, competition from Stickley's imitators, and the replacement of Craftsman with Colonial Revival furnishings as consumers' preferred representation of an autochthonous style. The crisis is easily read in the products offered in the late catalogs: fake leather "Fabrikoid" upholstery, fancy "best plate" silver service, Chinese Chippendale, Jacobean, and Colonial furniture suites. The rhetoric of utilitarian aesthetics continued to sputter, and classic Craftsman designs in fumed oak were still available. But in large part, the company tried to preserve its income by reinvigorating the fancy pieces of the Stickley-Simonds operation—Stickley's early venture, which made period pieces for high-end clients—and by tapping into the stylistic predilections of a market governed by the grammar of ornament.

Long accustomed to use *The Craftsman* as a promotional newsletter for his latest ventures and products, Stickley faced the problem of explaining the company's new direction to a readership of 20,000 (down from 60,000 in 1909) who would have trouble accepting an ornate "Craftsman" faux-Colonial or Stickley's "exact reproduction" of a mahogany Martha Washington chair. The early Craftsman enterprise demanded that its audience negotiate between the physical materials or original activities of workmanship and their represented forms; the late Craftsman enterprise put such correlations to the test by tying its products more and more tightly to the lexicons of the mass market, and by using *The Craftsman* as a rhetorical instrument for asserting the viability of the company's new direction. The strategies Stickley employed appear in an article published in October of 1914. The article drew on the diachronic notion of immanence established in the earlier phase of the company (by, for instance, Stickley's description of ammonia-fuming as the elicitation of a natural point of origin) but now set the emphasis on diachronicity in the scientific language of evolution:

> When [the American artist] Joseph Pennell was in Panama he stopped to admire the lock at Pedro Miguel. "How is it," he asked the engineer, "that you make your arches and buttresses as fine as those of a cathedral?" "Oh, that's done to save concrete," was the reply.
>
> Economy as the basis of beauty is not so strange as it may seem. It was through *elimination of the superfluous* that the loveliness as well as the strength of that Panama structure grew, and the same principle may be found at the root of every successful work whether or art or industry.
>
> Elimination is but another name for concentration, for the self-control that holds forces in command, governing and directing, preventing vacillation and insuring advance. Elimination does not weaken, but rather strengthens, wherever it is used. A good soldier discards everything but the essentials, for he cannot afford the least useless encumbrance; a runner trains away every ounce of superfluous flesh; a wise business man employs only vital workmen, permitting mediocrity—choking excess—no chance. Success depends ever upon the ability to choose wisely—another aspect of that all-prevailing law of the "survival of the fittest." (emphasis in original)[53]

Invoking the ability to "choose wisely" as the agent of practical aesthetics—"loveliness" combined with "strength"—the passage correlates such wise choices with the "survival of the fittest." In the late *Craftsman*, immanence depended not just on natural or environmental facts but on acts of choice and willful realization; in the passage just quoted, likening utilitarian design to the eliminative model of natural selection, selection flows from conscious human choices and deliberate acts of will. In its biological and sociological forms, evolutionary thinking around the turn of the century more often named inherent fitness. Pressures of the environment would eliminate those individuals who, in Herbert Spencer's words, were "least fitted to cope with the conditions . . . they [are] subject to."[54] The Craftsman model turns the equation around, rendering operations of selection ("elimination," "economy," and choice) as much acts of subjects themselves—the athlete in training, the shrewd businessman, the economical engineer—as of the environment to which they are subject. If the passage invokes evolutionary competition not just in its final sentence but in its general depiction of progress, it also gives the operations of nature over to the individual whose exceptional "self-control . . . holds forces in command, governing and directing, preventing vacillation and insuring advance." The very idea that elimination can be "used" suggests its personalization.[55]

The 1914 passage differs from the 1909 passage even as both direct an evolutionary model of natural design to activities of choosing. The 1909 passage focuses on the consumer's swift recognition of the real thing. That model is essentially positive, urging shoppers to choose the Craftsman style. The 1914 passage focuses on individuals who eliminate what is not useful. That model is essentially negative, modeling a process by which the wrong things are rejected rather than a process by which the right things are chosen. The later essay draws the lesson in its next paragraph, explicitly tying elimination to consumer behavior in a mass-market context:

> In every phase of life in America we are coming to recognize the importance of elimination, and especially is this true in the furnishing and decoration of our homes in what may be known as the American style. We are realizing that to create an environment of convenience and beauty, we must select, from the immense variety of articles, materials, colors, and designs, the few which are essential to comfort and harmony. As a lawyer discards from his argument all minor facts and details, as a painter eliminates from his canvas every needless tone and line, so we must eliminate from our rooms all fittings and colors which would mar the unity and restfulness of the whole . . . [A] sifting process, [a] disentangling and putting in order of many factors, is what the modern decorator keeps uppermost in his mind when putting together a room (69–70).

The economy that governs the individual object in the early, rectilinear Craftsman style is transferred to describe the decoration of an entire room. Acknowledging the persistence of an "American style" founded on an organic union of form and function ("convenience and beauty," "comfort and harmony"), *The Craftsman* locates this national aesthetic not in immanent things that might be positively chosen but in a process of negative selection that amounts to effective shopping in a world of greater stylistic abundance; "putting together" an American room out of an "immense variety of articles, materials, colors, and designs" is the labor of authenticity. If this sounds like Stickley pushing his own furniture in a competitive marketplace (that is, if the emphasis on proper selection implies that Craftsman furniture alone deserves consideration), such commercial intentions are only true insofar as Stickley's line had expanded to comprise exactly the sort of "immense variety" he invokes. The Chinese Chippendale and Jacobean models introduced in 1914—some of which were first presented in the essay I have been discussing—are only one aspect of rapid expansion in the Craftsman collection. Enameled black armchairs, painted colonial revival designs, wicker settees, and delicate nesting tables all made their appearance by 1915. Preferred materials included not just white oak and leather, but gray maple, gumwood, mahogany, canvas, velour, and the DuPont textile called Fabrikoid; many designs could be purchased in dozens of permutations of material and color. Stickley went so far as to advertise the adaptability of his products to virtually every décor: the Craftsman Building actually showed furniture in various combinations of period styles, and the 1915 Craftsman catalog offered furniture by a variety of manufacturers as complements to genuine Stickley pieces.

Thus, in the context of the essay as a whole, the "sifting process" cannot assume that a certain style of product would emerge. Rather, variety of design is the condition of the ability to obtain the few essential pieces for a given space. The horticulturalist Luther Burbank "develops thousands of plants in order that a perfect one may be found and brought to prominence. His whole method of work is along the lines of elimination, wise selecting" (75). The decorator, we are told, similarly develops "the power to choose rightly—just as Burbank can walk through large beds of flowers and see at a glance the ones to save and the ones to discard." The paradox, at least from the point of view of immanence, is that an original "American style" appears as an educated combination of extant terms rather than a discovery of new or essential ones. Originality is a function of possibility. The "thousands" of plants, "large beds of flowers," and "immense variety" of commodities are figures for the profusion out of which the singular will emerge; and they all serve, implicitly, to justify the mass-market phase of the Craftsman company not as the antithesis of an "authentic" or "genuine" aesthetic but as its guarantor.

This implication—that a commodity culture offers originality through the inspired management of resources—informs virtually all of Stickley's theory after 1913. In effect, the later Craftsman enterprise shifts the locus of authenticity from the individual piece to the decorative context, from the immanence of oak to the constructed environment, from the artisan to the consumer. Yet the terms of the effort had not changed from the days in which Stickley was describing ammonia fuming as a translation or *The Craftsman* was asking the readers of its fiction to consider the interplay of tactile and abstract meanings of workmanship. The Craftsman project correlated the organic, natural, physically inherent, or otherwise singular with processes of management, moralization, elicitation, abstraction, effect, and recognition. Stickley's depiction of the company's "evolution" settled the idea of evolution itself on willful choices, again closing a circle between the immanence or "fitness" of natural objects and the sensitivity of the subject, whether artisan or reader or consumer; in that regard, the derivative furnishings offered by the later company were no more a hoax, in Stickley's mind, than ammonia-fuming and quartersawn oak. The choice of Burbank, a horticulturalist, to model the selective process recapitulates the emphasis on the recognition of type also presumed of the workman. But what matters in the late essays in *The Craftsman* is less the inherent nature of a single board than how things are used. The 1914 essay concludes:

> Thus we see that in order to achieve real distinction and beauty in American furnishings, we must approach the undertaking from the standpoint of elimination, or judicious selection of objects, textures, and color harmonies. Sometimes the articles in a room will be perfect as to style and color, yet the result will appear awkward, coldly repellant. Or the interior may be *too* perfect, with an unpleasant air of aloof superiority. . . . These difficulties are often remedied by re-arrangement, the couch in better light, pillows placed more naturally, chairs in sociable relation, lamp placed on a different table, books with bronze book-end turned at more graceful angle, pictures hung in closer relation to the furniture. Those who undertake the work in this interested and earnest spirit will feel a kinship with that old Italian craftsman who, when asked what his ambition was, replied: "I should like those who examine the cupolas of St. Mark's five hundred years hence, to say, 'This was the work of a conscientious artist.' " (78, emphasis in original)

The contingency of decorative objects marks the essay as belonging to the magazine after 1912. In fact, decorative articles may be "perfect as to style and color," but the result will not cohere; in themselves, physical facts mean little compared to contriving for better light to fall on the couch or moving a lamp to a different table. Arrangement offers an American style of "real distinction," and the long list of design permutations—typical of the superlative language of possibility in the final years of *The Craftsman*—correlates originality with rich decorative prospects. The "permanent standard" of décor that was the Craftsman ideal is retained even as it is relocated: however improbably, a room in which the pillows and bookends have been brilliantly composed is an achievement in keeping with the five-hundred-year endurance of St. Mark's.

The strategy here is anticipated in general by ammonia-fumed white oak and in more concrete terms by an earlier image of Old World craftsmanship. Stickley had opened his 1904 catalog of metalwork by telling customers that "Craftsman artisans can trace a long ancestry of toil, their forefathers having for generations exercised the same trade in a single city, village, or hamlet of the old world." The blacksmith is typical: "projected against the firelight of the flaming forge, his sinewy frame satisfies the spectator with a sense of fitness, as he moves with quick, decisive gesture, directing the processes of the men who are shaping a large number of objects, widely differing in size and use: such as Lamps, Lanterns, Electroliers, Candlesticks, Umbrella Stands, Jardinieres,

Wine Coolers, Cigar Boxes, Serving Trays, Wall Plaques, Hinges, Drawer Pulls, Knockers, and Escutcheons."[56] The first sentence of this description captures the Old World continuity Stickley aims at, both in its medieval alliterative style and in its image of a sinewy body perfectly molded to the "long ancestry of toil" boasted by Craftsman artisans. But the alliterative breathlessness of the first two clauses becomes a different kind of breathless list by the end; the blacksmith turns out to be toiling away on umbrella stands, electroliers, jardinieres, cigar boxes, a whole host of late Victorian genteel goods. The commercial intentions are transparent: the list turns out to give the exact items, in the exact order, of the catalog that follows. Over the course of the passage, the self-sufficient craftsman, the man who might employ an apprentice or two but has a hand in all the work produced by his shop, evolves into a managerial figure whose "sinewy frame" and sure movement now fit him for the work of "directing the processes" of a large manufactory. The multiple tasks of production and the "quick, decisive" authority of the artisan-foreman distinguish him from the type of the deliberate, unrushed, and autonomous craftsman. This all looks a great deal like the paradox conventionally attributed to the Craftsman enterprise: as much as Old World continuity, Stickley's depiction of the blacksmith advertises the ability of his firm—under capable central leadership—to organize its resources and thus to produce a "large number of objects," a collection of "widely different" things. As impressive as the sinewy workman is the efficiency of the production process, the unceasing activity that produces so extensive and so various a line of goods.

But the mode of production described in the passage (and everywhere implicit in the commercial scale of the Craftsman company) controls its own excesses. For the emphasis on the number of the objects and their various "use" suggests the adaptation of perfect utility—having exactly the right thing—to marketplace profusion. Presenting customers with so many and such different goods connects the blacksmith's managerial prowess to the managerial prowess implicitly offered the consumer in the long list of product choices. The description of the blacksmith (perfectly adapted to his managerial work) and the list of genteel goods (each adapted to a different use) are thus not that different; there is a certain amount of bathos in the passage's fall from the sinewy Old World artisan to genteel Victorian consumption, but Stickley creates continuity by presenting the managerial idioms on which both kinds of activity are based. The 1914 passage about moving your lamps and shifting your pillows also generates a "kinship" between the consumer and the "old Italian craftsman" who built St. Mark's. The philosophy implicit in the earlier depiction of the blacksmith anticipated the philosophy that would become increasingly more important, as an explicit theory of selection and arrangement, as the Craftsman company had to turn to the period pieces constituting the Victorian grammar of ornament. When craftsmanship inheres not in objects themselves but in the total environment they constitute, a factory rapidly turning out pieces in the entire vocabulary of styles constitutes the authentic precisely to the degree that its products are so many and so various. Paradoxically, under the aegis of Stickley's founding notions of utility as an arrived-at point and of craft as a translation of material into effect, the excesses of mass-market production offer the consumer the flexible management of appearances on which originality, utility, and essence depend. From the "Craftsman" to the "Chinese Chippendale" there is not, perhaps, so much difference.

AFTER THE FACT: CRAFTSMAN HISTORICISM, 1914–1917

An abrupt shift in the audience presumed by *The Craftsman* occurred around 1914. The magazine began ascribing the American style to a labor of consumption that it associated, explicitly and stereotypically, with women—and, more particularly, with the ability to "plan interior decorations from one end of the house to the other" that the magazine coded as female. Here is the opening of a 1915 article on "making color schemes in furniture":

> There is something so peculiarly charming in the modern painted bedroom sets, something so winning that every woman instinctively pauses before the sets displayed for sale and mentally arranges a sleeping room after her heart's desire. With a set of any color whatsoever before a woman's eyes, she is immediately able to visualize a room that would be exactly to her liking. Her imagination leaps to suitable chintzes and rugs, to the fine details of feathered pen upon the stand, the lamp upon the wall, the books and flowers upon the table.[57]

Commodity superabundance, expressed as the availability of "any color whatsoever," appears as the catalyst for the creative management of home furnishings. The passage creates a causal link between the ability to create a distinctive interior—a room after the "heart's desire," "exactly to her liking"—and the emporium of goods "displayed for sale . . . before a woman's eyes"; the retail window is the site where originality begins. The article in which this passage occurs is about "making color schemes in furniture," but the "making" is specifically visual: women pause before sets, "mentally" arrange their bedrooms, "visualize" arrangements, and leap in "imagination" to future purchases.

The Craftsman catalogs reflected the new direction of Craftsman theory after 1913, when the different catalogs featuring furniture, lighting, metalwork, and textiles were consolidated into a single master catalog of interior furnishings. The move, as Bruce Johnson suggests, was a cost-cutting measure, but other evidence suggests that the master catalog was also part of a general effort to place Craftsman products in the context of the total home.[58] Earlier catalogs showed goods as singles or, at most, in lightly accessorized setting. The magazine and master catalogs of 1913 and 1915 (no 1914 catalog was issued), however, fit with Stickley's later emphasis on selection and arrangement by showing goods in groupings; in addition to the things for sale, Stickley staged interior scenes, as in figure 24, by using vases, rugs, pictures, tablecloths, and flowers. The formerly separate catalogs and the formerly separate pieces were woven together into visions of contextual decorative effects.

That the groupings were strategies for Stickley period styles in particular is dramatically demonstrated by the continued practice of showing classic Craftsman designs in isolation. Floral or basket displays often crowded the actual things for sale in Stickley's master catalogs, making it difficult to tell what is for sale and what is part of the general atmosphere, the lifestyle, with which the product is affiliated. This suggests the confusion of fantasy and reality often associated with consumer culture, but the more salient point here is that the master catalogs adapt a durable Craftsman theory of immanence to the process of selection, accommodating the real thing and its effect. Customers are implicitly urged to look at furniture, metalwork, lighting, and textiles as elements of the whole, even to the point of mixing classic Craftsman designs with reproduction Dutch, Jacobean, Bavarian, and "our own classic Colonial"; what mattered was not what things were, in the sense by which the real thing might be equated with provenance, physical singularity, or mode of production, but how they were used.[59] The correlation between this attitude and literary representation—the use of crafted things in particular to create the "sense of an interior" that Diana Fuss describes in nineteenth- and early twentieth-century literature—will emerge in the next chapter, but the simpler point about the late Craftsman enterprise is that it put tremendous emphasis on making good choices within a taxonomically coded structure of ornament. The formation of the Craftsman Interior Decorating Department in 1914 provided paying customers the services of travelling professional designers or, for free, custom drawings of possible arrangements. The Interior Decorating Department was led by a matriarchal figure whose "headquarters," the magazine explained, could be found on the fourth floor of the Craftsman Building; all inquires were to be directed to "Mrs. Cutting / The Craftsman Building / 6 East 39th St." Sometime between January and May 1914, Mrs. Cutting appears to have been promoted from hostess of the Craftsman Restaurant to titular head of the

FIGURE 24. Gustav Stickley, Craftsman furnishings, c. 1915.
(*The Craftsman* 27, no. 6 [March 1915])

Interior Decorating Department. In featuring her serendipitous name so prominently (a series of advertisements for new "Jacobean" and other new furnishings invited readers, in bold type, to "Ask for Mrs. Cutting"), one wonders if Stickley did not mean to suggest the patchwork process of simplification, the "elimination of the superfluous," at the center of the Craftsman theory of arrangement, selection, and evolution.[60] Whether or not Stickley intended the resonance between her name and the larger processes of "cutting" or "judicious selection" that he recommended, the department Mrs. Cutting headed became central to the Craftsman vision. "The decorator," Stickley wrote, "can be of real service to the homemaker. . . . The decorator is the key figure in modern design."[61]

As arbiters of originality, craft and consumption merged into a synthetic vision that flowed between Stickley's workshops and the retail floor. Stickley himself, who wrote a series of articles for the early magazine in the persona of the "Craftsman" ("the Craftsman . . . was aglow, mind and body; his pulses beating; his brain quickened to the joy and pride of having created something"), redefined himself as a buyer and as a designer: the introduction to his later catalogs announced that the contents were assembled from various well-chosen manufacturers, and the captions on spreads offered an "entire room designed by Gustav Stickley" rather than things explicitly made by him.[62] Whatever Craftsman products did appear, moreover, stressed the adaptability of their traditional forms to a variety of roles in the house, sacrificing even the logic of the 1904 passage about the blacksmith's range of products—that each piece had a definite and particular use—to decorative flexibility and modularity. Nesting tables were typical of the lightweight, modular pieces made in the final years of the enterprise. Gate-leg tables, davenports that could also serve as daybeds, bedroom chairs "equally suited" for the dining room or hall, sideboards that would look right not just in the dining room but in a "library, study, or den," china closets that could hold books (if silk curtains were drawn across the glass doors): the "interchangeable quality of furniture" was its best recommendation in the late *Craftsman*.[63] Stickley's refusal to pare wood away from his original pieces tied their massiveness to the unaltered (although enhanced) substance of nature, but the late furniture was made "light of weight" so that it could be drawn to the fireplace or the window or out on the porch.[64] Complaining, as ever, that copies are "fundamentally lacking in all that makes up the charm of an original," Stickley offered his neo-Colonial period pieces as practical and original in context if not in design. A 1915 table offered "artistic distinction"—a phrase that defined the late *Craftsman*—exactly because its uses were so unspecific: it could be placed in a library next to a reading chair or could "stand in a

FIGURE 25. Gustav Stickley, table and armchair, c. 1915.
(*The Craftsman* 24, no. 3 [December 1915]: 305)

hall, serve as a breakfast table or be taken out on the porch or sun room" (fig. 25).[65]

But the round table depicted could not be used very effectively in a hall. It is too large to be easily moved from the porch in case of bad weather. Its low stretcher rails prevent a breakfast chair from being drawn up close enough to save a diner from dribbling jelly into his or her lap. Stickley, however, insisted on variety whenever he discussed authenticity. In a pair of articles on the "new idea in home furnishing," sets of furniture come under attack as too suggestive of the standardized "output of a factory," despite the fact that early Craftsman pieces were nothing if not uniform.[66] An illustration of a "modern dining room" (fig. 26), moreover, reverses Stickley's original theory of this room almost completely. The decorative logic of the early *Craftsman* prescribed the dining room as the most coherent space in the house. Stability and solidity,

FIGURE 26. Gustav Stickley, dining room furnishings, c. 1915.
(*The Craftsman* 24, no. 2 [November 1915]: 202)

Stickley felt, were the effects most appropriate for the space in which family and friends come together, and so "nowhere more than in the dining room is evidenced the value of structural features."[67] Prominent wainscoting, built-in cabinets and sideboards, and a symmetrical set of table and chairs were typical (fig. 27).

In the early dining room, the pattern of the rug, the chandelier, and the matching chairs contain the table on all sides and force the eye to the center of the composition; use is mandated by the symmetry of the arrangement. By contrast, the 1915 dining room is simpler and more restfully economic on account of its impromptu, lightweight furnishings—an "interesting combination of three 'periods,' " Stickley writes in the caption. The text accompanying this image describes a pioneer age when one large room was reconfigured for the various functions of the day, and the image itself depicts lightweight chairs and a gate-leg table as furniture that can do double- or triple-duty to fit other needs. *The Craftsman*'s original advice about the dining room—that it, above all, should not be planned to "fulfill manifold functions"—is reversed. It is easy to imagine the table, with its leaves lowered, pushed back to the right of the door

FIGURE 27. Gustav Stickley, rendition of dining room, 1906. (*The Craftsman* 9, no. 4 [January 1906]: 569)

and composing nicely with the painting. Indeed, the dining room demands such adjustments, for otherwise the painting does not compose; the mental arranging described in the passage about the bedroom sets at the beginning of this section is in fact required by the viewer in this image. The chair rail on the wall invokes the same sort of decorative contingency as adaptable furniture and creative combinations of period styles; the detail originates in the need to protect the wall from scuffs and abrasions in an age of smaller homes, when chairs were moved from use in the center of the room to their waiting positions on the edges. The temporariness of the décor may be most explicitly conveyed by the way in which the table and chair block the door. Obviously impossible as a permanent arrangement and violating the clear sight lines that were an important principle of original Craftsman design (Stickley liked the front door to be placed in line with the other doors on the first floor, such that a person could see straight through the house to the landscape beyond), the setting is drawn like this to insist on the homemaker's spontaneous control over the interior.

In theory, immanence would seem a synchronic principle: form expresses the essence of an object at whatever moment one chooses to look at it. But the immanent virtues claimed for Craftsman furniture—that it was simple, original, tonally coherent, distinctively American—were diachronic, developed in time. In the late period, the link of form and function occurs not in a single, transcendently natural object but via the Darwinian idioms of selection (making good choices for the economy of the home as a whole) and adaptation (by which individual things, like gate-leg tables and davenports-daybeds, are reconfigured to meet the demands placed on them). By 1915, originality had to do with imagining new combinations of period furniture or by altering the appearance of things without touching their substance. Originality thus trades in history, in the past forms that constitute the décor of the present. The same china closet that could be used as a bookcase or a curio cabinet was right for the "modern home" because its extended legs gave it "lightness" and made cleaning under it a simple task, yet this "new note" of practical, utilitarian height was generated over the course of history: "In reality," *The Craftsman* explained, "this is a very old form, an evolution of the household chest that, gradually being raised from the floor, became a sideboard, a dresser, chiffonier and china closet."[68] The proposed teleology is spurious. Historically speaking, a chiffonier (a small- to medium-sized cabinet) is not necessarily a higher piece than a dresser (traditionally, a kitchen appliance for chopping food rather than, as in modern American English, a chest of drawers); eighteenth-century pattern books show sideboards, dressers, and china cabinets in various elevations from the floor, and Stickley's high version for the "modern home" was in fact anticipated by china cabinets that appeared on legs from their inception with the seventeenth-century china trade.

But Stickley bends the historical record to suggest that the contemporary usefulness of the piece is built on generations of furniture design stretching as far back as the folk form of the household chest. The idea that the practicality of the china cabinet is inherent in an "evolution" of the household chest is a diachronic claim that sums up the strategies of the late *Craftsman*, and it amounts to a modernist's defense of historicism. History was there not to be repeated or imitated but to constitute creativity as a usable past: "Study the good old things historically," Stickley urged in 1915, and "let them enlarge your appreciation and sympathy, then go ahead and create something that seems good to you in your own way."[69]

This is explicit in a passage from one of the last essays he wrote:

> Every cabinet-maker is entitled to gain the utmost from what every other cabinet-maker has accomplished. . . . But the final ornamentation, the lavish superstructure which gives a period its name, is not the thing that is worth imitating. When people know that I am making a new kind of furniture now they say to me, "What period will it be?" It perplexes them when I answer, "No period." I have never sought any period in my work. I am satisfied if it expresses what I believe to be progress in furniture making in America. . . . The furniture I am now making embodies the universal principles of cabinet making irrespective of countries or periods. There can be no design or construction without the employment of the basic elements of the square, the circle and the line. It is the manner of their combining that stamps the result as belonging to this or that period.[70]

The easy movement between "universal principles . . . irrespective of countries or periods" and "progress in furniture making in America" is not a contradiction but a philosophy. American design is in fact progress itself, not fixed "period." It reconstitutes basic elements and the accomplishments of "every other cabinet-maker" rather than reincarnating an historical aesthetic; composition replaces discovery or immanence. In 1909, Stickley had disparaged American Colonial furniture as a weak derivation of the "mother country," and said that he would have "little to do" with such work.[71] The "new kind of furniture" extolled in the late *Craftsman* belies this claim, but by now Stickley can offer his Colonial detailing—whether delicate turned legs or solid Jacobean paneling—as "no period" because the logic of selection and composition insulates him from blatant derivation.

This logic was anticipated by Emerson. Stickley's craftsman and Emerson's poet, I have suggested, came at the question of organic form from different directions but shared the effort to translate nature and thought, thing and idea, object and word. The poet and the craftsman also suffered the same fate: the contingency of all forms, what Emerson called the "onward trick of nature," proved too strong for theories promising an immanent correspondence between essence and expression.[72] For Stickley, the vagaries of the market shifted favor away from Craftsman oak and the classic Craftsman designs it inspired. Emerson's "fall," as famously described by Barbara Packer, was more immediately personal. The passing of his sorrow over his son Waldo's death ("the only thing grief has taught me is how shallow it is . . . [it] falls off from me and leaves no scar" [256]) occasions the essay "Experience," wherein Emerson wonders what, for the writer as for the father, is original and authentic. His frustration at the endless "change of objects" resolves, by the end, into something more patient:

> Our love of the real draws us to permanence, but health of body consists in circulation . . . inevitably does the universe wear our color, and every object fall successively into the subject itself. The subject exists, the subject enlarges; all things sooner or later fall into place. As I am, so I see; use what language we will, we can never say anything but what we are; Hermes, Cadmus, Columbus, Newton, Bonaparte are the mind's ministers. Instead of feeling a poverty when we encounter a great man, let us treat the newcomer like a traveling geologist who passes through our estate and shows us good slate, or limestone, or anthracite, in our brush pasture. The partial action of each strong mind in one direction is a telescope for the objects on which it is pointed. But every other part of knowledge is to be pushed to the same extreme, ere the soul attains her due sphericity. (271)

There are no objects, only subjects who receive bits and pieces of knowledge and work them into an organic whole: the strategy at work here anticipates Stickley's decorative version. Chippendale scrolls or Jacobean panels or fluted Hepplewhite legs—"what every other cabinet-maker has accomplished"—are elements of an original aesthetic in the same sense that the perceptions of Hermes and Cadmus and Newton guide Emerson's own version rather than making him feel the "poverty" of insignificance. Harold Bloom, interested in Emerson's anxiety of influence, takes a phrase from Wallace Stevens in calling this reconstitution of history the "freshness of transformation," but Emerson and Stickley pitch such operations not only as the rejuvenation of the self's originality but also as a way to reconstruct the originality of environment.[73] Burbank develops his flowers by piecing together "thousands" of others and, for Stickley, thus models the perfection of nature not as an immutable fact but as a subjective function of cultivation and selection. For Emerson, too, subjectivity—and particularly its limits, the inability of the mind to possess any one thing permanently—is the agent of the real: the "partial action" of past genius telescopes only certain features of nature and constructs essence diachronically, through the fragmenting vision—"a little chipping, baking, patching, and washing"—that, in Emerson's early essay "Nature," could not alter "an impression so grand as that of the world on the human mind."[74] By "Experience," the world made no grand impression, but the "beautiful estate" Emerson lost when he no longer grieved for Waldo is reconstructed through its details: the hard facts of anthracite and limestone and slate that, in the aggregate, constitute Emerson's natural home.

Stickley's natural home was more likely to be a bungalow than an estate, but its material simplicity and hands-on essence could likewise be reproduced—giving that word its full industrial value—through the profusion of decorative possibilities that was the very threat to Craftsman style. "The party-colored wheel must revolve very fast to appear white," Emerson wrote (260)—an aphorism about the resolution of abundance and heterogeneity into immanence that Stickley made applicable to his late "Chromewald" furniture, offered in a wide range of painted shades, by pressuring his readers to find the dominant "color note" of their homes and by offering them the array of choices required to cohere that tone. Wai Chee Dimock has seen "Experience" as an essay that locates a standard of sufficiency "at the pole" of superabundance: the complaint that initiates the essay is that Emerson, after more than two years, no longer feels overwhelmed by grief, and he never "gets" anything—his word—because he is like a "human black hole . . . forever unfilled and forever insatiable."[75] That the essential emerges only in the context of excess is also the point of the passage describing the "mind's ministers"—but where Emerson offers this as an epistemological fact (the long history of knowledge brings us ever closer to the real) and Dimock reads it as a social strategy (to assert that the self always requires more is to deflect penury away from questions of social injustice), Stickley takes it as a principle of consumer desire. By the last paragraph of the essay describing the cabinet-maker's reconstitution of history, Stickley's strategy has brought us back around to the shopper:

> In every home-maker is the artist's power to visualize a perfectly appointed home and the humble workman's willingness to patiently work out the details that would be troublesome enough without love of the work. To select the proper furniture, draperies, rugs and all the manifold little things that go to make up a livable, lovable home involves knowledge of materials gained only by study and experience, a sense of fitness and an inner feeling for beauty. If women approached home-making as an artist does his work we would have more suitable, lovely homes to leave as a valued legacy.[76]

The shopper's "sense of fitness" and "knowledge of materials" invoke the "humble workman" and the artisan's orientation to the immanent meaning of the medium. But this new incarnation of Stickley's favorite type possesses such virtues in order to negotiate the complexities of the decorative marketplace: making the Craftsman home means working with a vast array of consumer goods. The selective "economy" of choosing depends on these conditions. Transferring the immanence of nature produced by ammonia fuming to the immanent simplicity of decorative taste and the total home, Stickley adapts the Craftsman vision to the mass market by drawing on the gendered ideologies of homemaking. Period pieces become authentic in the sense that authenticity is reproduction, the reconstitution of what Stickley called an "infinite variety" of prefabricated forms and details into a simple and practical and essential whole.

The last sentence of the passage is even more telling than its explicit conflation of the workman and the consumer: the Craftsman home, described in 1909 as a "permanent way of building," now becomes a "valued legacy," one other element of a superabundance of forms and a generous, contingent history on which Stickley's idea of economy depends. The instinct for the fit use of materials that Cellini modeled as the artisan's quicksilver responsiveness, that Pugin identified with Gothic labor, and that Ruskin and Morris identified as a rich exuberance of creative artisanal adaptations became, for Stickley, a matter of the consumer's sensibility. But this must not be seen as the demise of the handicrafts vision, at least in the context of Stickley's whole career—and, I have argued, in the context of emerging epistemologies of craft in the nineteenth and twentieth centuries. Stickley certainly represents the fashionability of craft as a consumer style, as critics have long recognized. His vision, however, does not violate or make a mockery of artisanship by relocating it to an expensive building in Manhattan. Instead, Stickley's understanding of his project flows through the set of imperatives—of feeling and medium, instinct and telos, sensibility and immanence, type and practice—that structured the meanings of workmanship in his era and that made craft recognizable to his audience.

CHAPTER 5

THE SYNTAX OF THE EYE

Author, Artisan, and the "More Laboring Ages" in Henry James's *The Spoils of Poynton*

RESULTS "ALL OF THE SQUAREST": JAMES'S HOUSE OF FICTION

In brief, *The Spoils of Poynton* concerns a woman dispossessed of a collection of antiques made by the best artisans of the Old World. By a brutal legality, the collection falls to her son when her husband dies, and the woman, Adela Gereth, spends much of the novel trying to influence the son to break off an engagement to a woman of no taste for an engagement to a woman who appears to appreciate the rarity of the things. In his 1908 preface to the novel, James located its theme at the zenith of consumer desire for the crafts: *The Spoils of Poynton*, he wrote, records that "most modern of our current passions, the fierce appetite for the upholsterer's and joiner's and brazier's work, the chairs and tables, the cabinets and presses, of the more laboring ages" (xliii). Early reviews of the novel, first published in 1897, recognized this emphasis. The audience for *The Spoils of Poynton*, noted *The Critic*, would "include all that inner circle of devotees of the exquisite who find their solace for living in a cheap, hideous, machine made world, in owning and doting upon a few good examples of the craftsmanship of more leisurely or more artistic generations."[1] "Fortunately for Mr. James," *The Nation* remarked more succinctly, "it is fashionable to care for things, old things."[2] Devotees and collectors of the exquisite are almost always James's subject, of course, in one way or another. But this novel takes the theme, as another reviewer wrote, "conversely": the author's usual interest in a "person or persons" for whom things are "stage accessories" is here displaced by James's desire to "make people the accessories" of the marvelous collection of handmade furnishings.[3]

Against this background, however, the puzzlement of the novel for early readers was that the furnishings, while felt as the center of the drama, also seem abstract, ghostly, and poorly realized. They are presented in sweeping generalities, as "rare perfection" rather than as any very specifically perfect artifacts (7). The ekphrastic weakness of the novel, noted by almost every early and recent critic, may be one reason reviewers tended to describe the spoils in terms suggestive of their slightness at the same time as they identified them with the era's passion for antiques. In review after review, the objects appear as "bibelots," "bric-a-brac," and "priceless knickknacks" despite the fact that the novel is quite clear about their much more dramatic scale and setting. Poynton's furnishings are actually sparse: the things are arrayed in "clear chambers" and visible from "open doors where vistas were long and bland" (14). Many of the items are heavy and have to be moved, when the dispossessed woman steals them back from her son, by "men with mighty vans" (50); while there are bibelots and small things in the collection, James emphasizes furniture, "tables and chairs" (69, 73).[4] By describing a desire for craft that is also a literary abstraction of actual objects, a passion for furnishings that also seems to trivialize or minimize real things, the reviews of *The Spoils of Poynton* take us to the heart of the condition studied in *Talking Shop;* the ambiguous substance of the antiques reveals the definitional uncertainties attending craft as its modishness flowed through print media. Indeed, the most interesting aspect of this pattern, for my purposes, has to do with how reviewers traced the ekphrastic levity of the things to the correlative levity, the preciousness, of James's own literary craftsmanship. "He is," the reader for the *New York Times* reported skeptically, "still spinning his work out fine"; Trollope, the reader suggests, would have "wrought skillfully" with the same plot, but James's labor produces "a result which, if pleasing to one's finer senses, is yet scarcely tangible."[5] His craft "elaborates . . . miniatures," according to a scathing review in *The Spectator.*[6] Mervin Erie, writing for *The Bookman,* makes the same point in a more positive analysis of the novel: "The details of Mr. James's workmanship deserve close scrutiny," he writes, for "each situation is a miniature, each sentence a piece of thread lace. With what delicate insinuations he approximates his meaning!"[7] The bibelots and bric-a-brac that the reviewers identified with the collection itself reflected what was seen as James's authorial craftsmanship of miniatures and delicacies.

The Spoils of Poynton thus crystallized, for its initial readers, what I have presented in the preceding chapters as the intricate cultural drama of craft's transliteration. The novel celebrates handmade things and the appeal of a "few good examples of . . . craftsmanship." At the same time, however, those things evaporate into "unreal," "intangible," excessively profuse, or apparently lightsome artifacts through James's literary representation of them.[8] The language of craft, to put the same case in reverse, seems to run the risk of abstracting the material dimensions of handmade things at the same time as the novel asks us to understand the passion, in a "machine made world," for things made by "the hands of rare artists" (14). The text is my subject in this final chapter of *Talking Shop* because it so pointedly focuses the relation of words and things in the context of the era's acquisitive desires for handicrafts artifacts. While dealing with antiques rather than contemporary crafts, old things rather than new ones, James's novel revolves around the questions of craft's legibility with which Hawthorne, Pugin, Cellini's readers, and the partisans of Arts and Crafts Movement in the United States and the United Kingdom also grappled.

This chapter ultimately argues that *The Spoils of Poynton* develops alternatives to some of the quandaries of representing handicraft in, and as, text. But I want to begin by suggesting that *Spoils* focused such quandaries for James himself, whose own understanding of his literary practice mirrored the concerns of reviewers that his craft poorly represented the more substantial artifacts made by Old World braziers and joiners. James's concerns, however, had less to do with his finely spun prose than with another, albeit related anxiety: that the efforts of the literary artisan were analogous to the taxonomic energies of the marketplace, translating handcrafted furnishings into lexicons of style, type, and class. In the last decade of his novel-writing career, James indeed seems to have been drawn to the imagery of craft at moments when he was thinking about combinations and collections. Consider, to begin with, a curious sentence in a letter he wrote in 1899 to the French author Paul Bourget, on the occasion of Bourget's preparation of his collected works: "*Heureux homme*," James congratulated the novelist, "to be building and gilding, carving and colouring, yourself, already, your marble, your mosaic sarcophagus."[9]

This is not the kind of congratulations Bourget might have hoped to receive. The sentence stutters its way toward the image of an entombed, prematurely dead author. Pulling up in multiple clauses, James seems to resist his morbid conclusion. The halting effect punctuates the inexorable momentum of a sentence that begins with the happy autonomy of the literary craftsman and ends with his final act of laying his literary corpus to rest. The letter interests me for two reasons: because James thinks of building and gilding when he thinks of Bourget's editorial work on his collection, and because that association appears to have threatening implications. The association itself, to take the first of these concerns, is characteristic—for James returned to the image of the literary craftsman when he came to build and gild his own mosaic sarcophagus, the New York Edition of his collected fiction (1907–9). The prefaces James wrote for the collected volumes are sustained reflections on literary technique, and they are full of the language of workmanship—a language that bears the mark of having originated in the context of the author's retrospective ordering and disposition of his completed novels and tales. In the preface to *The Wings of the Dove*, for instance, the "house of fiction" is built of "solid blocks of wrought material, squared to the sharp edge."[10] The figure of workmanship invoked here involves the procedure by which a block is made perfectly rectangular. The "sharp edge" is what artisans call the reference plane, the face initially worked to be level and smooth; the author, in James's formulation, is like the woodworker who flattens this one side and then, using traditional methods or (by 1908, when James wrote the preface for *The Spoils of Poynton*) a mechanical planer, trues the other sides of the block square to the original surface.

By contrast, James might have analogized craft to freeform sculpture or handiwork by eye—in the sense that Emerson, for instance, compared the poet's imaginative transport to the sculptor's ability to express an "essence in his mind" or a vision lodged "on the retina of his eye."[11] But the images of literary craftsmanship in James's prefaces consistently describe work ordered in relation to other work. In the preface for *The Wings of the Dove*, James goes on to attribute the "firmness" and "smoothness" of his "constructional block[s]" to the fact that much of his fiction appeared in magazine installments, as elements in a series of pieces (46, 49). Describing a "world of periodicals and editors," of rigid "conditions of publication," James saw his finest workmanship in his ability to adapt to the editorial style of the magazine and to write novels in well-shaped episodes of consistent length. The "prescriptions" of the serialized novel, he claimed, "often operate as a tax on ingenuity"—an ingenuity characteristic of the "expert craftsman who likes to be taxed" so that his technical prowess might exert itself most fully (41).

Results that are "all of the squarest" thus originate in the reference planes provided by serialized fiction (49); the "building-up" of a novel involves the relations handled by the master craftsman (43). Recent scholarship has stressed such patterns in early industrial-era aesthetics. Two influential books with similar titles—Bill Brown's *The Sense of Things: The Object Matter of American Literature* and Diana Fuss's *The Sense of an Interior*—describe how industrial culture developed affective models of aesthetic coherence (founded on "passionate acts of . . . selecting [and] situating," the kind of work James imagines for the writer and that Stickley imagines for the consumer) as an alternative to understanding goods as individually fetishized "objects of consumption."[12] Although Fuss and Brown do not expressly discuss artisanship, James's representation of craft appears to fit nicely into this model. The artisan's eye for reference planes echoes what Fuss describes as a kind of proprioceptive "sixth sense," an "inner mechanism that allows a body to orient itself in space" and that handles relational matters of "distance and proximity."[13] That sense makes furnishings something more than commodities, humanizing objects by suggesting the individual who arranged and related them—and, we might add, who made them. I have argued that nineteenth- and twentieth-century models of artisanship stressed the artisan's instinct for the labor and for the medium as an affective "sense," to use the word shared by Brown and Fuss, that distinguished craft from the impersonality of industrial manufacture.

The problem with reading James's depiction of craft in this way—as an alternative, in effect, to the commodity fetish—is that James felt so anxious about his own equation of craft and relational models of labor and coherence. James may have appreciated the "expert craftsman" for his practiced ability to imagine surfaces or bits of writing in relation to one another, as constituent pieces of an aesthetic whole—but, as the letter to Bourget intimates, he also recoiled from describing aesthetic cogency or coherence as an ideal of crafted objects. He recoiled, I am going to be suggesting over the course of this chapter, for the good reason—the absorption of craft into words, texts, and lexical systems—that informs *Talking Shop* as a whole. Because the industrial era taxonomized virtually every traditional detail of workmanship (a ball-and-claw foot, say) as an example of a certain marketable type ("Chippendale"), James's depictions of the artisan's eye for cogency are haunted by the specter of that cogency's commodification as this or that style. If we can glimpse this problem in James's supercilious congratulations to an author who builds and gilds the definitive representation of himself and his work (Bourget's *Oeuvres Complètes*), it is more explicit in *The Spoils of Poynton*. For the novel presents a character who represents the exact dilemma. Mrs. Brigstock, the mother of the woman of no taste who stands to become the possessor of the artifacts, tours the collection of handicrafts items made by the best artisans "of the more laboring ages" while clutching and consulting a decorative magazine (xliii). Her relational, taxonomic "formula of admiration" is that every antique she sees appears " 'in the style' of something else" (18).

Mrs. Brigstock thus exemplifies a typical attitude toward craft that, I will argue, is the central drama of material objects in *The Spoils of Poynton*. In the age of Jones's *Grammar of Ornament* and of decorative magazines (*House Beautiful*, *Decorator and Furnisher*, and *House and Garden* all originated in the late nineteenth century), craft was sold to the middle class as much in terms of patterns as of practice. Nineteenth-century decorative publications created and depended upon elaborate vocabularies of workmanship, as in this description of a mirror from Henry Shaw's *Specimens of Ancient Furniture* (1836): "This splendid example of the French fashion in the times of Charles the Second [shows] the connecting link between the Elizabethan style and that of [James the Second], though it should be observed that in the time of our Charles the First, the frames were being worked on a bevel from thence to the wall."[14] The complicated matrix of historical details, spanning countries as well as centuries, required a relational understanding of crafts history that was as much a part of the era's "sense of an interior"—to borrow Fuss's phrase—as the eye that cohered surfaces instinctively and affectively. Indeed, the relational sensibility for décor historicized by Fuss and Brown might be said to have depended on the marketplace for stylistic coherence as much as it resisted the consumerist fetishization of individual objects. *The Spoils of Poynton* is, I think, the record of this paradoxical condition. In its depiction of a beautiful collection of crafted objects, it is about the appeal of situating surfaces relative to one another (a fundamental condition of handicraft itself, as the New York Edition argues) at the same time as it is constantly aware that such operations easily fall victim to the taxonomic salesmanship of the age.

James's attitude toward the relation of names and things in the preface to *Spoils*, in fact, reveals a disturbing correspondence between the novelist and Mrs. Brigstock. Her formula is to equate décor and description. The rendering of objects in words is, of course, also the practice of the author, and thus the preface to the novel anticipates the drama of the plot as a commentary on the craft of fiction. James describes his decision to write a novel about great works of artisanship: "On the face of it the 'things' themselves would form the very center of such a crisis; these grouped objects, all conscious of their eminence and their price, would enjoy, in any picture of a conflict, the heroic importance. They would have to be presented, they would have to be painted—arduous and desperate thought; something would have to be done for them not too ignobly unlike the great array in which Balzac, say, would have marshaled them: *that* amount of workable interest at least would evidently be 'in it' " (xliii; emphasis in original). Literary refinishing—marshalling and painting the antiques—seeks to present the " 'things' themselves," but is also, at the same time, "an arduous and desperate thought" operating at one remove from the original. As in the other prefaces and the letter to Bourget, the act of writing is understood as an act of arranging and grouping—but that act appears as already too imitative for the stated purpose of incarnating the antiques. The subjunctive mood of the passage draws the lesson: the spoils "would" ("on the face of it") "have to be painted . . . in any picture of a conflict" that the author might mount. Emphasizing how the author would paint the spoils in the context of a hypothetical picture, the language opens gaps between the actual crafted objects—the "upholsterer's and joiner's and brazier's work," the rare antiquities of the "more laboring ages"—and the objects of literary craft (xliii). There is a hint of this problem in the preface to *The Wings of the Dove*, where the word "craft" appears in its two senses: to define those "constructional blocks" of fiction created by the "expert craftsman," but also to characterize the "dissimulation," the "usual craft" (now with the sense of "crafty"), of the author who obfuscates, "displaces," or—a figure James explicitly draws from the lexicon of painting technique, where it describes a method of blurring—"dodges" his central themes (46–47).

The preface to *Spoils*, however, goes on to more fully describe the problem of craft's craftiness, when it comes to the idea of the writer as artisan. The quoted passage only begins to introduce the language of workmanship that defines this preface in particular. James fantasizes about a story "hammered into a sacred hardness," an "indestructible" accomplishment of a "master-builder" who "builds and piles high, laying together the blocks quarried in the deeps of his imagination" (xl, xlii). The difficulty with all this, as it emerges, is that language is neither as stable nor as tangible as a stone edifice, and that James's very definition of craft as the coherence of "grouped objects" builds literary things only in relative and representational terms. If *The Spoils of Poynton*, as Thomas J. Otten has detailed, is concerned with the tactile properties of objects, the novel's preface is concerned with the more fundamental problem, for the writer, that words are not tangible and can only present, at second hand, the things themselves.[15] The preface indeed opens by describing a "mismeasurement" whereby a story about objects (the "citadel of the interest" would be the "Things, always the splendid Things") insistently loses itself to language (xliii, xlvi). Beginning as a short story, a "little workable thing" about the "valuable furniture of a fine old house," the piece gets longer and longer (xli). By the time it became the novel—its title changed from *The Old Things* to *The Spoils of Poynton*—its "sole impression" appears to James to be not that of craft but "that of length" (xliv).

Overwhelmed by words, James can only imagine (again subjunctively) the novel he did not write, the novel in which the spoils would have been "figured and constituted, with each identity made vivid, each character discriminated":

> The rendered tribute of these honors, however, no vigilant editor could be conceived as allowing room for; since, by so much as . . . [the novel] should suggest the gleam of brazen idols and precious metals and inserted gems . . . by just so much would the muse of "dialogue," most usurping influence of all the romancingly invoked, be routed without ceremony. . . . The spoils of Poynton were not directly articulate, and though they might have, and conse-

> quently did have, wondrous things to say, their message fostered around them a certain hush of cheaper sound—as a consequence of which, in fine, they would have been costly to keep up. In this manner Fleda Vetch, maintainable at less expense—though even she, I make out, less expert in spreading chatter than the readers of romance mainly like their heroines today—marked her place in my foreground. (xlvi)

The apparent antipodes here (author and editor, one striving to depict the things and the other stressing character and dialogue) are illusory. For James is his own "vigilant editor." He stops himself from describing the spoils, turns himself to dialogue; he projects that the things "would . . . be routed" if they became too prominent. Preparing the New York Edition, James is even more literally his own editor. This conflation of the roles of author and editor exactly suggests the nature of the Jamesian craft of fiction, as it is described in the prefaces. Authorship adjusts, adapts, relates, and presents; its technical accomplishment is relative rather than original, contextual rather than autonomous.

It is also, the passage just quoted suggests, therefore cheap and tawdry. The substitution of dialogue—talk about the things, in relation to them—for their "directly articulate" preeminence introduces a "cheaper sound." Dialogue appears at "less expense" than the actual antiques; it is less "costly," a phenomenon of popular fiction and sentimental, garrulous heroines. Talking around the authenticity of the spoils, literary workmanship cheapens the things it would incarnate. In the preface to the novel, the craft of fiction appears to raise certain problems for the crafted objects.

MAKING TALK: CRAFT AND THE CONVERSATION PIECE

The "arduous and desperate thought" that the literary artisan—Bourget, Balzac, James—is really just a taxonomist, a collector and stylist of represented antiques and reprinted fiction, thus appears so threatening because it collapses the distance between the writer's practice and Mrs. Brigstock's "formula of admiration." Mrs. Brigstock is the boorish mother of the woman (Mona Brigstock) who stands to inherit the spoils by marrying their legal inheritor (Owen Gereth). And no one could be more adept at "spreading chatter" at the expense of objects than Mrs. Brigstock. She "pronounce[s]," stylistically, on "whatever she sees" (17). She "turns up the underside of plates" to identify their maker (18). She classifies in order "to show how much she had seen" (23). Seeing, however, really means reading and naming: Mrs. Brigstock consults her magazine's "patterns for antimacassars" when she might, just by raising her head, take in the real thing (18). Her own home, Waterbath, is a riot of decorative objects that are really texts. The walls are hung with illuminated manuscripts (12) and excerpts from "society papers" (22).

Mrs. Brigstock's foil is Mrs. Gereth, who collected the objects at Poynton but stands to lose them, by a patrilineal inheritance law, to her son Owen. The novel's drama is neatly represented in Mrs. Gereth's withering comment about Mrs. Brigstock's design magazine, that "precious publication" (23). As the Brigstocks are leaving Poynton, Mrs. Gereth implores Mona not to let her mother forget "the female magazine with the what-do-you-call-'em?—the grease-catchers" (23). Grease-catchers, to be sure, are a different order of objects than chairs and tables. Mrs. Gereth is making a joke at the expense of the Brigstocks by referring to the purpose of antimacassars, covers for upholstered chairs that prevent pomade, commonly made of macassar oil, from transferring to the fabric; the Brigstocks, she is implying, are slimy. But Mrs. Gereth's theatrical loss for words, her refusal to remember the name of the "what-do-you-call-'em" furnishings, also distinguishes her taste from the decorative lexicon of the woman who translates everything into this or that style. The décor at Poynton, by contrast, can never be put into words. The things are, James says repeatedly, "mute." The spoils are "written in the syllables" not of language but of "color and form" (14). Their "tongues" are those of their origins "in other countries" (14); they are relics of crafts eras when the only arbiters of style were the original conceptions incarnated by the "hands of rare artists" (xliii). "Everything at Poynton was in the style of Poynton" (18).

It is significant that the most memorable item at Poynton, however, is named: the Maltese Cross. But that name is a misnomer. The geographic tag refers not to the style of the cross or to its provenance, but to the place where Mrs. Gereth, by an "odd and romantic chance," first heard of its existence (49). By defining the ivory crucifix with a title that is "technically incorrect" (49), Mrs. Gereth undermines the relation of word and thing, style and "style," assumed by Mrs. Brigstock. In point of fact, a Maltese cross is a conventional design—it has four arms of equal length, generally indented at each end. The Maltese Cross at Poynton, however, eludes its relation to stylistic convention. Mrs. Gereth's is finely wrought, "a masterpiece of delicacy," where Maltese crosses, especially as popularized around 1900 by the Arts and Crafts Movement, are normally plain and robust (49). More to the point about language that I want to make here is that the adjective "Maltese" is a convention only of the Gereths, a word that "had always been applied at Poynton" (49) to recall the place where the idea of the object—not the object itself, materially or stylistically—first appeared. For Mrs. Brigstock, a Maltese cross would be in the style of Malta, in the same sense that a Rococo room could be identified by serpentine wall sconces or a Queen

Anne hall table would have scallop-shell carving, slipper feet, and batwing hardware. For Mrs. Gereth, the Maltese Cross relates to Malta as a place without being Maltese as a style, in the same sense that Louis XV—who "thumbed" the things at Poynton, whose actual touch alighted on their surfaces (14)—is a flesh-and-blood king before he is a bombé chest or an ormolu table.

The two ways of construing "Maltese" or "Louis XV"—as stylistic tags promising to typify the objects they describe, or as a place or a person—represent polarized ways of thinking about what James describes as his central subject in the novel: that "fierce appetite" for the "chairs and tables, the cabinets and presses" of a more artisanal culture (xliii). As a place and a person, Malta and Louis XV are imagined at Poynton only in terms of the singular historical moments—a vision that comes in Malta or the thumb of the king on the spoils—that make the antiques desirable. Mrs. Gereth operates with a sense of space that is relational without being taxonomic. In Malta, she imagines an object (*not* a Maltese cross, conventionally speaking) that will fit beautifully into her assembled interior. Her appreciation of the "upholsterer's and joiner's and brazier's work" is likened by James to the original moment of creation, to the touch of the artisan, because she thinks of her whole collection in terms that are singular and private rather than typical and public. The antiques, Mrs. Gereth explains, are "*me*": "with the brush of a finger, I could tell one from another . . . they know me, they return the touch of my hand" (31).

Mrs. Gereth's model is, of course, affectively compelling; Bill Brown calls it "a matter of aura, not artifacts."[16] But I hope to have already suggested that the novel cannot effectively defend this way of thinking. As revealed in the preface, James found Mrs. Gereth's attitude unsustainable by any novelist, however much James appreciates her taste and satirizes her adversary's vulgarity. For the novel, as a genre, forces the "fierce appetite" for crafted things into the representational logic of a marketplace devoted to workmanship as a matter of words. Gervase Wheeler, the American author of *Homes for the People* (1855), typifies Victorian epistemologies of workmanship when he describes old furnishings as "specimens" that would "make talk," in polite society, on subjects other than "politics, dress, fashion, and scandal"; they were "curiosities," historical "relics" that could be discussed in drawing rooms and libraries.[17] Wheeler's populism, as directed to the middle and upper classes (his first book, *Rural Homes*, offered "simple" country estates of nine or ten rooms), motivated his attempt to name old things as something for Victorians to talk about other than dress or fashion. But the language of craft constituted its own fashion by the mid-nineteenth century, as Thorstein Veblen assumed in tracing the perversion of the "instinct of workmanship" into conspicuously consumed "old styles" of handicrafts objects.[18] In this context, the handmade old things described by James as his subject—and ultimately translated into a novel that left the impression of "dialogue"—appear as Wheeler's discussable "curiosities"; James, in fact, uses the word "curiosity" twice in the surrounding text. Critical interest in the novel, however, has largely been motivated by either the effect that "obscure[s] particular objects," or by the "fierce appetite" on its own terms.[19] Scholars have imagined the spoils within the abstracting logic of the commodity fetish (Armstrong); as projections of fundamentally psychological conditions (Sarris); as "real" things subject to "spoiling" by their implication in an invidious, competitive culture of acquisition (Koenigsberger).[20] The most talked-about problem in *The Spoils of Poynton* is that the objects appear to fade behind the ability to arrange them or the desire to possess them. But the context of the "fierce appetite" James describes, the terms of its emergence, is the introduction of a technical language of workmanship into Victorian décor—a language that, detailing styles and forms of artisanship with taxonomic specificity, concretizes the meaning of craft as "curiosities."[21]

The Spoils of Poynton, then, turns on a paradox of desire, of "appetite." James likes old things that act on the aesthetic imagination as groupings (suddenly imagining, at Malta, the perfect thing for the Poynton collection even if one won't actually find it in, or especially *as*, Malta), but this same logic of relational aesthetics suggests the classificatory consumerism that positioned crafts objects in exemplary groupings. The central questions raised by *The Spoils of Poynton*, in the preface and in the contest between Mrs. Brigstock and Mrs. Gereth, seem to me something like these: How might James imagine furnishings as literary objects without appearing, like Mrs. Brigstock, to transliterate real things into the grammar of ornament, a language of pattern? How might qualities James clearly admired—Mrs. Gereth's taste, Balzac's idealized ability to incarnate things in a "great array," a "sense of things" operating outside of the common marketplace—be accommodated to a fictional world of popular editors, usurping dialogue, reprinted novels, opportunistic editions of Collected Works, and textually reproduced antiques?

One of James's responses to these questions was Fleda Vetch, the heroine of *The Spoils of Poynton*—who, the passage about the "vigilant editor" tells us, "marked her place in my foreground" only once James realized that his very genre, the novel, was poorly compatible with the "hush" demanded of antiquities. Fleda is thus imagined by James, explicitly, as a reaction to the foundational problem of writing about crafted objects. How Fleda negotiates the imperatives of dialogue and of silence, when it comes to rare furnishings, will become my subject shortly. But consider first how the novel's "foreground," as it was imagined in the New York Edition and its preface, includes not just Fleda Vetch but a remarkable frontispiece (figure 28). Each volume of the New York Edition has a photographic frontispiece, and James collaborated closely with Alvin Langdon Coburn, the photographer, on many of the shots; he was particularly explicit about the image for *The Spoils of Poynton*.[22] The objects depicted in that image appear, as one interpreter puts it, "superior and remote."[23] For most readers of the novel, these *are* the spoils, or at least very much like them. The sentinel-like effect of the screen, the geometric positioning of the items, the chairs arrayed for display rather than conversation, and the image's emphasis on visual appreciation all suggest the values of inaccessibility, rarity, and speechlessness associated with Poynton.

In fact, however, these were some of the most talked-about objects of the era—and they are not all, as it happens, very rare. The objects, for one, are from the Wallace Collection, the story of which bears a striking resemblance to the drama narrated in *The Spoils of Poynton*. When Richard Wallace died in 1890, he left a marvelous assembly, the best outside of France, of Louis XIV and Louis XV antiques. Unlike Mr. Gereth in *The Spoils of Poynton*, Wallace left them explicitly and legally to his wife—who bequeathed them, and the house in which they are arranged, to the nation of England. In the 1870s, the Wallaces had refurbished Hertford House as an ideal setting for French antiques; among other renovations, Wallace hung wallpapers, installed cornices and period details, and arranged lighting to show the pieces to best effect. England, however, refused the gift on the grounds that Hertford House was not zoned as a museum and could not therefore enter the public trust. The woman was therefore allowed to bequeath the things, but not if she bequeathed the house as well; the novel's interest in the relationship of things to context—the spoils to Poynton, individually crafted items to larger groupings—is anticipated in the legal drama that threatened to break up the collection. Years of strange litigation ensued, in which the trustees for the collection and the house had to sue the nation to accept the gift. The matter was finally resolved when the house was rezoned as a museum.[24]

This history is relevant to *The Spoils of Poynton* in general because James wrote the novel during the period of litigation, when the fate of the antiques was being worked out. The things depicted in the frontispiece were the subject of a fascinating story in their own right—even before the reader discovers that the story implies another, *The Spoils of Poynton* itself. The frontispiece thus presents superior and remote objects that are not too superior to be talked (or written) about. The provenance of the collection is even more pointedly relevant to the novel because the legal dispute turned on two different ways of presenting the

FIGURE 28. Alvin Langdon Coburn, frontispiece for Henry James, *The Spoils of Poynton* (New York: Scribner, 1908)

material past. Implicit in the government's decision to accept only the things, and to accept them into some already-zoned museum, is the probability that the antiques (if they even stayed together as a collection) would have ended up as specimens behind cordons. They would be housed as examples, in the Brigstock sense, rather than in the carefully composed setting of the house that the Wallaces had renovated as the perfect context for the pieces. As disputed, the items in the photograph thus anticipate the question driving *The Spoils of Poynton*; they image the threat of interiors atomized as specimens.

That threat is adverted by the rezoning of Hertford House. And yet just as James chooses things layered with narrative context and narrative possibility, the photograph does not unequivocally endorse the idea that these objects—the Wallace spoils—are superior to the typology, representation, and construction of historicity. For the objects are not uniformly genuine, superior, remote, or rare. The clock is genuine Louis XV; it was made by Joseph Coteau in 1763. The vases are real; they are Sèvres porcelain of 1772. But the other items, as detailed in Peter Hughes's catalogs of the Wallace Collection, are historical reproductions.[25] In requesting permission for Coburn to shoot this setting in particular, James remembered a "divine little chimney piece with all its wonderful garniture, a couple of chairs beside it, and a piece on either side, of the pale green damask on the wall."[26] The chimney piece, the object James most particularly remembered, is a hasty imitation of the Louis XV style. Constructed quickly for the renovation of Hertford House in the 1870s and left unfinished on the inside, the chimney piece is a theatrical prop. The ornate pier mirror, too, is a gilt-wood Victorian reproduction of the gilt-bronze that would have been used in the age of Louis XV. As representations of the wondrous spoils made by Old World artisans and touched by the king, James remembers the bogus.

Or, more precisely, he remembers the bogus as the center of an authentic scene. It is not that the presence of the ersatz constitutes a hoax, belying the vision of rarity and remoteness. Rather, James offers an image that is composed indistinguishably of real antiques and represented ones; like Fleda, who begins as an ally of Mrs. Gereth but ends up also defending the interests of the Brigstocks, the frontispiece represents a tenuous accommodation between two ways of understanding craft and collections. It is not certain, of course, that James knew the divine little chimney piece was a fake. But he had reviewed the paintings in the Wallace Collection in 1873, and certainly knew the history of Hertford House; it is hard to imagine that he did not have a sense of the theatricality of the choice. More than thirty years before the preparation of the New York Edition, in fact, James had described the Wallace Collection precisely as a study in the relationship of individual objects to their stylistic or taxonomic groupings. Reviewing a display of Wallace's paintings in London's East End (during the period when Hertford House was under renovation), James opened his comments with the claim that the collection "pretends as little as possible to be instructive or consistent, to illustrate schools"—and went on to use the pieces in the collection as a way of taxonomizing, in the following order, the typology of English landscape painting, the paradigmatic principles of French pictorial subjects, and the nature of Dutch realism.[27] In the review, the paintings appear on the one hand entirely typical (certain works appear the "very model" of national traits, as "specimens" or "representative[s]"), and on the other hand, superior to the merely representational ("Comparisons are odious," James states breezily as he catches himself admiring the essential Englishness of one of Wallace's Reynolds).[28]

Such questions were inherent in the Wallace Collection, the epicenter of a public drama about objects and their settings; the very fact that James first saw the paintings while they were being shown in an East End warehouse (soon to become the Bethnal Green Museum) raises the issue. In the frontispiece, in 1908, James drew on this history to anticipate the drama of the novel itself. Indeed, the language James used to prescribe the setting is telling. The letter requesting permissions recalled the chimney piece, but it also stresses everything as being arrayed along "pale green damask on the wall." The same emphasis—on the damasked wall as a plane of visual coherence—appears in another letter about the setting, this one to Coburn himself. James asked Coburn to "take the beautiful subject *obliquely*, won't you?, with as much of the damask on the wall as possible" (emphasis in original).[29] The point, then, was to use the wall and damask as the cohering surface for the whole composition; James wanted the shot taken obliquely so that the pieces would appear as part of a perspective, a "beautiful subject." In stressing the damask and the oblique perspective, James gave stylistic coherence to a setting that is not, itself, quite genuine or uniformly authentic. The frontispiece, shot along an angle to blend the things into one another and into the room, eliding the real and the represented, generates an experience, an effect, of historical authenticity. In the picture, to put it most briefly, French things are indistinguishable from French style.

THE "TOUCH OF THE AIR" AND THE VOLUBILITY OF DESIGN

The beautiful subject of the frontispiece is a narrative matter, not just a material one, to the degree that it implies both a backstory and the story to follow; it is also a narrative matter because it turns on constructions of authenticity which, in the Victorian age, were increasingly understood in terms of a classificatory grammar of ornament. Moreover, in prescribing that the things should blend into their environment—and in using the obliquity of the perspective to render the real and the represented, the Louis XV and the "Louis XV," indistinct—James tapped into Coburn's particular photographic predilections and stipulated a visual effect that others, including Stickley, would also claim as the epicenter for a model of craft as effect. Like Alfred Stieglitz and Edward Steichen, Coburn aimed to photograph mood in the early twentieth century; the softly focused, gray atmospheres of the so-called Pictorialist strain of photography were produced by such techniques as stretching gauze over the camera lenses or saturating the paper with platinum salts. The effects produced by Coburn around the time he worked on James's New York Edition mirror the diffuse light characteristic of turn-of-the-century visual art—particularly the paintings of Thomas Dewing, Dwight Tryon, and James McNeill Whistler—and also, more suggestively for my purposes, constituted an element of Stickley's project in the late stages of the Craftsman enterprise. Returning briefly to that enterprise, as it began reinventing the classic Craftsman style in the 1910s, will help contextualize the strategies implicit in James's instructions to Coburn.

One of Stickley's late lines of furniture, the previous chapter explains, depended on an expanded color palette. But to distinguish these variously painted "Chromewald" pieces from the stark contrasts of the style promoted by the Viennese Werkstäate—a modernist outlet of the international craft movement best known for its appreciation of color blocks and black-and-white furnishings—Stickley depended on analogies between color and the tonal atmosphere provided by a musical key. Noting that "it has been developed and proved by a New York artist, named Muratta[,] that there is an actual scale of color corresponding exactly with the scale of music," Stickley asserted that "all colors are in exquisite and infinite harmony with all others if only this scale is understood."[30] Stickley misspells the name of Hardesty Maratta, an obscure New York artist best known for mentoring the Ashcan painter Robert Henri, but he accurately describes Maratta's musical theory of color. By mixing paints only according to certain "intervals," Maratta claimed, the painter could arrive at a series of colors (the "set palette") that would span the whole spectrum but all have the same tonal value. The paradigmatic example of a set palette, too basic to be used in actual practice but illustrative of the principle, began with three shades: red, yellow, and blue. These would be mixed in equal quantity to arrive at six shades: red, orange, yellow, green, blue, and purple. The six were then mixed neighbor with neighbor to produce twelve usable shades, none of which was allowed to be mixed again.[31] Painting—as Henri in particular did—only with shades achieved according to this version of a musical key, the artist would be guaranteed what Maratta and Henri called the "supercolor" or the "color of the whole."[32] The system sought a tonal homogeneity that nonetheless (if the artist started the process of producing the set palette with quite different colors) allowed for the entire spectrum of colors required to paint the gritty, everyday scenes of real life that the Ashcan painters preferred.

One can see why Stickley was attracted to Maratta's theory. Notions of the "supercolor" adapted the appeal of ammonia-fumed oak, a typologically cogent medium, to the wide range of finishes and styles that the market demanded and that Stickley introduced as part of the Craftsman brand. Accommodating polychromatic variety and immanence, the heterogeneity of decorative historicism and a tonal effect of authenticity, atmospheric evenness became for Stickley a business model. Stressing that it was the homeowner's role to "think out the color arrangement from the entrance to the top floor," Stickley explained how nature blends an "infinite variety" of shades into a "single unifying quality of atmosphere."[33] Period pieces seemed compatible with the "luminous quality" of Craftsman oak, or with the "deep mellow brownish glow" of his original hand-hammered metal hardware, when well-chosen by a good decorator.[34] Recalling the diffusion common to Pictorialism in photography, Tonalism in painting, and the Maratta system of color, *The Craftsman* likened the home to a "many-hued opal" in which the individual colors are indefinite but a "soft fire transcends them all"; if a "vase of strong color" is needed to "give tone," that tone must also not be stark, but "softened" by details that blend the whole.[35]

James's instructions to Coburn name the obliquity of the angle, not color, as the agent of a similar effect. But in asking Coburn to feature as much of the "pale green damask" as possible, James also ensured that the atmospheric density for which Coburn was known would characterize this image in particular. In the fronstispiece, then, James imagines what Stickley also did: décor that is reproduced without being tawdry, objects of the more laboring ages—or, rather, in the *style* of the more laboring ages—that are not merely a specimen of this or that period. And yet if the image constitutes a rebuttal of Mrs. Brigstock's vulgarity while also suggesting one strategy for cohering style according to the taxonomic terms of the market, that coherence is one thing in Coburn's medium. It is another thing in the novel itself, wherein the problem anticipated by the preface—that style becomes not just visual unity but words and names for that unity—is more particularly inherent to the written medium and to the writer's craft.

Indeed, the wall that gives coherence in the frontispiece is immediately converted, at the beginning of novel, into a wall that doesn't. The first thing we learn about Mrs. Gereth, visiting the Brigstock mansion, is that she has been "kept awake for hours by the wall-paper in her room" (1). In a house in which everything becomes text, yards of "pasted paper" set the standard of the décor; at Poynton, where wainscoting predominates and "the panels and the stuffs were themselves the picture" (a style of wall covering recommended by, among others, Edith Wharton in *The Decoration of Houses*), there is "not an inch" of wallpaper (14). That Waterbath should be smothered in paper is, of course, only an analogy for its inexorable translation of things into text. For this paper is not printed with actual words, even as the novel's opening does use the image to stress its central problem—the problem that novels and novelists deal, in effect, with printed versions of traditional details. The opening appears even more apt when one considers that wallpaper was the virtual epicenter of Victorian lexicons for representing and taxonomizing style. *Decorator and Furnisher* ran an entire series on wallpaper, employing a corps of reviewers who would review "rococo" papers or visit wallpaper manufacturers to examine "Venetian, Renaissance, and Heraldic designs, brave with a feudal splendor."[36] The language of style that Henry Shaw generated through his "specimens" could be even more bewildering when applied to a medium in which the design, apart from any requirements of structure, was everything: the motifs of a new paper might be "almost entirely French Renaissance in character," yet even so with "Louis XVI and Empire" conventions sprinkled liberally into one of the "most modern" wallpapers imaginable (21).

The achievement of the frontispiece is thus inverted in the novel's opening image of vulgarly printed—and probably explicitly stylized—décor. But *The Spoils of Poynton* works back toward the negotiation of design and print, craft and narrative, by easing Fleda Vetch into the foreground of good taste. Consider, first, how Fleda initially appears as an acolyte of Mrs. Gereth and an extension of her silent habits of appreciating old things. Fleda's first visit to Poynton is soundless: " '*Now* do you understand how I feel?' Mrs Gereth asked when in the wondrous hall, three minutes after their arrival, her pretty associate dropped on a seat with a soft gasp and a roll of dilated eyes. The answer came clearly enough, and in the rapture of that first walk through the house Fleda took a prodigious span. She perfectly understood how Mrs. Gereth felt—she had understood but meagerly before, and the two women embraced with tears over the tightening of their bond" (13). Three kinds of language are absent or inefficacious here. First, James does not describe the spoils that prompt the scene. Throughout the novel, the central objects get much less detailed treatment than the vulgar things at Waterbath or Mr. Vetch's house—where, for instance, "old brandy-flasks and match-boxes, old calendars and hand-books, mixed with an assortment of pen-wipers and ash-trays" (99) present a clearer picture of a collection than, as the spoils are described, "all France and Italy with their ages composed to rest" (14) or "old, chastened, figured, faded France" (53). Second, the words Mrs. Gereth has used to describe Poynton have not availed; three months of learning about the spoils cannot prepare Fleda for their material force. Third, that force is entirely physical even after the fact. Fleda's answer to Mrs. Gereth's question comes "clearly enough" not verbally, but viscerally, in "tears," a "soft gasp and a roll of dilated eyes."

Fleda's allegiance to Mrs. Gereth and her taste, however, does not hold. The typically Jamesian complexity of her changed allegiance involves the fact that Fleda falls in love with Owen Gereth, Mrs. Gereth's son, who legally inherits the spoils but doesn't really care about them—at least not until his fiancée, Mona Brigstock, makes his possession of the spoils a condition of their marriage. Fleda, acting out of some combination of extreme ethical devotion to Owen's engagement and morbid fear of her own passions, begins defending Mona's desires and arranging for Owen (who feels most, it seems, for Fleda) to possess the spoils as his dowry. One method by which Fleda advances Owen's claim is by subtly turning Mrs. Gereth's aesthetic appreciation to objects and scenes other than those at Poynton; the best example is a little cottage, Ricks, where Mrs. Gereth, now dispossessed, takes residence. As critics have often noted, the very shabbiness of Ricks appears as a charming alternative to the recherché vistas of Poynton. But what matters from my point of view is how Fleda's enthusiasm for Ricks—which appears alternately as a genuine recoil from Mrs. Gereth's imperious taste and as a strategic play to divest Mrs. Gereth of her interest in the spoils—involves the novel's central questions about language, craft, and collections. On the first visit to Ricks (originally owned and decorated by a deceased aunt of Mrs. Gereth's), words initially appear, as they do in the preface and at Poynton, to give the lie to décor: " 'It's charming!' [Fleda] exclaimed . . . , turning back again into the small prim parlor from a friendly advance to the single plate of the window" (35). Fleda is not being totally candid. In contrast to the fixed focus of her "dilated eyes" at Poynton (13), here the first sight of the parlor causes her to flee to the window, where the vision outside ("four iron pots on pedestals, painted white and containing ugly geraniums, ranged on the edge of a gravel path and doing their best to give it the air of a terrace") in turn forces Fleda to "instantly avert . . . her eyes" and turn back in (35). The things on which Fleda cannot focus her eyes are defined by their own attempt to trick the eye: iron pots painted to look like terra cotta, geraniums simulating a terrace, a house in the "deepest depths of Essex" contriving to "look suburban," walls "guiltless of cornice" but with that architectural detail represented by a "little band of crimson paper glued round the top of the other paper, a turbid gray sprigged with silver flowers" (35).

The white lie that opens the scene ("It's charming") mimics the general effect of translation produced by the cottage, the slipperiness through which an architectural cornice becomes one represented on printed paper. That is not so different, in its duplicity, than Waterbath or its walls. But if her eyes must fail Fleda in the presence of so much mimicry—and if the scene opens with a statement that is a misrepresentation—Fleda, and the novel itself, suddenly begin changing tack. While Mrs. Gereth broods with a "soundless moan" (36), Fleda spends the hour (the novel's critical hour, I think) imagining, if not always actually articulating, what might be said for the things. She wants to tell Mrs. Gereth that a beam "papered over"—the novel's well-established pun on decorative grammars and the craft of fiction—is "rather picturesque" (35). Even when her first impulse is that she would be able to "say nothing for mantle-pieces and doors," Fleda manages it, in a sense: she is moved to invent the story projected in the deceased aunt's things. Those things testify not to themselves, like the antiques at Poynton, but to the narrative of a life lived "shyly, yet with some bruises," to the history of a woman "sensitive and ignorant and exquisite" (36). "That too," Fleda thinks, was a "kind of origin, an atmosphere for relics and rarities, though different from the sorts most prized at Poynton" (36). If Poynton is the occasion for silence, Ricks is the occasion for narrative and prolixity. "Fleda . . . repeated to [Mrs. Gereth] more than once the indulgent fantasy about the maiden aunt—she was so sure she had deeply suffered" (36–37).

Mrs. Gereth will have none of Fleda's fantasy. Her reticence is not broken until the end of the scene, when after a "brooding hour" she only allows that "something can be done with it" (36). That something will have to do not with the story of the aunt who had deeply suffered ("I thoroughly hope she did," Mrs. Gereth remarks [36]) but with what, objectively, she might do with the place. Foiled by Mrs. Gereth's silence, Fleda's volubility seems forced and her story of the maiden aunt seems maudlin. Indeed, the comparison to Poynton in the passage is inexorable and makes the melancholy story seem like a compensation, like the "cheaper sound" of that invented language that routs the spoils in the preface. Fleda recognizes this, stopping herself just in time from actually saying, out loud, that the place is picturesque; such a statement, she realizes, "would be weak" (36).

But the final visit to Ricks, near the end of the novel when Mrs. Gereth has actually moved there and renovated the cottage, is less ambiguously committed to the possibilities for cohering narrative around objects. Fleda goes to see Mrs.

Gereth with the commitment that this time she will not hold back: if she likes Ricks, she "would utter it to her companion without reserve" (170). She does like it, very much, and it is worth quoting at length because the scene itself is so entirely without reserve:

> Fleda broke out before she even sat down. . . . "Where on earth did you put your hand on such beautiful things?"
>
> "Beautiful things?" Mrs. Gereth turned again to the little worn bleached stuffs and the sweet spindle-legs. "That's the wretched things that were here—that stupid starved old woman's." . . .
>
> Fleda took the highest line and the upper hand, and as Mrs. Gereth, challenging her cheerfulness, turned again a lusterless eye over the contents of the place, she broke into a rapture that was unforced, yet that she was conscious of an advantage in being able to feel. She moved, as she had done on the previous occasion, from one piece to another, with looks of recognition and hands that lightly lingered, but she was as feverishly jubilant as of old she had been anxious and mute. "Ah the little melancholy tender tell-tale things: how can they *not* speak to you and find a way to your heart? It's not the great chorus of Poynton; but you're not, I'm sure, so proud or so broken as to be reached by nothing but that. This is a voice so gentle, so human, so feminine—a faint far-away voice with the little quaver of a heart-break. You've listened to it unawares for the arrangement and the effect of everything. . . . It's your extraordinary genius; you make things "compose" in spite of yourself.
>
> "The impression [is] somehow of something dreamed and missed, something reduced, relinquished, resigned; the poetry, as it were, of something sensibly *gone*." Fleda ingeniously and triumphantly worked it out. "Ah, there's something here that will never be in the inventory!"
>
> "Does it happen to be in your power to give it a name?" Mrs. Gereth's face showed the dim dawn of an amusement at finding her seated at the feet of her pupil.
>
> "I can give it a dozen. It's a kind of fourth dimension. It's a presence, a perfume, a touch. It's a soul, a story, a life. There's ever so much more here than you and I." (emphasis in original; 171–72)

A dozen names, where not one word could be found for Poynton. In fact, the voice of the "tell-tale" things prompts more than a dozen; Fleda's language piles on top of itself, building up lists, asking and answering rhetorical questions, spiraling out into her major dialogic performance in *The Spoils of Poynton.* The passage moves breathlessly through images of naming, speaking, listening, singing, and telling. That fact in itself marks the difference between this moment and the earlier encounters with décor in the novel, but even more striking is the timing of all these words. At Poynton, Fleda sinks mutely into a chair at the sight of such authenticity. At Ricks, on the first visit, narrative is compensatory, a forced reparation for the trickery of the eye and the imitativeness of the furnishings. But here, in a point-by-point inversion of Fleda's mute sinking into a chair at Poynton, Fleda "broke out even before she sat down." Words are neither suppressed in the physical experience of the spoils nor apologetic, after the fact, for the material inauthenticity of the maiden aunt's home. Instead, words emerge simultaneously with the sight of the things. The dialogue that in the preface is a "cheaper sound" is, here, not too cheap a language for fiction. A story flows from the visual effect even before Fleda actually touches the objects or (an essential difference from earlier scenes) raises the question of what the things, in themselves, really are. For the first time in the novel, language and objects appear synchronous.

That is not to say that the things themselves are irrelevant. Fleda's question to Mrs. Gereth—"Where on earth did you put your hand on such beautiful things?"—is loaded with the standards of provenance that define the effect of the spoils. That question, about the physical origins of beauty, occasions a language of touch reminiscent of the characterization of Poynton; the image of Mrs. Gereth putting her hand on beautiful things recalls antiques made by the "hands of rare artists," pieces so genuine that they were "thumbed" by Louis XV and that Fleda "finger[s] fondly" (14). The difference is that here, origins are not immanent, obvious, or sensuous. The desire to know origins, the experience of rare beauty, instead flows from the overall effect of the room. Mrs. Gereth's accomplishment is in that sense similar to that of the frontispiece—an effect of marvelous rarity inherent not in things but in their composition. Consider too how Fleda touches the things. "She moved," this passage tells us, "as she had done on the previous occasion, from one piece to another, with looks of recognition and hands that lightly lingered." The reference to the "previous occasion" refers not to the first visit to Ricks, but a visit Fleda makes just after Mrs. Gereth has stolen the spoils and moved them to the cottage. Then, the very tips of Fleda's fingers had "thrilled at the touch of an old velvet brocade, a wondrous texture she could recognize, would have recognized among a thousand, without dropping her eyes on it" (47).

Both passages invoke the recognition implicit in the lightest touch. But the nature of the recognition is different. The later passage restores the "look of recognition" that the first passage—claiming that Fleda need not drop her eyes to the brocade—disavows. This difference, focusing the experience visually, suggests the transformation the passage enacts in the nature of touch itself. Fleda touches the spoils, in the first passage, to discover what she already knows they are. She touches the maiden aunt's things, in the second passage, with a sense of wonder that these beautiful things really are the same ones that once appeared so sad. Both touches confirm the substantial identity of the pieces, but where stroking the spoils brings reassurance that nothing has changed, running her hands over the maiden aunt's things brings wonder at the aesthetic experience they have been made to produce. The experience of tactility at Ricks is in that sense atmospheric, a created regard for the marvel of the pieces, as well as inherently sensual. Authenticity, Fleda says, is "in the very touch of the air" (173).

The sensuousness of things, their tactile appeal, flows from their context, from their aesthetic effect. The passage retains the experience of things as rare objects—an experience also embedded in Fleda's first question—even as it transforms the nature of that experience into visual coherence and narrative content. This distinguishes the decorative "poetry" of Ricks from the voice of Waterbath, where everything is only a reference. Ricks does not become a Chippendale or Elizabethan or Louis XV fantasy. But it is composed from those imitation furnishings collected by the maiden aunt, extended in this passage to include the "spindle-leg" furniture that defined the popular cottage styles of Colonial Revival, Georgian, and Queen Anne. And it does involve the translation of décor into words. Mrs. Gereth's triumph, however, is to join the narrative effect of reproduction, as defined by the novel and inherent in the craft of fiction, to the appeal of sensuous décor, rare origins, and authentic composition.

The sentimentality of Ricks, on the first visit, is defined in opposition to the elegant austerity of Poynton. But the effect of Ricks on this later visit is not so polarized. Rather, that effect comes, in a sense, *from* the spoils. The "poetry, as it were, of something sensibly *gone*" (emphasis in original) is the poetry of the missing spoils. Irrevocably lost to Mrs. Gereth, the antiques are reflected, as a subjective experience, in her arrangement of Ricks. "Sensibly gone" is a kind of pun, or rather an oxymoron: it describes the sensation of things palpably missing, both there and not there.

The spoils thus remain the sensible arbiters of taste even as the novel works out the possibilities of a language of imitation. It is the spoils that give authenticity to Ricks, the spoils to which Fleda's touch is compared, the spoils that allow Mrs. Gereth to be so brilliant. The standard of the genuine is still the knowledge of real things even when those things are absent. Just as Fleda's regard for Ricks appears both genuine and a strategic effort to manipulate Mrs. Gereth, James refuses to wholly endorse the resolution—signified by Ricks—

toward which the novel tends. Indeed, the novel's final chapters work hard to retain the standard set by the spoils even while transforming its terms. At Ricks, Fleda and Mrs. Gereth wait desperately for the *Morning Post* to print a wedding announcement despite the fact that they know perfectly well Owen and Mona are marrying; it is as if the fate of the spoils is only sealed by the description, in print and in society papers like those plastered to the walls of Waterbath, of the "unique collection of artistic curiosities" that the paper will announce Owen Gereth brings to the union (173). Yet if the rendering of the collection in newsprint marks its literal and metaphorical incorporation into a world where crafted objects become words, the novel disallows Fleda and Mrs. Gereth from transliterating the spoils. First Fleda cuts short Mrs. Gereth's suggestion that " 'we can always, as time goes on, talk of them together.' " " 'Always?' she said, turning again to her friend. 'Never!' " (161) The only reference to the spoils between the two women in the final pages is a single invocation by Mrs. Gereth of "what we don't, you know, by your wish, ever talk about" (177).

And then James cuts short Fleda's near-transgression of her own advice. Owen, acting out of the exact regard for the theater of memory and reference that makes Waterbath "perversely full of souvenirs," has asked Fleda to travel to Poynton to take a "remembrance," a "symbol," a "token" (178–80). Fleda indulges the idea of the keepsake as a token of Owen's "signed desire." She likes one item in particular because Owen "had named it" (180). That item is the only one at Poynton that is referred to with a conventional name: the Maltese Cross.

But Poynton burns down before Fleda can take the memento. The novel's final scene is remarkable for drawing together so many established images. Disembarking the train to go seize the object that is the equivalent of a name, a "signed desire," Fleda steps into the smoke from the distant fire. The stationmaster tells her Poynton has been lost. Fleda sinks into a chair, exactly as she had when she first encountered Poynton. Incredulously, she queries the stationmaster in terms that also refer back to an earlier scene, this one the triumphal episode at Ricks: "Poynton's *gone*?" (emphasis in original; 184)

The stationmaster's response is telling: "What can you call it, miss, if it ain't really saved?" (184) That Poynton is really gone—unequivocally gone—is different than "the poetry of something sensibly gone" that characterizes Mrs. Gereth's success at Ricks. For the spoils at Ricks are only partially gone. Their presence remains; their memory gives the cottage its authentic voice even as the novel crafts memorials—and we might think back to the letter to Bourget here—by remembering, recalling, and rearranging. But James will not let the spoils themselves, the actual things, become stories, Brigstock possessions, Waterbath keepsakes, testaments to signed desire, examples of this or that style, or any other occasion for narrative. *The Spoils of Poynton* confronts the relations of crafted objects and language more directly than any other example discussed in *Talking Shop*. It epitomizes my subject because its resolution is so jubilant, at least as regards Fleda's volubility about Mrs. Gereth's accomplishment of feeling for—or through—imitative period styles and the sense of the past that they prompt. But *The Spoils of Poynton* also epitomizes my subject because it holds back so pointedly about the full implications of translating crafts into words. Cellini's canonizers, I have suggested, celebrated his narrative of the wide-ranging artisanal sensibility but also sought ways to restore associations between his representation of craft and its classic, embodied standards of learned expertise; similarly, Hawthorne's fiction accords durability to a language of workmanship while also fearing that such operations were merely the kinds of projections he associated with the Brook Farmers. In all of the chapters of *Talking Shop*, the definition of workmanship flows between its translatable idioms of sensibility, feeling, or typology and its phenomenological realities as an experience, a way of working, a trade, or a set of objects made by uniquely skilled hands. For James, the last line of defense for the materiality of the things themselves is the stationmaster. Gone, as he says, is gone. When it comes to the spoils, at least, there is no other name for it.

CONCLUSION

RESOUNDING SILENCE

The stream of discourse about craft traced in this book depends—for its drama, its significance, and its legibility—on silence; reticent artisans and soundless artifacts appear in every chapter as the fixed points against which the language of artisanship resounds. The "mute" objects at Poynton set the stakes of Fleda Vetch's ability to give a "dozen names" to Mrs. Gereth's approximation of the effect of those objects.[1] Longfellow's taciturn artisan, Michelangelo, upbraids his protégé Benvenuto Cellini for his excessive prolixity—a correction that ultimately leads, in Longfellow's play, to Benvenuto's superb balancing of voice and hand when he casts the *Perseus*. Hawthorne's Drowne speaks "modestly" of his labor and falters when asked to explain his works, even as Copley and the townspeople enthuse, gossip, and predict (wrongly) that he has turned craft into life.[2] Not unlike Drowne, at least to the degree of stressing the practical, Stickley framed his Craftsman enterprise as originating in natural facts and material realities—taking it as his secondary rather than his primary charge to adapt those realities to a vocal marketplace that, he claimed, needed artisans as "translators."[3] Horatio Greenough, to return to an example from the opening of *Talking Shop*, screened his literary efforts behind the persona of Horace Bender precisely because he imagined the paradigmatic stonecutter as a taciturn figure whose labor could not be described in the "Encyclopedia or Conversations Lexicon" and whose habit was to "hang the lip" when questioned.[4] At the same time, having set up the image of the silent artisan, Greenough cited the practical experience of "many years" as justification for his daring to "utter a few words of discontent"—a few words that, in the eight years between Greenough's first publications and his death, actually extended to a twenty-six-chapter volume (with a second volume promised) liberally sprinkled with quotes in French, Latin, and Italian.[5]

Silence and reticence thus anchored the meaning of craft as a private relation with the medium even as a public discourse of artisanship flourished. The ideological adaptability of the handicrafts between 1840 and 1920, as I have presented it, was structured by the interlacing of traditional definitions of artisanship, ideally untranslatable, and emerging definitions of artisanship within and as print culture. Practice and publication, labor and translation, objects and their expressible types, converged in the culture of craft. The stakeholders in that culture included partisans seeking a renascence of traditional methods; design taxonomists who developed classifications and grammars of historical workmanship; publishers and retailers who marketed emerging languages of artisanship and décor; consumers who depended on patterns of recognizability and legibility to guide them to handicrafts goods; and, perhaps most self-conscious about the implications of transliterating a manual practice, writers of fiction. For Hawthorne, among the latter constituency, the falsity of celebratory stories about craft seemed patent, especially after his experiences at Brook Farm; and yet he also found ways to tap the handicrafts past for a guiding historical narrative—particularly focused around gravestone engraving—about things of greater quality and more substantial durability "than at present."[6] For James, the cultural practices under which craft emerged as a mass-market language led him to wonder, in his novel about the modishness of artisanal things, if his own fiction therefore rang with a "cheaper sound." Mirroring these concerns while raising them in the context of craft's emergence as a value system, *The Craftsman* appears as perhaps the most important archive of relevant fiction in the era. Its contributors epitomized the two imperatives of artisanship's popularization by charting an intricate course through craft's moral translatability and its association with such wonderful skills as, sufficient unto themselves, required no translation into other tongues.

The artifacts most important to these diverse constituencies of the crafts movement ranged widely, comprising objects and texts, sculpture as well as furnishings, things produced and things consumed, canonical as well as obscure pieces, irregular as well as rectilinear styles. What links all of these forms as expressions of craft, I have argued, is precisely the fact that they presented craft as expression: an outward-looking form of cultural production that could only become so by virtue of its accommodation to inward-looking notions of craft's virtuosity, organized around its self-containment, around the reticence of its objects, or around jobs well done for their own sake. The adaptations I have described were rarely total. What allows James to indulge in a mass-market version of the crafted effect is the countervailing animus of the spoils as sui generis, so much so that he would rather burn down Poynton than allow any one of the antiques to be removed from the collection of authenticities as a sign, symbol, or souvenir. But the point is that James does create the context for validating a vulgar language of workmanship—that of the "Colonial" in particular, and of historical reproduction in general—through a reformed sensibility for the furnishings of the "more laboring ages," if not through its actual relics.

As an element of the epistemological history of craft, this pattern demands a different set of assumptions about workmanship's focal points than definitions centered by the self-containment of artisanal labor or the one-to-one authenticity of craftsperson and medium. But readjusting the template makes visible (or, to use a more appropriate metaphor, readable) a number of ways in which craft, as understood in the period between 1840 and 1920, helped shape the emphasis on the affective life of objects that recent scholarship has convincingly uncovered in modern literature and culture. For one, easing craft away from the workshop and the body—in effect, allowing craft a wider influence as a kind of expressiveness that crosses fairly easily between its sites of reception and sites of production—reveals the implication of workmanship in what Bill Brown and Diana Fuss have historicized as western culture's investment in a "sense" of things in the late nineteenth and early twentieth centuries. Craft, translated into a qualitative aspect of both people (a way of being, an artisanal sensibility) and things (a style, an appreciable effect, a name), seems to me a uniquely crucial medium for creating the affective aspect of "built space" that Brown and Fuss describe.[7]

In stressing the expressiveness, translatability, and sensibility associated with craft and its objects, I hope also to have made clear that I mean something quite different than did Veblen in his emphasis on the semiotics of artisanship. For Veblen, those semiotics were "pecuniary" and "honorific"; craft, he asserted in 1899, had become a vector of conspicuous consumption.[8] The argument of *Talking Shop* is not incompatible with Veblen's, but it complicates the artificiality he imputes to the migration of things from the realm of craft to the realm of consumption. Instead, I have suggested that the imperatives of craft and consumption were not clearly distinct. Craft's advocates saw that their advocacy depended on artisanship's translatability to realms outside the workshop and outside the skills of the body—not just because they wanted to sell their goods in the consumer market, but more importantly, I have argued, because the technical operations of the workshop and of the body could be reproduced by machines. Handicrafts advocacy therefore revolved around a definition that emphasized not skill or technique but standards of subjectivity, feeling, and legibility. Operating by such standards, artisanship transitioned readily into a variety of nameable aesthetic styles, from the "Gothic" and the "Craftsman" to the derivative types promoted in the late *Craftsman*. By the same standards, too, artisanship flowed through a wide-ranging print discourse that variously emphasized artisanal ways of being and the articulacy of crafted objects. And yet however fully the era developed a "sense" of craftedness, my most important contention has been that it did so multilaterally, correlating artisanship as transliterated with the immanence of the medium, the immediacy of the process, and the material durability of the product. A sense of craftedness could not have made sense, we might say, under any other conditions.

WALT WHITMAN'S TYPES OF CRAFT

Given the complexity of the negotiations involved, where we want to draw the boundaries of artisanship's translatability—the points beyond which it has moved too far from the Platonic virtuosity of the artisan's narrow calling or the silent authority of Michelangelo's labor at St. Peter's—will likely remain an open question. The cultural landscape of handicraft's transliteration is crisscrossed with lines in the sand. John Addington Symonds drew one of those lines between posterity and Cellini's introductory note when he excised from his translation the bald confession that an amanuensis penned a text subtitled *Scritta Da Lui Medesimo* (Written by His Very Same Self). Hawthorne drew other lines in the sand when he cautioned against the false promises about craft poured into the ears of Giovanni, Owen Warland, and Drowne's fellow Bostonians. (Readers of *The Scarlet Letter* and "Chippings with a Chisel" are also cautioned not to put all their trust in a narrative of craft's ideally transformative quality—symbolized by Hester Prynne's fanciful embroidery of the *letter* A—because the language of craft, as Hawthorne understands it, must also serve the imperatives of solidity and permanence.) Yet other lines were drawn by James, burning the spoils; by Stickley, continuing to depict traditional Craftsman furnishings in isolation even as his catalogs came to feature decorative settings; and by Morris, worrying that the emphasis of the Arts and Crafts Movement on individually and singularly "expressive" furnishings meant that only the rich could afford them.

All of these figures managed, in one way or another, to compromise. Their often conciliatory approaches to craft's emergence as a public discourse and a consumable idea have shaped the main theme of this book. But what, I want to ask in closing, do we want to make of cultural phenomena that seem to put up little or no defense against the representational volubility of craft? Is there an end stage to the phenomenon I have described? Have the lines in the sand, which at least serve to orient the landscape of craft toward its traditional principles, been entirely washed away in a culture of Starbucks coffee and supermarket bakeries wherein the language of the "artisanal" resounds with implausible ubiquity?

The obvious place to focus these questions is in the mass-market culture of the handcrafted everywhere visible today. But I would like to begin by looking in some detail at a literary passage from the period I have been discussing, a passage that anticipates an era—perhaps our own—in which the representation, the expressiveness, of the craft seems to have come entirely unmoored from the crafter:

> When the psalm sings instead of the singer,
> When the script preaches instead of the preacher,
> When the pulpit descends and goes instead of the carver that carved the supporting-desk,
> When I can touch the body of books, by night or by day, and when they touch my body back again,
> When the sacred vessels, or the bits of the eucharist, or the lath and plast, procreate as effectually as the young silver-smiths or bakers, or the masons in their over-alls,
>
> . . . .
>
> I intend to reach them my hand, and make as much of them as I do of men and women.[9]

The lines are Whitman's, from the conclusion of his 1856 "Poem of the Daily Work of the Workmen and Workwomen of These States." In themselves, removed from the context of artisanal epistemologies of their era and from the context of the rest of the poem, the lines seem to me quite vexing; they appear to carry Whitman's delight in practices of representation to the extreme of animating the made environment at the cost of those who made it. Such a supercilious reading does not have only to do with the obfuscation of labor that Marx and his successors have taught us to see, because Whitman himself would have experienced the obscuration of the tradesman in the most concrete of ways. Artisanal labor in Whitman's New York was being rapidly transformed by the subdivision of labor, out-of-shop contracting, and the spatial division of shops into a front room where goods were displayed and a back room where work was performed.[10]

We might think, in this context, that Whitman would be more inclined to locate the artisans themselves in his foreground. Instead, reproducing the spatial reorganization of displayed goods and hidden workers, he concludes the poem by bringing forward—and, through his religious iconography, spiritualizing—the object that appears in place of the person who produces it. The third line presents the most surprising and vivid example. The carver is represented by the "supporting desk," by which Whitman presumably means the lectern; this piece appears itself subordinate to the larger pulpit which "descends" to meet the poet. The chain of substitutions (that is, the things that replace the lectern's carver as the center of the poet's interest) can be further extended if one is willing to read "pulpit" in its common metonymical sense;

the word was used to represent preachers, not just the physical platform, as early as 1570. The chain might be extended yet again if we recall from the previous line that preachers are themselves represented by their scripts. Depending on how far the reader wishes to take the sequence (the most extreme reading would stress the sequential replacement of the carver by supporting-desk, pulpit, preacher, and then script), what the poet encounters directly is more or less abstracted. But the striking fact is that there is any substitution at all, in a poem addressed to workmen and workwomen. The poet who professes, earlier in the piece, to "stand as nigh as the nighest that works in the same shop" seems to have given up that charge (122). He becomes, in effect, the audience for a culture of craft in which the actual craftsperson is distant and invisible.

It is hard not to wonder at the poet's easy preparedness for a future when psalms, sermons, and books will carry the voice of craft—a future when these forms, which Whitman intends to take by the hand, will appear viable correlatives for actual "men and women." At the same time, however, such a pointedly skeptical reading depends on a presumed gap between the realm of reception (the point where the poet stands, hearing the psalms and the sermons, looking into books, and contemplating the "sacred vessels") and the realm of production (where things are produced from the body, whether that body is singing, preaching, carving, plastering, or silversmithing). This is the precise gap that, I have argued, appears unsustainable in the wider context of crafts theory, crafts advocacy, and crafts-centered literature as it flowed through the nineteenth and early twentieth centuries. And indeed, it may be that the poem itself—understood as a whole—asks us to read the stanza in the context of the new standards of workmanship that Whitman's era generated; in this reading, the poem proposes an angle of vision oriented not to the axioms of craft's embodiment but to the interwoven threads of production and representation, craft and print, within nineteenth-century discourses of workmanship. Consider the fifth and sixth lines of the poem's opening section, which reveal its relevance to the themes traced in this book as Whitman's initial *recoil* from talking shop:

> I was chilled with the cold types, cylinder, wet presses between us.
> I pass so poorly with paper and types, I must pass with the contact of
>   bodies and souls. (121)

"Types," in the context of craft's print discourse, can be read as pun. It refers to printer's type but also to the more general condition that I have described throughout the preceding pages: the orientation of a textual culture of artisanship to typological classification. Through his autobiography, Cellini became the type of the universally capable artisan, represented by "such hands" as he possessed. Stickley idealized white oak as a type. Advocates for the Gothic established irregularity as the typological expression of the artisanal. The punning title of Ruskin's chapter "The Nature of Gothic" stands for the adaptation of crafted matter to type: it describes both an essentialized quality (Gothic's fundamental nature) and the lashing of that quality to the immanence of a natural medium (the hard stone provided *by* nature to northern European stoneworkers, on which the development of the Gothic depended).

Obviously, Whitman's assertion about the "cold types" of printed accounts, interceding between the poet and "workmen and workwomen," does not comprehend the later examples of Ruskin or the Arts and Crafts Movement. But the cold types to which Whitman might have been responding were already legion by 1856, including literary enthusiasm for utopian farming and craft communities; the early decades of Cellini's popularization; craft-centered discourses of nation building; Greenough's efforts to give birth to a "new language" of building (Whitman, like Greenough and Hawthorne, was published in *The United States Magazine and Democratic Review*); and the early development of taxonomic grammars of originally artisanal styles. Writing about the trades, moreover, had an even more specific dimension for Whitman. Complaining at the beginning of the poem that "you may read in many languages" yet "read nothing" of workmen and workwomen, Whitman identifies the "daily papers," among other examples, as agents of craft's obscuration and as apparent outlets for the "cold types" of printed accounts of labor (126). The advent of the New York dailies in the 1830s in fact turned journalism toward the trades, replacing the staples of the upper-class weeklies—news of ships and their passengers arriving and departing, financial reports, pious editorials—with "local news that would interest an audience of artisans" as well as notices, for instance, about meetings of journeymen's associations or the Mechanic's Fair.[11] Many of the founders of the dailies had roots in the organized crafts movements of the 1820s. Benjamin Day of the *New York Sun* identified politically with the short-lived Workingmen's Party (1829–31), on behalf of which he had worked in 1830 on a paper called the *Daily Sentinel*. Another force in New York publishing, George Henry Evans, moved from Fanny Wright's polemical *Free Enquirer* (a publication to which Whitman's father, a carpenter, subscribed) to unveil the *Workingman's Advocate* in 1829, a paper that "would be the voice of New York's artisanal radicalism" during Whitman's years as an apprentice newspaperman.

The poem, read against this background, has a clear proposition: to present a different "daily work"—to quote the title—than the *other* "dailies," the newspapers. As he says at the outset, Whitman seeks to resist the chilly typological modalities, the "cold types," through which the textual culture of craft was more generally articulated (121). But that prospect is complicated for the exact reason that it was also complicated for Hawthorne, Greenough, James, and the editors of *The Craftsman;* all contended with the paradox that, in the nineteenth century, the writer's own medium structured the force of craft. As the poem develops, Whitman's grandest catalog of labor—over sixty lines naming the tools and processes of every imaginable craft—develops an accretive, collective sense of artisanal effort that includes and depends on what the poem initially abjures: "the four-double cylinder press, the hand-press, the frisket and tympan, the compositor's stick and rule, type-setting, making up the forms" (134). The four-double cylinder press refers to the rotary "lightning press" introduced in the early 1840s by Richard Hoe, an essential technology for the rise of the dailies, but the more interesting aspect of the line concerns its backward glance to the punning meaning of "types" in the text's first invocation of the cylinder press. For the effect of the catalog is precisely to set "type" and make "forms" as the poem aggregates the "usual routine" of workmanship in Whitman's city (131).

As exhibited within (and as) the rotary action of the huge catalog itself, the cylinder, the press, and the type-setting process now appear not cold but enlivened by "all the work of newspaper counters, folders, carriers, news-men" (134). The catalog crescendos by returning to the print imagery of the poem's opening, praising rather than resisting "daily and weekly newspapers, / The columns of wants in the one-cent paper" (137). By naming so many tools and actions, Whitman's literary depiction of workmanship differs from, say, Cellini's—whose *Life*, as I have suggested, sets surprisingly few scenes in the workshop. But Whitman nonetheless writes himself into a different, more textually animated position than the one with which he begins. The disavowal of cylinders and types at the outset transforms into a viable representation of craft as language, a trajectory that Whitman, in fact, seemed to embrace more and more surely as he wrote and rewrote this poem between 1856 and 1891. In the editions of *Leaves of Grass* published in 1856 and 1860, the line about the "cold types . . . between us" appears as I have already quoted it. But in 1867 and 1871, it appears in parentheses, as if insisting on its past tense; the effect of the line as an aside reinforces that Whitman "was chilled" but is now warmed. In the final editions of 1881 and 1891, the line has disappeared altogether, its attenuation across time mirroring the attenuation of Whitman's frustration over the course of the poem.

My point is this: that the final stanza, in which artisans are removed bodily from the site of craft's reception by the poet, can be seen in the context of the fundamentally literary trajectory at the heart of the poem. How, the poem is asking, can one write about craft? In this context, the concluding visions of scripts preaching themselves, of songs singing without singers, of pulpits more fully vitalized than their carvers, and of books reaching out as hands resolves the initiating condition: that the poet has been chilled by the text, the "wet cylinder," between him and the trades. What to make of this trajectory remains, for me, a harder case to evaluate—in terms of the future it projects—than many of the other examples in *Talking Shop*. Whitman's catalog of tools and procedures, of course, is vigorously substantial. But unlike the carefully negotiated positions I have described in my chapters, Whitman concludes with a celebration of artisanship's volubility itself; the defenses of materiality visible in other cases seem to shatter in the poet's vision of a prolix future in which words and representations will appear "instead" of singers, carvers, silversmiths, and masons. Naming an intention to someday be as sociable with such representations as with craft's actual practitioners, Whitman's enthusiastic future may, from our perspective today, in fact look foreboding. Even so, in the light provided by the whole poem and by its moment in the cultural history of handicrafts, where Whitman arrives is probably best understood not as the abyss between labor and its products; the alienation of the crafts worker does not finally appear a fair pattern to discover in his words. Rather, Whitman dramatizes the vigorous textuality operative *within* the culture of craft. His poem swings toward, not away from, the standards of workmanship as they emerged over the course of the age. What we think of the entirety of that swing, in this particular case, is a different issue from the condition of craft itself to which Whitman is most pointedly responding.

MARTHA STEWART'S RESTORATION HARDWARE

As Whitman's poem modeled and patterned, the future of craft would offer an exuberant vocabulary as a type. From the proliferation of the adjective "artisanal" itself to a host of retailers and products—Plow and Hearth, Pottery Barn, the new Stickley Company (a remnant of the company started by Gustav Stickley's brothers), Kettle Chips, Craftsman-branded Sears appliances, and "handcrafted" Starbucks beverages—consumer culture today is always talking shop. Whitman, of course, did not imagine Pottery Barn. Allen Ginsberg's famous depiction of Whitman as a doddering, estranged lecher in the modern supermarket begs the question I asked in the previous section: How well does Whitman's optimism fit our own day? The language of craft has become fractal and profuse—but more particularly, I want to close by suggesting that the interwoven patterns of translatability, legibility, and sensibility traced in this book have been fully integrated, not just into the quantity, but into the terms, of mainstream discourse. This development was, I think, practically inevitable. Because they were often acting against the machine, the authors and artisans I have studied essayed to situate craft's standards outside of the workshop and the body, outside of skill and technique. The solutions they articulated to the obviously thorny problems of that migration set a precedent that has reached us in stranger form than even Stickley, a most enthusiastic entrepreneur, could have foreseen.

Consider the name of a company founded in 1980 in a California home and now a mass-market retailer with more than a hundred stores. Restoration Hardware recurs on the one hand to the traditional meaning of the word "hardware," which began to appear in print in the eighteenth century. Originally tied to the metalworker's craft, "hardware" described the functional components made by the blacksmith or bronze caster for use on furnishings or cabinets. The "branches of hardware" described by Thomas Pennant in his *Tour in Scotland and Voyage to the Hebrides* (1776) include locks and hinges, to which one might add latches, drawer pulls, catches, escutcheons, castors, corners, knobs, handles, and hasps.[12] These things were added to a piece after it was completed; thus, nails, in the meaning still preserved among cabinetmakers and carpenters, are not hardware. They are fasteners, along with screws and bolts. Hardware includes those things purchased for the purpose of finishing the piece, often after the stain or varnish or oil—or, for that matter, ammonia vapor—has been applied.

Of course, nails today are purchased in hardware stores. The term in that context has expanded to include fasteners, washers, pipe, insulation, and—extending to the entire category of goods sold in hardware stores, if not often named individually as hardware—tools, garden hose, fertilizer, flashlights, paint, and padlocks. Restoration Hardware connotes both meanings. The company made its start with period hardware, including lighting fixtures, hooks, pulls, and knobs in styles ranging from the Queen Anne to the Colonial. At the same time, the store sounds, in the more modern sense of its title, like it might sell two-by-fours and framing hammers; it does in fact sell paint and a few tools. The two aspects of the name "Restoration Hardware" capture the relations I have traced in *Talking Shop*. A scene of restoration, of revitalizing and reproducing prior styles of workmanship, invokes simultaneously the idioms of production ("hardware" as the raw materials of construction, as sold in hardware stores) and the idioms of consumption and aesthetic coherence ("hardware" as those authentic period details that, traditionally applied after the construction, give style and unity). The history of the word interconnects a variety of relations: it refers to construction and to effect, to origination and to presentation, to building and to buying. These are the precise values that the products sold by Restoration Hardware also aim to cohere. Whether "crafted from the finest materials" or "crafted of 100-year-old reclaimed pine timbers from buildings in Great Britain," the items are made by "artisans" who make legible the various styles of the past—in, for instance, an "18th-century French Rococo-style mirror, elaborately hand-carved in rustic pine" or "a mid-19th-century second empire bed design, hand-carved with elaborate moldings."[13]

The effect of the company's name is doubled by the fact that "restoration" also connotes both devotion to an original and the copying of a look. In both parts of the company name, the initial act of construction flows into the consumer goods that give final aesthetic unity to pieces and homes. The meanings that circulate in both ideas—restoration and hardware—relate scenes of original production to later moments of finish and stylistic coherence. In that sense, "Restoration Hardware" captures the circularity of the earlier examples of the language of craft that I have presented. Stickley's unique way of handling white oak crafted relations between immanence and typological lexicons, between origins and ends. James's prefaces and fiction weave together the appeal of original construction and secondhand composition, of real things and things that become words, stories, arrangements, and novelistic as well as decorative compositions. Hawthorne begins with the idea that one must transcend the brutally iterative processes of what Pugin called a "mere trade," but he also, writing in the context of the nineteenth-century marketplace, seeks to write his way back into the durability and sense of permanence that such processes offer. The most popular artisanal text of the nineteenth century, Cellini's *Life*, makes workmanship a popular narrative by dislocating it from the tedium of the workshop, even as his canonizers pitched the autobiography to nineteenth-century readers by stressing the relations between the author's larger-than-life public persona and his private, workmanlike devotion to his medium, to telos, and to practical purposes.

All of these examples reflect the bidirectional aspect of craft's invigoration as public discourse, a pattern that historicizes how the rhetoric of Restoration Hardware and companies like it can move so easily between the registers of the hand and the image, of production and reception. In 2009, the company profiled a series of its individual manufacturers—figures featured as artisans who also, in one way or another, are explicitly described as operating in the public world of craft's historical lexicons and contemporary discourse. One of the profiled artisans, for instance, is described as an "antiques dealer/reproductionist"; he is depicted in a room full of examples from his "handmade, reproduction steamer trunk collection."[14] The handcrafted flows seamlessly into a period style, with the manufacturer inhabiting, at once, three points on the spectrum of production and consumption: he is "artisan," "reproductionist," and "dealer." This combination is potent for the same reason that the company name is suggestive: it allies the appeal of craft as labor (embodied in the persona of the artisan) to the manifestation of craft as style (about which the antiques dealer/reproductionist is presumably expert).

The example of Restoration Hardware is in some ways too easy, for one could not pick a manufacturer more obviously invested in the artisanal as an aesthetic effect and in craftsmanship as a vocabulary for catalog copy. But my point is that there may be less distance to travel than we might think between, on the one end, the nineteenth century's praise of Cellini as a tradesman before the age of reproduction and, on the other, Restoration Hardware's praise of the "reproductionist" himself. Models of authenticity that stress the bodily provenance of handmade things do not, I think, fully account for how crafts revivalism actually managed the idea of authenticity: as an affective capacity and a composition as much as an act of construction, as a sensibility produced and perpetuated through narrative and through language as much as a material practice founded on the iterative activities of everyday labor. Literature, in the model I have advanced, is not just a field in which we might find attitudes about craft. It is central to craft's meaning in the past two centuries, in the sense that the articulation of such meaning in terms of the author's medium was fundamentally at stake.

Even so, it remains unquestionably surprising to find Martha Stewart tracing her interest in craft-centered entertaining to having "read all the classics."[15] "What remained most vivid to my memory," she writes in describing the genesis of her career, "were the banquet scenes in Sir Walter Scott, the Roman punch dinners in Edith Wharton, and the country weekends in Tolstoy's *Anna Karenina*. Entertaining always seemed natural to me, a matter of taking something very appealing to me—a favorite dish, a holiday, an activity—and making it bigger" (1). The dinners in eighteenth- and nineteenth-century literature do not, of course, seem obviously tied to the literary culture of artisanship I have been tracing. But for Martha Stewart, entertaining is fundamentally a craft because it is predicated on using homemade foods or table settings and simply "making [them] bigger"; what she describes seeing in literature is not just a culture of upper-class consumption but one of production, a scene that can be emulated by taking everyday dishes or activities and performing them on a larger scale.

Her own books and articles, largely ghostwritten, establish as few distinctions between production and consumption as her reading of the classics. There is a sense in which the patterns central to this study—the translatability of craft across multiple media, its dependence on expressiveness and a notion of sensibility, its adaptation to public discourse and the consumer sphere—reach their culmination (and perhaps their breaking point) in the artisanal idioms of Martha Stewart Living Omnimedia. Values associated with a mainstream culture of the "handmade," a word that appears everywhere in Stewart's enterprise, anchor what her brand publishes, broadcasts, streams, discusses, and sells. Her basic ethics suggest that we cook with produce from our own gardens, improvise entertainments from things near to hand, and make dozens of domestic items, from candles and handwoven floor runners to quilts, pillows, socks, blankets, and aprons. The obvious heir to the values of domestic household industry idealized by Horace Bushnell's 1851 sermon on the "age of homespun," Martha Stewart has also suffered more for that mythology than any of its other public advocates. The titillation of her arrest and imprisonment for securities fraud, according to commentators delighted that she got her comeuppance, has to do with the presumed gaps between the homey values she sells and the corporate world in which she operates. The assumption that originality and good taste are available through a consumerist notion of handicrafts—the same paradigm promoted by Stickley—appeared when she was on trial as the mask of greed, of a hard-driving corporatism that would stop at no fakery to profit.

For those who put the case that way, Stewart's conviction revealed the chasm between an image and a reality. *Mutatis mutandis*, it revealed what Hawthorne had also been at pains to show in the fiction he wrote just after returning from Brook Farm: that assertions of craft's virtues were really just bourgeois projections and instruments of a misleading idealism. But the apparent paradoxes of craft's representation are also principles, as I have argued they were for Hawthorne and for the crafts advocates of the nineteenth and early twentieth centuries. Consider how Stewart's *Entertaining* (1982) follows the pattern set by her nineteenth- and twentieth-century forebears, from the advocates for Gothic workmanship to Stickley; like those writers (although with a metastasized market share) Stewart predicates the legibility of her craft-centered life on values of subjectivity and adaptation rather than on repetitive processes, merely durable or lasting goods, and narrow relations with the material world. For one, the natural environment Stewart presents herself as inhabiting, wherein she cooks "simple peasant dishes" from the abundant produce of a garden planted with "six varieties of cabbage," puts a premium on good choosing—rather than on necessity—by running everywhere to abundance: everything in the garden "grows bigger than life," and her model of country living (in which she and her husband were "dependant on what we . . . created") comprises "the house, the first barn, the second barn, the flower garden, vegetable gardens, orchards, the chickens and turkeys and sheep" (4–6). Sunday meals in her childhood involved dishes made with "ten different vegetables" and "five fresh fruit desserts"; when her father took his skiff out on Barnegat Bay, he returned with "not one but eighty fish, not two dozen but twelve dozen crabs" (2).

One hundred and forty-four crabs and eighty fish is a peculiar kind of homey self-sufficiency. But Martha Stewart's logic of handcraftedness presumes, as its operational principle, an extraordinary range of material and textual resources. Mirroring Gustav Stickley's promotion of a "large number of items, widely differing in size and use" as the good result of the blacksmith's exertions on behalf of the adaptive homemaker, Stewart's romantic account of a neighborly gathering—an instance, as she frames it, of a bygone localism—requires owning enough plates and flatware to improvise the décor around the company, the weather, the occasion, the season. A dinner party might require "enough qualifying dishes to establish a Chinese theme," or, in the characteristic language of accumulation in *Entertaining*, "glasses of many hues, a few special cobalt, amethyst, and teal goblets, and an odd enough assortment of side dishes to make interesting, suggestive tables"—not because all these things would be set on a single occasion, but because they are the resources on which the dual imperatives of originality and expedience are founded. Stewart does not stress luxury goods; she claims to possess "nothing particularly valuable" (21). Yet the aggregative nature of decorating, the need to have a profusion of resources to work from scratch, sets the standard of a organic décor in the rituals of prolific consumption.

To be sure, the idioms of an idealized craft-based domesticity here do not look, visually, like the idioms of artisanship promoted by Ruskin and Morris or like the settings that Stickley imagined in the late *Craftsman*, but the principles are correlative. The distinction Martha Stewart makes is not between simplicity and consumption or between essence and excess but—the logic evident in craft revivalism as it flowed through the nineteenth and early twentieth centuries—between authentic settings and merely expensive objects, between improvisation and iteration, between expressiveness and enactment. Distinguishing her compositions from the "elaborate technique" of bygone modes of entertaining, just as the craft movement urged its followers to do in the fields of stonecutting or furniture-making, *Entertaining* yokes the domestic crafts of its author to a longer arc of thinking and writing about the handmade. As affective capacity rather than fixed method or learned expertise in one medium, artisanship translates far better than we may have presumed; the volubility of Fleda Vetch, when she experiences the Poynton-like effect of Ricks, marks how culture in the past two centuries has spun the textual discourses of craft's meaning around the legibility of wood or stone, the lexicons of style, and the literary vitality of workmanship. The goods demanded by Martha Stewart's settings or sold at Restoration Hardware are different in kind from Gothic stone or Craftsman oak but, orienting workmanship to expression, atmosphere, and personality, they are not entirely different in character. Cellini's ability to work in every media, just because he has such an instinctively artisanal sensibility, reaches the farthest edge of handcraftedness in Martha Stewart Omnimedia. We can draw the lines of fakery through many points in this history, from the moment Cellini begins dictating to the sickly son of Michele Goro to the moment Martha Stewart appeared in court. But these lines cannot hold in a culture that has become so habituated to talking shop. The processes by which things are made, in the notion of authenticity that informs modern definitions of workmanship, appears less important than what is done with and through them, than the vigorously communicative culture of craft of which they are a part.

NOTES

INTRODUCTION

1. Greenough, "American Architecture," in *Travels*, 136. The two essays that appeared in *The United States Magazine and Democratic Review* were "Remarks on American Art" (July 1843) and "American Architecture" (August 1843).

2. Greenough, "Remarks on American Art," in *Travels*, 122.

3. Greenough, "Relative and Independent Beauty," in *Travels*, 197.

4. Greenough, "Aesthetics at Washington," in *Travels*, 18.

5. Greenough, "American Architecture," in *Travels*, 139.

6. Emerson, *English Traits*, 6; Emerson to Greenough, 6 September 1852, in *Letters of Ralph Waldo Emerson*, 330.

7. Greenough, "Fourier et Hoc Genus Omne," in *Travels*, 63–64.

8. Greenough, "Criticism in Search of Beauty," in *Form and Function*, 99. This twentieth-century collection contains some essays, including this one, not printed in the *Yankee Stonecutter.*

9. Greenough, "Aesthetics at Washington," in *Travels*, 32.

10. Greenough, "American Architecture," in *Travels*, 141 (on nature's "truer laws"), and 133 ("storied relief," "eloquent statue").

11. Greenough, "Relative and Independent Beauty," in *Travels*, 197.

12. Greenough, "The Stonecutter's Creed," in *Travels*, 184.

13. Greenough, Preface to *Travels*, x.

14. Greenough, "American Architecture," in *Travels*, 137.

15. Sennett, *Craftsman*, 91–106. For a discussion of Greenough's influences, see Crane, *White Silence*, 147–66, and Metzger, *Emerson and Greenough*, 143–44n7.

16. Lubbock, *Craft of Fiction*, 1–2.

17. James, *Spoils*, xliii, 18.

18. Chippendale, *Gentleman and Cabinet-Maker's Director*, iii; Sheraton, *Cabinet Dictionary*, title page.

19. Speltz, *Styles of Ornament*, title page.

20. In this sense, grammars of ornament might be understood as instances of what Mark Seltzer has described as the "body-machine complex" in late nineteenth-century culture. Seltzer, *Bodies and Machines*, 4.

21. Quoted in Rigal, *American Manufactory*, 10, 29–30.

22. Sewell, *Work and Revolution*, 221.

23. Wilentz, *Chants Democratic.*

24. Ulrich, *Age of Homespun*, 6.

25. Orvell, *Real Thing*, xv.

26. Knight is quoted in Brandt, *Craftsman and the Critic*, 179.

27. Bushnell, "Age of Homespun," in *Work and Play*, 48–52, 71.

28. Veblen, *Theory of the Leisure Class*, 159, 162.

29. Lears, *No Place of Grace*, 75, 78.

30. Plato, *Republic*, I, 345d. Following philosophical convention, I cite the page number and section letter from the Stephanus edition of 1578; the translation I am using, by G. M. A. Grube, includes the Stephanus pagination in the margins.

31. Veblen, *Instinct of Workmanship*, 33, 237.

32. Sennett, *Craftsman*, 296.

33. Crawford, *Shop Class*, 194.

34. Greenhalgh, "Complexity," 199.

35. On "tacit knowledge," see Sennett, *Craftsman*, passim, but especially 94–95, and Crawford, *Shop Class*, 166.

36. Risatti, *Theory of Craft*, 106.

37. Greenhalgh, "The Genre," 24. For a particularly good discussion of how collaboration between artisans and the market has shaped craft, see Livingstone, "Art Manufacturers."

38. G. Brown, *Domestic Individualism*, 63–64.

39. Bromell, *Sweat of the Brow*, 37.

40. Benjamin, "The Storyteller," 85, 91, 93.

41. Denning, *Cultural Front*, 244.

42. Hapke, *Labor's Text*, 13.

43. Hapke's literary history unfolds the steady emergence of the worker as a realist subject; her monograph charts the development of "real" labor from antebellum obscurity (when, Hapke writes, the "the workingman who remains who and what he is . . . continues to wait in the wings" [47]) to a triumphant depression-era unveiling (Ibid., passim, but see especially chapter 9).

44. Seltzer, *Bodies and Machines*, 4.

45. *Craftsman* 25:2 (November 1913), 5a.

46. Stickley, "Invitation," 110.

47. Stickley, "Craftsman Woods and How We Finish Them," 186.

48. Stickley, "Invitation," 110.

49. Hewitt, *Gustav Stickley's Craftsman Farms*, 130.

1. THE GHOST WRITER

1. Cellini, *Autobiography [Life]*, 464. I use Symonds's 1887 translation (as reprinted by the Modern Library in 1927) both because it is the most widely available of the five printed between 1771 and 1910, and because Symonds's explanation of how he handled Cellini's vernacular prose will become one of my major subjects. However, I cite George Bull's 1956 translation (New York: Penguin, 1998) when discussing a introductory poem and note by Cellini that do not appear in Symonds's translation. The title appears in Symonds's Italian source as it did in manuscript (*La Vita di Benvenuto Cellini*), and I have

chosen to render it consistently as *The Life of Benvenuto Cellini* despite the fact that publishers of Symonds's edition variously give it as the *Autobiography* or the *Memoirs*.

2. Crawford, *C. R. Ashbee*, 348. Crawford's description refers most particularly to Cellini's popularity within the British Arts and Crafts Movement of the late nineteenth century. My own interests concern Cellini's emergence as a representative figure outside as well as inside the craft movement.

3. Wilde, "Decay of Lying," 27; Symonds, Introduction, xlii. All in-text references to Symonds are from this piece unless otherwise denoted.

4. Symonds, *Renaissance in Italy*, 3:321, 330–51.

5. Hubbard, *Little Journeys*, 111.

6. Sennett, *Craftsman*, 68.

7. M. Cole, "Cellini's Blood," 232n10, 219.

8. Sennett contrasts Cellini's craftsmanlike predilections with his desire to become an artist, an endeavor that inevitably led him into courtly "intrigues of patronage" and forced him into a larger public role than he might have preferred (Sennett, *Craftsman*, 71). My own aim is to situate Cellini's negotiation of private and public spheres not in the breaking points of craft and art but in the double imperatives of workmanship.

9. Zandy, *Hands*, xi.

10. Hawthorne, "Rappaccini's Daughter," 119.

11. Hawthorne, *French and Italian Notebooks*, 321.

12. Ibid., 353.

13. Hawthorne, *Our Old Home*, 192.

14. Hawthorne, *French and Italian Notebooks*, 375; Hawthorne, *Marble Faun*, 105.

15. Spofford, "In a Cellar," 167.

16. Gilman, "Hand-craft and Rede-craft," 74.

17. Culme, " 'Benvenuto Cellini,' " 296.

18. Balzac, *Comédie Humaine*, 523.

19. Thackeray, *Novels by Eminent Hands*, 513.

20. Addison, *Arts and Crafts*, 10.

21. Hubbard, *Little Journeys*, 114, 99. Hubbard began publishing a series of short paperbacks called *Little Journeys to the Homes of the Great* in 1894; the number containing the chapter on Cellini appeared in 1902, under the title *Little Journeys to the Homes of Eminent Artists*. I am citing from an edition of the entire series published by the Roycroft Press in 1912.

22. Ashbee, "Introductory Account," ix.

23. On Cellini and drawing, see M. Cole, "Benvenuto Cellini's Designs," 798.

24. "Cellini, Benvenuto," *Encyclopedia Americana*, 6:174.

25. Cellini, *Autobiography*, trans. Bull, 1.

26. While the introductory note is quoted from Bull's translation, I revert here to in-text citations from the Modern Library edition of Symonds's translation of the *Vita*.

27. Here and elsewhere, I have consulted Bianchi's *Vita* (1866) for the Italian text. The English, as in the rest of the chapter, is Symonds's translation (22, 93).

28. See Amelang, *Flight of Icarus.*

29. For a classic overview of the Renaissance workshop, see B. Cole, *Renaissance Artist at Work.*

30. Longfellow's translation of Dante's *Divina Commedia* would have made use of Bianchi's well-known commentaries on that work, and so it is difficult to imagine that he did not know Bianchi's *Vita.* Even if he only read the *Life* in English, however, Thomas Roscoe's 1822 edition was likely Longfellow's source, and Roscoe does include the introductory note in an appendix.

31. Emerson, "Michael Angelo," 231.

32. Longfellow, *Michael Angelo,* 104.

33. Cellini, *Autobiography* [*Life*], trans. Symonds, 76.

34. Longfellow, "Village Blacksmith," 14–15.

35. Cortissoz, "Benvenuto Cellini," xii.

36. Lears, *No Place of Grace,* 91.

37. Pope-Hennessy, *Cellini,* 178.

38. Cairns, *Berlioz,* 2:505. My discussion of the operatic version of the *Life* relies on Cairns's detailed account of Liszt's adaptations, as well as Schmidgall's discussion of the original in *Literature as Opera.*

39. Liszt's press release appeared on 20 March 1852 and is quoted in Cairns, *Berlioz,* 2:473.

40. Benjamin, "The Storyteller," 85.

41. Dormer, "Language and Practical Philosophy of Craft," 222.

42. Heidegger, "Building Dwelling Thinking," 323, 326.

43. Vasari, *Lives of the Artists,* 116.

44. My source for the original is Milanesi's edition of Vasari, *Vite,* 336.

45. Ashbee, "Cinquecento Jewelry," 152.

46. Ashbee, "Introductory Account," ix. The remaining page references in this paragraph refer to "Cinquecento Jewelry."

47. Chard, "Sculptor as Potter," 246.

48. "Tiffany & Co. at the St. Louis Exhibition," 179.

49. Schopfer, "The Silversmith's Art," 341; "Some Recent Examples of Gorham Silverware," 447.

50. Kirby, "Clay Modeling," 490.

51. Marx, *Eighteenth Brumaire,* chap. 7.

52. I return here to Cortissoz's "Benvenuto Cellini," xi, xiii.

53. Adams, *Education,* 12, 382.

54. Adams to Barrett Wendell, 12 March 1909, in *Letters of Henry Adams,* 6:237–38.

55. Adams to William James, 17 February 1908, in *Letters of Henry Adams,* 6:119–20.

56. Veblen, *Instinct of Workmanship,* 33.

57. Hoffman, *Sloyd System,* 23.

2. LEGENDS OF LABOR

1. Hawthorne, *Scarlet Letter*, 24.

2. See Male, Jr., "Dual Aspect of Evil," and Cappello, " 'Rappaccini's Daughter' as Translation."

3. "Rappaccini's Daughter" was first published in 1844. Hawthorne read Cellini's *Life* sometime before 1842, the year in which the first reference to the autobiography appears in his notebooks. See Hawthorne, *American Notebooks*, 242.

4. The dodgy nature of the daguerreotype is discussed in Trachtenberg, "Seeing and Believing."

5. See Trachtenberg, "Seeing and Believing," and Gilmore, *American Romanticism*, passim, but especially 74.

6. Michaels, *Gold Standard*, 85–112.

7. Bell, "Hawthorne and the Real," 18.

8. Gilmore, *American Romanticism*, 16–17. Bromell's comment on "spiritualizing labor" in the next sentence is from *By the Sweat of the Brow*, 101.

9. G. Brown, *Domestic Individualism*, 64, 77, 81.

10. Hawthorne, *Blithedale Romance*, 1.

11. Maibor, *Labor Pains*, 71.

12. Weinstein, *Literature of Labor*, 55, 53.

13. Hawthorne, *Scarlet Letter*, 204.

14. Hawthorne, *House of the Seven Gables*, 2.

15. *Graham's* and *Godey's* were both well known for their pictorial engravings, giving another dimension to Holgrave's choice of these magazines as his target publications for the legend of Alice Pyncheon.

16. Hawthorne, "Great Stone Face," 42.

17. Buell, "Hawthorne and the Problem of 'American' Fiction," 76.

18. "Rappaccini's Daughter" and *The Scarlet Letter*, moreover, both feature lovers who cannot touch as well as objects (the vase and the letter) symbolic of the possibility, or the history, of erotic consummation.

19. Hawthorne, *Fanshawe*, 454.

20. All of the quotes from *The Scarlet Letter* are from the final paragraph (204).

21. Like Buell, the other scholar to analyze the heraldic ending of *The Scarlet Letter* in detail reads its difficulty as a correlative for the novel's more familiar trajectory of reassigning the letter's meaning. See Mayhook, " 'Bearings Unknown to English Heraldry.' "

22. Hawthorne, "Drowne's Wooden Image," 320.

23. Hawthorne, "Artist of the Beautiful," 472.

24. See Kaplan and Boris, *"Art That Is Life."*

25. Morris, "Lesser Arts," in *Hopes and Fears for Art*, 9.

26. Hawthorne to Sophia Peabody, 18 October 1841, in *The Blithedale Romance*, ed. Cain, 424.

27. Bromell goes on to argue that Hawthorne offers a different model of women's

work; his reading of female "generativity" as a model of earthly production differs from the mainstream of critical thinking about the "spiritual ministry" of labor performed by Hester Prynne or Phoebe Pyncheon. Bromell's interest in Hawthorne's alternative model of labor anticipates a cultural transformation that I will be describing in later chapters: the explicit packaging of the crafts aesthetic for female audiences in the later years of the American Arts and Crafts Movement.

28. Wineapple, *Hawthorne*, 71.

29. Fourier, *Selections*, 165. See Hapke, *Labor's Text*; Bromell, *By the Sweat of the Brow*; Lears, *No Place of Grace*; and David E. Shi, *Simple Life*.

30. Green, *Friar Bacon and Friar Bungay*, 12.

31. Hawthorne, "Chippings with a Chisel," 409.

32. Quoted in Moore, *Salem World*, 26.

33. See Tolles, *Architecture in Salem*, 113–14; Moore, *Salem World*, 24.

34. See Ulrich, *Age of Homespun*; Downing, *Cottage Residences*, v.

35. Cobden-Sanderson, *Arts and Crafts Movement*, 29–30.

36. Morris, "Lesser Arts," 17.

37. Benjamin, "Work of Art," 221.

38. Wigglesworth, *Day of Doom*, 36. Jenks is quoted in Dean, *Memoir*, 7–8n1.

39. Hawthorne, *House of the Seven Gables*, 3.

3. THE NATURE OF GOTHIC

1. Vitruvius, *De Architectura*, 2.

2. Dormer, "Language and Practical Philosophy," 222.

3. Waugh, *Brideshead Revisited*, 38.

4. Pugin refers to the baker's shop in two of his books. See *Contrasts*, 46; and *Present State of Ecclesiastical Architecture*, 101 and 101n.

5. Walker and Pugin, *Examples of Gothic Architecture*, 28n. *Examples of Gothic Architecture* was begun by the two Pugins but completed by Walker and A. W. N. Pugin after the elder architect's death. In the preface, Walker describes A. W. N. Pugin as having contributed the sketches, while he composed the text.

6. The description of the oriel window is Walker's, correlating to two sketches of the oriel window made by Pugin (Walker and Pugin, *Examples of Gothic Architecture*, 11).

7. Pugin, *True Principles*, 33.

8. Reynolds, *Nineteenth-Century Architecture*, 38.

9. Hawthorne, "Chiefly about War Matters," 310.

10. Hawthorne, "Jonathan Cilley," 271.

11. "The 'Noble Forehead' Fallacy," 419.

12. Brown, *Domestic Individualism*, 69–77.

13. See Trachtenberg, "Seeing and Believing," 464.

14. Veblen, *Theory of the Leisure Class*, 137, 159–64.

15. Veblen's furniture is described by Jorgenson and Jorgenson, *Thorstein Veblen*, 75; Edgell, *Veblen in Perspective*; and Lubin, "Recollections of Veblen," 133.

16. Veblen, *Instinct of Workmanship*, 3.

17. As it happens, Gustav Stickley, the best-known representative of simple furnishings in Veblen's America, was a close collaborator of Veblen's sometime friend Oscar Lovell Triggs—president of the Chicago Arts and Crafts Society, faculty colleague of Veblen's at the University of Chicago, and contributor to Stickley's *Craftsman* magazine.

18. Veblen, *Theory of the Leisure Class*, 162.

19. Veblen, *Instinct of Workmanship*, 38.

20. Spretnak, *Resurgence of the Real*; Fox, *Against the Machine*.

21. McKibben, *Age of Missing Information*, 30–34.

22. Stickley, "Danger of Too Much System," 494.

23. Stickley, "Home Training in Cabinet Work," 516; Stickley, "Cabinet Work for Home Workers," 169–84.

24. See "Craftsman Metal Work," 162–64. Stickley was responding to the wider trends in crafts pedagogy—as character-building rather than vocational—that I describe briefly in chapter 2.

25. "Tools and Tables for Carving," 550.

26. Stickley, "Danger of Too Much System," 493.

27. Crawford, *C. R. Ashbee*, 36.

28. Morris, Introduction, 1.

29. Ruskin, *Stones of Venice*, vol. 2, 168.

30. Cobden-Sanderson, *Arts and Crafts Movement*, 29–30.

31. Morris, "Lesser Arts," 17.

32. Quoted in Naylor, *Arts and Crafts Movement*, 170.

33. See Bradley, *William Morris and His World*, 67–68.

34. Voragine, *Golden Legend*, 127.

35. The role of St. George is not as clearly cast, for Jane Burden became Dante Gabriel Rossetti's lover while Morris's wife. One might wonder in this regard about the bierlike aspect of the piece, superimposed on its aspects of uplift and its triumphal reorientation of the St. George story. There may be a sense in which the design itself, carrying a painting that narrates the winning of Jane Burden, reflects some of Morris's notoriously equivocal attitude toward the affair and toward his marriage. Such speculation would demand that Philip Webb, Morris's partner in the design, be himself reflecting on the affair—which is not entirely improbable, as it was the infamous open secret of the pre-Raphaelites.

36. Wallace, "Todd Hoyer and Hayley Smith," 30.

37. Holzapfel is quoted in Wulff, "An Ingrained Aesthetic," 26.

38. Benjamin, "Art in the Age of Mechanical Reproduction," 221.

39. Krenov, *Fine Art of Cabinetmaking*, 20.

40. See Pye, *Nature and Art of Workmanship*, passim, but especially chapter 2.

41. In that sense, it is the opposite of the "hard, gem-like flame" that closes Pater's *Renaissance*. Pater's flame marks the "unstable, flickering, inconsistent" nature of aesthetic impression. The difference in the two kinds of aesthetic subjectivity is that Pater's version

is founded on the impossibility of reproducing aesthetic experience, while Waugh's version is founded on aesthetic experience's diachronic continuity—indeed, the relation of aesthetics and reproduction is exactly my larger point in discussing the scene. See Pater, *Renaissance*, 151–52.

4. IN THE AMERICAN GRAIN

1. Stickley, "Thoughts Occasioned by an Anniversary," 42.

2. Cobden-Sanderson uses these terms throughout *The Arts and Crafts Movement*.

3. Sargeant, "John Ruskin," 3. While much of this chapter will deal with Stickley's contributions to the magazine he published, *The Craftsman* was largely a communal endeavor and included pieces by a wide range of authors and many anonymous contributions, especially after 1913. Because the late *Craftsman* (1911–16) will become my major subject in the second half of this chapter, I would take this opportunity to say that some of the material quoted is not definitely attributable to Stickley—even if clues of style and sentiment often make such an assumption reasonable. In any case, the chapter is less about Stickley himself, in a psychological or biographical sense, than about the strategies by which his furnishings were offered to the public. In the sense that Stickley and his cadre of editors and writers all created the Craftsman phenomenon, and for the practical purposes of discussing that phenomenon, I will treat some unattributed material as Stickley's own. The notes and bibliography, however, will not attribute to Stickley any piece that does not carry his name explicitly.

4. Ruskin, *Stones of Venice*, vol. 2, 203.

5. Stickley, "Als Ik Kan," 232.

6. Stickley, *Catalog of Craftsman Furniture*, 1912, 4.

7. The most sardonic treatment of Stickley's career is Sanders's *Complex Fate*, which likens Stickley's aggressive promotion of his brand to the narcissistic capitalism of Donald Trump. Hewitt's *Gustav Stickley's Craftsman Farms* soft-pedals its exposé of Stickley's contradictions by practicing Clifford Geertz's notion of "thick description": practically organized around the limits of Stickley's utopian vision for Craftsman Farms (a property in New Jersey where he sought to promote communal living and back-to-the-land ethics), Hewitt's goal is to explain all sides of the Craftsman enterprise, including its inconsistencies and ironic reversals. Studies that place Stickley in a larger historical context, on the other hand, tend to take the instability of the crafts revival as a premise rather than a conclusion. Lears's *No Place of Grace* and Orvell's *Real Thing* see the paradoxes and reversals of Stickley's enterprise in dialectical terms: by promising the rustic life of the frontier to a suburban workforce, the crafts revivalists provided a synthesizing vision that abetted the emergence of corporate culture (Lears) or opposed a visionary "humanistic synthesis" of the authentic and the salable to "the forces of mass advertising that increasingly were governing the marketplace" (Orvell, *Real Thing*, 166, 161).

8. Stickley, "Thoughts Occasioned by an Anniversary," 42.

9. Stickley, "Important Announcement," ix.

10. Stickley, "Outline of Furniture-Making," 156.

11. Stickley, "Treatment of Wall Spaces," 146; Stickley, "Our Native Woods," 185.

12. Stickley, "Thoughts Occasioned by an Anniversary," 54.

13. Stickley, "Our Native Woods," 187.

14. More formal woods like maple, cherry, and mahogany are called diffuse-porous because the grain continues to grow throughout the year, minimizing the difference between earlywood and latewood; the grain of these species is more regular because of the nature of the tree's annual growth. But these woods, in Stickley's mind, were either not native or too firmly associated with genteel parlor furnishings. Stickley's approach to oak thus sought ways to minimize variation while retaining the "strong-fibered, open-textured" appeal of the species that he saw as correlative with probity and honesty. Stickley, "Our Native Woods," 185.

15. Stickley, "Cabinet Work for Home Workers," 177; Stickley, "Structure and Ornament," 396; Stickley, "Thoughts Occasioned by an Anniversary," 48.

16. Stickley, "Our Native Woods," 185.

17. Stickley, "Cabinet Work for Home Workers," 174; "Structure and Ornament," 396.

18. Stickley, "Cabinet Work for Home Workers," 174.

19. Seltzer, *Bodies and Machines*, 3–5.

20. Stickley, "Our Native Woods," 185.

21. Kaplan, *"The Art That Is Life"*, 216. Riordan's articles for *The Craftsman* covered his own educational experiments as well as reporting on similar efforts across the country.

22. Stickley, "Structure and Ornament," 396.

23. Stickley, "Thoughts Occasioned by an Anniversary," 47–48.

24. Mayer, *In the Arts and Crafts Style*, 36.

25. See Schafter, *Order of Ornament*, 22–43.

26. Ibid., 73.

27. Summerson is quoted by Schafter in the same passage.

28. Wheeler, *Rural Homes*, 207; Kirkland, "World's Fair," 325.

29. See McNerney, *American Oak Furniture*; also Swedborg and Swedborg, *American Oak Furniture*.

30. Eastlake, *Hints on Household Taste*, 6.

31. See Mumford, *Brown Decades*.

32. Wharton, *Age of Innocence*, 71.

33. Stickley, "Cabinet Work for Home Workers," 178.

34. Stickley, "Thoughts Occasioned by an Anniversary," 119.

35. Emerson, "Poet," 223–24, 237.

36. Ruskin, *Stones of Venice*, vol. 1, 134.

37. Stickley, "Structure and Ornament," 392.

38. Indeed, by calling his taxonomy a "grammar," Schafter claims, Jones projected his hope that readers would take the book as a guide for making original decorative statements. See Schafter, *Order of Ornament*, passim, but especially 72–78.

39. Stickley, "Flood of Fiction," 195–96.

40. Sanders, "Gift of Angelo," 181.

41. Richards, "Brother of the Cross," 97–98.

42. Richards, "Master Workman," 850.

43. While popular histories of the Craftsman enterprise describe Stickley's earnest regard for originality, scholarly accounts tend to see that position as a sham and a marketable image. In stressing the typological foundations of Stickley's theories, I hope to suggest that his project neither incarnated nor sold out the authentic; rather, the Craftsman enterprise depended on relays between terms normally seen in opposition.

44. Sweet, "Bridge Keeper," 216.

45. Bailey, "Regeneration of Benvenuto," 539, 543.

46. Harboe, "Taming of the Bear," 34–35.

47. Root, "Angel in the Stone," 523.

48. Joor, "Lover of the Beautiful," 76.

49. By the "Arts and Crafts Movement," Triggs meant the American handicrafts revival. The name given by Cobden-Sanderson to the English movement was widely carried over to the United States. See Triggs, *Chapters in the History*, 178–79.

50. The terms of his claim are not unfamiliar. The case for industrial advancement and economic expansion in political discourse has often been made on behalf of the interests of labor and the American worker. In general, the craft movement was not opposed to machines. Horace Traubel, Walt Whitman's biographer and a resident at the Rose Valley craft community, spoke for many handicrafts advocates in refusing to distinguish "between the hand holding a tool and the hand guiding a machine"; sounding like Triggs on a microeconomic scale, Traubel urged workers in small shops to accept the forward momentum of the "historic line" and not remain theatrically devoted to traditional skills. Stickley wrote a series of articles on the "right use of the machine," and, like Triggs, named Carnegie as his model of the "enlightened industrialist." See Traubel, "Keeping in the Historic Line," 250. On Stickley's ideas about Carnegie, see Smith, *Gustav Stickley*, 37–38.

51. Stickley, "Outline of Furniture-Making," 156.

52. See Smith, *Gustav Stickley*, 157–58.

53. "The Development of an American Style," 69.

54. Spencer, *Herbert Spencer on Social Evolution*, 168.

55. "Insure," not "ensure," was a standard Victorian usage for "guarantee."

56. Stickley, "Hand-Wrought Metal Work," 1.

57. "Artistic Opportunities in Painted Furniture," 596.

58. B. Johnson, "1912," 65.

59. Stickley, *Craftsman Catalog of Interior Furnishings*, 1915.

60. Advertisement, *Craftsman* 27:3 (December 1914).

61. "Increase of Home Building in America," 240, 203.

62. The early third-person articles constituted a series called "Chips from the Craftsman Workshops." See "Chips," 315.

63. "'Hercules of the Forest,'" 309–11. See also "Ethics of Home Furnishing" and "New Idea in Home Furnishing: No. 1: The Dining Room."

64. "Development of an American Style," 77.

65. "Hercules of the Forest," 309–10.

66. "New Idea in Home Furnishing: No. 1: The Dining Room," 202; "Hercules of the Forest," 304–11.

67. "Dining Room as a Center of Hospitality," 140.

68. "Hercules of the Forest," 309–10.

69. "Most Valuable of All Arts," 531.

70. Stickley, "Furniture Based upon Good Craftsmanship," 531–32.

71. Stickley, "Outline of Furniture-Making," 151.

72. Emerson, "Experience," 259.

73. See Bloom, "Freshness of Transformation."

74. Emerson, "Nature," 22.

75. Dimock, "Scarcity, Subjectivity, and Emerson," 85, 99.

76. Stickley, "Furniture Based upon Good Craftsmanship," 538.

5. THE SYNTAX OF THE EYE

1. "*The Spoils of Poynton*," 301. Because *Spoils* was often reviewed in more general articles, I cite the title of each review in the notes. The reviews were mostly anonymous.

2. "Recent Fiction," *Nation*, 18.

3. "Mr. Henry James's Latest Tendency," 296.

4. See "Books of the Week" and "Recent Novels" as well as Erie, "*The Spoils of Poynton*," 258; "Current Fiction," 126; and "Recent Fiction," *Dial*, 307. The reference to "priceless knickknacks" appears in "Mr. Henry James's Latest Tendency," 296.

5. "Henry James: His New Novel," 1.

6. "Recent Novels," 309.

7. Erie, "The Spoils of Poynton," 259.

8. The reference to the spoils as "unreal" appears in "Current Fiction," 127.

9. Edel, *Henry James*, 5:321.

10. James, *Wings of the Dove*, 42.

11. Emerson, "The Poet," 232.

12. B. Brown, *Sense of Things*, 146, 5.

13. Fuss, *Sense of an Interior*, 17.

14. Shaw, *Specimens of Ancient Furniture*, 27.

15. Otten, "*Spoils of Poynton* and the Properties of Touch."

16. B. Brown, *Sense of Things*, 147.

17. Wheeler is quoted in Banham, Macdonald, and Porter, *Victorian Interior Style*, 38.

18. Veblen, *Theory of the Leisure Class*, 163.

19. B. Brown, *Sense of Things*, 147.

20. Armstrong, *Phenomenology of Henry James*, 191–203; Sarris, "Fetishism in *The Spoils of Poynton*"; Koenigsberger, "Alchemy and Apprcciation," 35.

21. The handicrafts curiosity is in this sense a particularly charged example of the mementos and souvenirs described by Susan Stewart. For Stewart, souvenirs are interesting because they memorialize a prior authenticity (the fact of having really been there), transforming that "directly lived" primary experience into a narrative not of consumption but of production, a story of self-authorship signaled by the gimcrack on the mantle. Crafts objects, relics of preindustrial authenticity translated into a grammar of ornament, focus Stewart's point in an especially literal way. See Susan Stewart, *On Longing*, 139, and passim.

22. See Edel, *Henry James*, 5:333–38. James describes his work with Coburn in the preface to *The Golden Bowl*.

23. Richards, Introduction, xxvi.

24. The story of the Wallace Collection is best told in Baldry, *Wallace Collection*.

25. Hughes, *Wallace Collection: Catalogue*.

26. Quoted in Edel, *Henry James*, 5:337–38.

27. James, "Wallace Collection," 68.

28. Ibid., 71–73, 69.

29. James to Coburn, 9 December 1906, in *Letters of Henry James*, 6:431.

30. "Increase of Home Building in America," 203.

31. Maratta's system is described in Homer, *Robert Henri and His Circle*.

32. See the excerpt from Henri's *Art Spirit* in Sloane, *Primary Sources*, 110.

33. "Development of an American Style," 75.

34. Stickley, "Cabinet Work for Home Workers," 175.

35. "Development of an American Style," 75. Other relevant articles on color in late years of *The Craftsman* include "More Color in the Home"; "The Magpie Note"; and "Artistic Opportunities in Painted Furniture."

36. "Wallpaper Reviews," 21–24.

CONCLUSION

1. James, *Spoils of Poynton*, 14, 172.

2. Hawthorne, "Drowne's Wooden Image," 314.

3. Stickley, "Structure and Ornament," 392.

4. Greenough, "Fourier et Hoc Genus Omne," in *Travels*, 63–64.

5. Greenough, *Travels*, 15, 146.

6. Hawthorne, *Scarlet Letter*, 25.

7. B. Brown, *Sense of Things*, 178.

8. Veblen, *Theory of the Leisure Class*, 161–64.

9. Whitman, "Poem of the Daily Work," 139. In the first edition of *Leaves of Grass*, in 1855, Whitman placed an early version of the poem, untitled, immediately after the long work that came to be called "Song of Myself." The poem appears in other versions in later editions.

10. See Wilentz, *Chants Democratic*, 113–42. On a similar reorganization of workshops in upstate New York, see Johnson, P., *Shopkeeper's Millennium*, 38–42.

11. Burrows and Wallace, *Gotham*, 523–24. See also p. 529, on Evans's *Workingman's Advocate* (mentioned at the end of this paragraph).

12. Pennant, *Tour in Scotland*, 11.

13. See the Restoration Hardware Catalog, Holiday 2009, preface, 32, 73, 64.

14. Restoration Hardware Catalog, June 2009.

15. Stewart, *Entertaining*, 1.

BIBLIOGRAPHY

Adams, Henry. *The Education of Henry Adams*. Edited by Ernest Samuels. Boston: Houghton Mifflin, 1973.

———. *The Letters of Henry Adams*. Vol. 6, 1906–1918. Edited by J. C. Levenson, Ernest Samuels, Charles Vandersee, and Viola Hopkins Winner. Cambridge: Harvard University Press, 1988.

Adams, John Quincy. *Memoirs*. Edited by Charles Francis Adams. New York: AMS Press, 1970.

Addison, Julia deWolf. *Arts and Crafts in the Middle Ages*. Boston: L. C. Page, 1908.

Amelang, James S. *The Flight of Icarus: Artisan Autobiography in Early Modern Europe*. Palo Alto: Stanford University Press, 1998.

Annas, Julia. "Virtue as a Skill." *International Journal of Philosophical Studies* 3:2 (September 1995): 227–43.

Armstrong, Paul. *The Phenomenology of Henry James*. Chapel Hill: University of North Carolina Press, 1983.

"Artistic Opportunities in Painted Furniture." *The Craftsman* 28:6 (September 1915): 596–98.

Ashbee, C. R. "Cinquecento Jewelry." *Art Journal* (1893).

———. "An Introductory Account of the Origin and Object of the Treatises and of Cellini's Position as Craftsman and Author." In Benvenuto Cellini, *Treatises on Goldsmithing and Sculpture*, trans. Ashbee, ix–xiv. London: Guild of Handicraft Press, 1888.

Bailey, Carolyn Sherwin. "The Regeneration of Benvenuto." *The Craftsman* 11:5 (February 1907): 539–44.

Baldry, A. L. *The Wallace Collection at Hertford House*. London: Goupil, 1904.

Balzac, Honoré de. *La Comédie Humaine of Honoré de Balzac*. Translated by Katharine Prescott Wormeley. Boston: Little, Brown, 1899.

Banham, Joanna, Sally Macdonald, and Julia Porter. *Victorian Interior Style*. London: Studio Editions, 1995.

Bell, Millicent. "Hawthorne and the Real." In *Hawthorne and the Real*, ed. Millicent Bell, 1–21. Columbus: Ohio State University Press, 2005.

———, ed. *Hawthorne and the Real*. Columbus: Ohio State University Press, 2005.

Benjamin, Walter. "The Storyteller." In *Illuminations*, edited by Hannah Arendt, 83–109. New York: Schocken, 1968.

———. "The Work of Art in the Age of Mechanical Reproduction." In *Illuminations*, edited by Hannah Arendt, 217–51. New York: Schocken, 1968.

Black, Henry Campbell. *Law Dictionary*. St. Paul, MN: West, 1910.

Bloom, Harold. "The Freshness of Transformation." In *Emerson—Prophecy, Metamorphosis, Influence: Selected Papers from the English Institute*, edited by David Levin, 129–48. New York: Columbia University Press, 1975.

"Books of the Week." *Outlook*, 27 February 1897. Review of Henry James, *The Spoils of Poynton*.

Bradley, Ian. *William Morris and His World*. New York: Scribner, 1978.

Brandt, Beverly K. *The Craftsman and the Critic: Defining Usefulness and Beauty in Arts and Crafts–Era Boston*. Amherst: University of Massachusetts Press, 2009.

Bromell, Nicholas. *By The Sweat of the Brow: Literature and Labor in Antebellum America*. Chicago: University of Chicago Press, 1993.

Brown, Bill. *A Sense of Things: The Object Matter of American Literature*. Chicago: University of Chicago Press, 2003.

Brown, Gillian. *Domestic Individualism: Imagining Self in Nineteenth-Century America*. Berkeley: University of California Press, 1990.

Buell, Lawrence. "Hawthorne and the Problem of 'American' Fiction: The Example of *The Scarlet Letter*." In Bell, *Hawthorne and the Real*, 70–87.

Burrill, Alexander. *Law Dictionary*. New York, 1871.

Burrows, Edwin G., and Mike Wallace. *Gotham: A History of New York City to 1898*. Oxford: Oxford University Press, 1999.

Bushnell, Horace. "The Age of Homespun." In *Work and Play*, 39–76. London: Alexander Strahan, 1864.

Cairns, David. *Berlioz*. Vol. 2, *Servitude and Greatness, 1832–1869*. Berkeley: University of California Press, 2003.

Cappello, Mary. " 'Rappaccini's Daughter' as Translation." *Philological Quarterly* 65:2 (Spring 1986).

Cellini, Benvenuto. *Autobiography*. Translated by George Bull. New York: Penguin Books, 1986.

——. *Autobiography [Life] of Benvenuto Cellini*. Translated by John Addington Symonds. New York: Modern Library, 1927.

——. *La vita di Benvenuto Cellini*. Edited by Brunone Bianchi. Florence, 1866.

Chard, Louise C. "A Sculptor as Potter." *The Craftsman* 3:4 (January 1903): 244–46.

Chippendale, Thomas. *The Gentleman and Cabinet-Maker's Director*. London, 1754.

Cobden-Sanderson, T. J. *The Arts and Crafts Movement*. Hammersmith: Hammersmith Publishing Society, 1905.

Cole, Bruce. *The Renaissance Artist at Work: From Pisano to Titian*. New York: Harper and Row, 1983.

Cole, Michael. "Benvenuto Cellini's Designs for His Tomb." *Burlington Magazine* 140 (December 1998): 1149.

——. "Cellini's Blood." *Art Bulletin* 81:2 (June 1999).

Cortissoz, Royal. "Benvenuto Cellini: Artist and Writer." In Benvenuto Cellini, *The Life of Benvenuto Cellini*, xi–xxx. New York: Brentano's, 1906.

Crane, Sylvia E. *White Silence: Greenough, Powers, and Crawford*. Coral Gables: University of Miami Press, 1972.

Crawford, Alan. *C. R. Ashbee*. Yale University Press, 1985.

Crawford, Matthew. *Shop Class as Soulcraft: An Inquiry into the Value of Work*. New York: Penguin, 2009.

Culme, John. " 'Benvenuto Cellini' and the Nineteenth-Century Collector and Goldsmith." In *Art at Auction*, 293–96. London: Sotheby's, 1973–74.

"Current Fiction." *The Literary World*, 17 April 1897. Review of Henry James, *The Spoils of Poynton*.

Dean, John Ward. *Memoir of Rev. Michael Wigglesworth*. Albany, 1871.

Denning, Michael. *The Cultural Front: The Laboring of American Culture in the Twentieth Century*. London: Verso, 1996.

Dimock, Wai Chee. "Scarcity, Subjectivity, and Emerson." In *Revisionary Interventions into the Americanist Canon*, edited by Donald Pease, 83–99. Durham: Duke University Press, 1994.

Dormer, Peter. "The Language and Practical Philosophy of Craft." In *The Culture of Craft*, 219–30. Manchester: Manchester University Press, 1997.

Downing, Andrew Jackson. *Cottage Residences*. New York: Wiley and Halsted, 1856.

Eastlake, Charles Locke. *Hints on Household Taste*. American Edition. Boston, 1878; reprint New York: Dover, 1969.

Edel, Leon. *Henry James*, Vol. 5, *The Master: 1901–1916*. Philadelphia: J. P. Lippincott, 1972.

Edgell, Stephen. *Veblen in Perspective*. New York: Sharpe, 2001.

Emerson, Ralph Waldo. *English Traits*. New York: AMS Press, 1968.

——. "Experience." In *Selections from Ralph Waldo Emerson*, 254–74.

——. *The Letters of Ralph Waldo Emerson*. Vol. 8, 1845–1859. Edited by Eleanor M. Tilton. New York: Columbia University Press, 1991.

——. "Michael Angelo." In *Natural History of Intellect and Other Papers*, 213–44. Boston: Houghton Mifflin, 1904.

——. "Nature." In *Selections from Ralph Waldo Emerson*, 21–56.

——. "The Poet." In *Selections from Ralph Waldo Emerson*, 222–41.

——. *Selections from Ralph Waldo Emerson*. Edited by Stephen Whicher. Boston: Riverside Editions of Houghton Mifflin, 1957.

The Encyclopedia Americana: A Library of Universal Knowledge in Thirty Volumes. New York: Encyclopedia Americana Corporation, 1918.

Erie, Mervin. "The Spoils of Poynton." *The Bookman: A Review of Books and Life*, May 1897.

"The Ethics of Home Furnishing." *The Craftsman* 29:4 (January 1916): 412–20.

Fourier, Charles. *Selections from the Works of Fourier*. Edited by Julia Franklin. London: Sonnenschein, 1901.

Fox, Nicols. *Against the Machine: The Hidden Luddite Tradition in Literature, Art, and Individual Lives*. Washington, DC: Shearwater, 2002.

Fuss, Diana. *The Sense of an Interior: Four Writers and the Rooms That Shaped Them*. New York: Routledge, 2004.

Gibson, Katharine. *The Goldsmith of Florence: A Book of Great Craftsmen*. New York: Macmillan, 1929.

Gilman, Daniel C. "Hand-craft and Rede-craft: A Plea for the First Named." *Scientific American Supplement* 497 (July 1885).

Gilmore, Michael. *American Romanticism and the Marketplace.* Chicago: University of Chicago Press, 1985.

Green, Robert. *Friar Bacon and Friar Bungay.* Edited by Daniel Seltzer. Lincoln: University of Nebraska Press, 1964.

Greenhalgh, Paul. "Complexity." In Greenhalgh, ed., *The Persistence of Craft*, 195–208. New Brunswick: Rutgers University Press, 2003.

——. "The Genre." In Greenhalgh, *Persistence of Craft*, 18–27.

Greenough, Horatio. *Form and Function.* Edited by Harold A. Small. Berkeley: University of California Press, 1947.

——. *Letters of Horatio Greenough to his Brother, Henry Greenough.* Edited by Frances Boott Greenough. Boston, 1887.

——. *The Travels, Observations, and Experience of a Yankee Stonecutter.* New York, 1852.

Hapke, Laura. *Labor's Text: The Worker in American Fiction.* New Brunswick: Rutgers University Press, 2001.

Harboe, Paul. "The Taming of the Bear." *The Craftsman* 12:1 (April 1907): 34–8.

Hawthorne, Nathaniel. *The American Notebooks.* Columbus: Ohio State University Press, 1972.

——. "The Artist of the Beautiful." In *Mosses from an Old Manse*, 447–75. Columbus: Ohio State University Press, 1974.

——. *The Blithedale Romance.* Oxford: Oxford University Press, 1991.

——. *The Blithedale Romance.* Edited by William Cain. Boston: Bedford, 1996.

——. "Chiefly about War Matters." In *Tales, Sketches, and Other Papers*, 299–345. Boston: Houghton Mifflin, 1878.

——. "Chippings with a Chisel." In *Twice-Told Tales*, 407–18. Columbus: Ohio State University Press, 1974.

——. "Drowne's Wooden Image." In *Mosses from an Old Manse*, 306–20. Columbus: Ohio State University Press, 1974.

——. *Fanshawe.* In *The Blithedale Romance and Fanshawe.* Columbus: Ohio State University Press, 1964.

——. *The French and Italian Notebooks.* Columbus: Ohio State University Press, 1980.

——. "The Great Stone Face." In *The Snow Image and Uncollected Tales*, 26–48. Columbus: Ohio State University Press, 1974.

——. *The House of the Seven Gables.* Oxford: Oxford University Press, 1991.

——. "Jonathan Cilley." In *Tales, Sketches, and Other Papers*, 264–75. Boston: Houghton Mifflin, 1878.

——. *The Marble Faun.* New York: Thomas Crowell, 1902.

——. *Our Old Home.* New York: Houghton Mifflin, 1912.

——. "Rappaccini's Daughter." In *Mosses from an Old Manse*, 91–128. Columbus: Ohio State University Press, 1974.

——. *The Scarlet Letter.* Oxford: Oxford University Press, 2007.

——. *The Snow Image and Uncollected Tales.* Columbus: Ohio State University Press, 1974.

——. *Twice-Told Tales.* Columbus: Ohio State University Press, 1974.

Heidegger, Martin. "Building Dwelling Thinking." In *Martin Heidegger: Basic Writings*, edited by David Farrell Krell. New York: Harper and Row, 1977.

"Henry James: His New Novel That Shows He Is Still Spinning His Work Out Fine." *The New York Times*, 20 February 1897.

" 'Hercules of the Forest': The Second of a Series on the New Idea in Home Furnishing." *The Craftsman* 29:3 (December 1915): 302–11.

Hewitt, Mark Alan. *Gustav Stickley's Craftsman Farms*. Syracuse: Syracuse University Press, 2001.

Hoffman, B. B. *The Sloyd System of Woodworking*. New York: American Book Company, 1892.

Homer, William I. *Robert Henri and His Circle*. Ithaca: Cornell University Press, 1969.

Hubbard, Elbert. *Little Journeys to the Homes of Eminent Artists*. East Aurora, NY: Roycroft Press, 1912.

Hughes, Peter. *The Wallace Collection: Catalogue of Furniture*. London: Trustees of the Wallace Collection, 1996.

"The Increase of Home Building in America." *The Craftsman* 26:2 (May 1914): 202–03.

James, Henry. *The Letters of Henry James*. Edited by Leon Edel. Cambridge: Harvard University Press, 1974.

——. *The Spoils of Poynton*. New York: Oxford University Press, 1982.

——. "The Wallace Collection in Bethnal Green." In *The Painter's Eye: Notes and Essays on the Pictorial Arts by Henry James*, edited by John L. Sweeney, 67–78. Cambridge: Harvard University Press, 1956.

——. *The Wings of the Dove*. New York: Penguin, 1986.

Johnson, Bruce, "1912: The Final Year of Glory." Introduction to *Craftsman Furniture Made by Gustav Stickley at the Craftsman Workshops*. Durham: Knock-on-Wood Publications, 1989.

Johnson, Paul. *A Shopkeeper's Millennium: Society and Revivals in Rochester, New York, 1815–1837*. New York: Hill and Wang, 1978.

Jones, Owen. *The Grammar of Ornament*. London, 1856.

Joor, Harriet. "A Lover of the Beautiful." *The Craftsman* 9:1 (October 1905): 73–80.

Jorgenson, Elizabeth and Henry Jorgenson. *Thorstein Veblen: Victorian Firebrand*. New York: Sharpe, 1999.

Kaplan, Wendy. *"The Art That Is Life": The Arts and Crafts Movement in America, 1875–1920*. Boston: Museum of Fine Arts, 1987.

Kirby, C. Valentine. "Clay Modeling: An Appreciation of Its Value." *The Craftsman* 5:5 (February 1904): 490–97.

Kirkland, Caroline. "The World's Fair." *Sartain's Magazine* 8:5 (May 1851).

Koenigsberger, Kurt. "Alchemy and Appreciation: The Spoiling of the Real in *The Spoils of Poynton*." *Studies in the Novel* 30 (1998).

Krenov, James. *The Fine Art of Cabinetmaking*. New York: Sterling, 1992.

Lears, Jackson. *No Place of Grace: Antimodernism and the Transformation of American Culture, 1880–1920*. Chicago: University of Chicago Press, 1981.

Livingstone, Karen. "Art Manufacturers of the Twenty-First Century." In Greenhalgh, *Persistence of Craft*, 37–48.

Longfellow, Henry Wadsworth. "Michael Angelo." In *Judas Maccabaeus, Michael Angelo, and Translations*, 51–176. Boston: Houghton Mifflin, 1911.

———. "The Village Blacksmith." In *The Complete Poetical Works of Henry Wadsworth Longfellow*, 14. Boston, New York, and Chicago: Houghton Mifflin, 1893.

Lubbock, Percy. *The Craft of Fiction*. London: Jonathan Cape, 1921.

Lubin, Isador. "Recollections of Veblen." In *Thorstein Veblen: The Carleton College Seminary Essays*, ed. Carlton Qualey, 131–47. New York: Columbia University Press, 1968.

"The Magpie Note in New American Furniture." *The Craftsman* 28:5 (August 1915): 478–85.

Maibor, Carolyn. *Labor Pains: Emerson, Hawthorne, and Alcott on Work and the Woman Question*. London: Routledge, 2004.

Male, Roy R., Jr. "The Dual Aspect of Evil in 'Rappaccini's Daughter.' " PMLA 69 (1954).

Marx, Karl. *The Eighteenth Brumaire of Louis Bonaparte*. Translated by Daniel De Leon. New York, 1897.

Mayer, Barbara. *In the Arts and Crafts Style*. San Francisco: Chronicle Books, 1992.

Mayhook, J. Jeffrey. " 'Bearings Unknown to English Heraldry' in *The Scarlet Letter*." *The Nathaniel Hawthorne Journal 1977*. Edited by C. E. Frazier Clark, Jr. Detroit: Gale Research, 1980.

McKibben, Bill. *The Age of Missing Information*. New York: Penguin, 1993.

McNerney, Kathryn. *American Oak Furniture*. Paducah, KY: Collector, 1984.

Metzger, Charles R. *Emerson and Greenough*. Berkeley: University of California Press, 1954.

Michaels, Walter Benn. *The Gold Standard and the Logic of Naturalism*. Berkeley: University of California Press, 1987.

Mills, Robert. *Guide to the Capitol of the United States, Embracing Every Information Useful to the Visitor, Whether on Business or Pleasure*. Washington, 1834.

Moore, Margaret. *The Salem World of Nathaniel Hawthorne*. Columbia: University of Missouri Press, 2001.

"More Color in the Home: Painted Furniture Inspired by Peasant Art." *The Craftsman* 28:3 (June 1915): 245–54.

Morris, William. Introduction to *The Nature of Gothic*, by John Ruskin, i–v. Hammersmith: Kelmscott Press, 1892.

———. "The Lesser Arts." In *Hopes and Fears for Art*, 1–37. New York: Longmans, Greens, 1903.

"Mr. Henry James's Latest Tendency." *The Chap-Book: A Miscellany and Review of Belles Lettres*, 15 February 1897.

Mumford, Lewis. *The Brown Decades: A Study of the Arts in America, 1865–1895*. New York: Harcourt, Brace, 1931.

Naylor, Gillian. *The Arts and Crafts Movement*. Cambridge, MA: MIT Press, 1971.

"The New Idea in Home Furnishing: No. 1: The Dining Room." *The Craftsman* 29:2 (November 1915): 201–03.

"The 'Noble Forehead' Fallacy." *The Medical Age*, September 23, 1886.

Orvell, Miles. *The Real Thing: Imitation and Authenticity in American Culture, 1880–1940.* Chapel Hill: University of North Carolina Press, 1989.

Otten, Thomas J. "*The Spoils of Poynton* and the Properties of Touch." *American Literature* 71 (1999).

Pater, Walter. *The Renaissance.* Oxford: Oxford University Press, 1986.

Pennant, Thomas. *A Tour in Scotland and Voyage to the Hebrides.* London, 1790.

Plato. *The Republic.* Translated by G. M. A. Grube, revised by C. D. C. Reeve. Indianapolis: Hackett, 1992.

Pope-Hennessy, John. *Cellini.* New York: Abbeville Press, 1985.

Pugin, A. W. N. *Contrasts; or, A Parallel between the Noble Edifices of the Middle Ages, and Corresponding Buildings of the Present Day.* [1841]. Leicester: Leicester University Press, 1969.

——. *The Present State of Ecclesiastical Architecture in England.* London: Charles Dolman, 1843.

——. *The True Principles of Pointed or Christian Architecture.* London: John Weale, 1841.

Pye, David. *The Nature and Art of Workmanship.* Cambridge: Cambridge University Press, 1968.

"Recent Fiction." *The Dial*, 16 May 1897.

"Recent Fiction." *The Nation*, 1 July 1897.

"Recent Novels." *The Spectator*, 27 February 1897.

Reynolds, David Martin. *Nineteenth-Century Architecture.* Cambridge: Cambridge University Press, 1992.

Richards, Bernard. Introduction to *The Spoils of Poynton*, by Henry James, xxxix–l. New York: Oxford Univ. Press, 1982.

Richards, Burton. "The Brother of the Cross." *The Craftsman* 11:1 (October 1906):97–9.

——. "The Master Workman." *The Craftsman* 9:6 (March 1906): 850–53.

Rigal, Laura. *The American Manufactory: Art, Labor, and the World of Things in the Early Republic.* Princeton: Princeton University Press, 1998.

Riordan, Raymond. "Interlaken, An Outdoor School Where Boys Through Their Own Efforts Learn How to Think and Work." *The Craftsman* 22:2 (May 1912): 177–86.

——. "Lincoln Memorial School: A New Idea in Industrial Education." *The Craftsman* 22:6 (September 1912): 611–18.

——. "A Visit to Craftsman Farms: The Impression It Made and the Result: The Gustav Stickley School for Citizenship." *The Craftsman* 23:2 (November 1912): 151–64.

Risatti, Howard. *A Theory of Craft.* Chapel Hill: University of North Carolina Press, 2007.

Root, Katharine Metcalf. "The Angel in the Stone." *The Craftsman* 9:2 (January 1906): 522–29.

Ruskin, John. *The Stones of Venice*, Vol. 1. New York, 1891.

———. *The Stones of Venice*. Vol. 2. New York: Collier, 1900.

Sanders, Barry. *A Complex Fate: Gustav Stickley and the Craftsman Movement*. New York: Wiley and Sons, 1996.

Sanders, Helen Fitzgerald. "The Gift of Angelo." *The Craftsman* 11:2 (November 1906): 181–86.

Sargeant, Irene. "John Ruskin." *The Craftsman* 1:2 (November 1901): 1–12.

Sarris, Fotios. "Fetishism in *The Spoils of Poynton*." *Nineteenth-Century Literature* 51 (1996).

Schafter, Debra. *The Order of Ornament, The Structure of Style*. Cambridge: Cambridge University Press, 2003.

Schmidgall, Gary. *Literature as Opera*. New York: Oxford University Press, 1977.

Schopfer, Jean. "The Silversmith's Art." Translated by Irene Sargeant. *The Craftsman* 5:4 (January 1904): 337–57.

Seltzer, Mark. *Bodies and Machines*. New York: Routledge, 1992.

Sennett, Richard. *The Craftsman*. New Haven: Yale University Press, 2008.

Sewell, William. *Work and Revolution in France: The Language of Labor from the Old Regime to 1848*. Cambridge: Cambridge University Press, 1980.

Shaw, Henry. *Specimens of Ancient Furniture*. London, 1836.

Sheraton, Thomas. *The Cabinet Dictionary, Containing an Explanation of all the Terms Used in the Cabinet, Chair, and Upholstery Branches, With Directions for Varnishing, Polishing, and Gilding*. London, 1803.

Shi, David. E. *The Simple Life: Plain Living and High Thinking in American Culture*. Oxford: Oxford University Press, 1985.

Sloane, Patricia, ed. *Primary Sources: Selected Writings on Color from Aristotle to Albers*. New York: Design Press, 1991.

Smith, Mary Ann. *Gustav Stickley, The Craftsman*. Syracuse: Syracuse University Press, 1983.

"Some Recent Examples of Gorham Silverware." *The Craftsman* 7:4 (January 1905): 447–59.

Speltz, Alexander. *The Styles of Ornament*. Translated by David O'Conor. Berlin: Bruno Hessling, 1906.

Spencer, Herbert. *Herbert Spencer on Social Evolution*. Edited by J. D. Y. Peel. Chicago: University of Chicago Press, 1972.

Spofford, Harriet. "In a Cellar." *The Atlantic Monthly* 3:16 (February 1859).

"*The Spoils of Poynton*." *The Critic*, 1 May 1897.

Spretnak, Charlene. *The Resurgence of the Real: Body, Nature, and Place in a Hypermodern World*. New York: Perseus, 1997.

Stewart, Martha. *Entertaining*. New York: Clarkson Potter, 1982.

Stewart, Susan. *On Longing*. Durham: Duke University Press, 1993.

Stickley, Gustav. "Als Ik Kan: The Old Crafts and the Modern Factories." *The Craftsman* 20:2 (May 1911): 231–33.

———. "Cabinet Work for Home Workers." In *Craftsman Homes*, 169–84.

——. *Catalog of Craftsman Furniture*. Syracuse: Craftsman, 1909.
——. *Catalog of Craftsman Furniture*. Syracuse: Craftsman, 1912.
——. "Chips from the Craftsman Workshops." *The Craftsman* 6:3 (June 1904): 315–17.
——. *Craftsman Catalog of Interior Furnishings*. Syracuse: Craftsman, 1915.
——. *Craftsman Homes*. Syracuse: Craftsman, 1909.
——. "Craftsman Metal Work." In *Craftsman Homes*, 162–64. Syracuse: Craftsman, 1909.
——. "The Danger of Too Much System in Education." *The Craftsman* 15:4 (January 1909).
——. "The Development of an American Style of Home Furnishing Founded upon Beauty, Comfort, and Simplicity." *The Craftsman* 27:1 (October 1914): 69–78.
——. "The Dining Room as a Center of Hospitality and Good Cheer." In *Craftsman Homes*, 137–41.
——. "The Flood of Fiction." *The Craftsman* 5:2 (November 1903): 195–97.
——. "Furniture Based upon Good Craftsmanship." *The Craftsman* 29:5 (February 1916): 531–38.
——. "Hand-Wrought Metal Work." Syracuse: Craftsman, 1904.
——. "Home Training in Cabinet Work." *The Craftsman* 10:4 (July 1906): 514–18.
——. "An Important Announcement: Our Plans for the Coming Year." *The Craftsman* 12:6 (September 1907): ix–xii.
——. "An Invitation to the New Opening of the Craftsman Building." *The Craftsman* 25:1 (October 1913): 110–11.
——. "The Most Valuable of All Arts." *The Craftsman* 28:6 (September 1915): 527–31, continued on pg. 615.
——. "1912 Craftsman Furniture Catalog." Syracuse: Craftsman, 1912.
——. "Our Native Woods and the Craftsman Method of Finishing Them." In *Craftsman Homes*, 185–93.
——. "An Outline of Furniture-Making in this Country: Showing the Place of Craftsman Furniture in the Evolution of an American Style." In *Craftsman Homes*, 151–59.
——. "Structure and Ornament in the Craftsman Workshops." *The Craftsman* 5:4 (January 1904): 391–96.
——. "Thoughts Occasioned by an Anniversary: A Plea for a Democratic Art." *The Craftsman* 7:1 (October 1904): 42–64.
——. "The Treatment of Wall Spaces." In *Craftsman Homes*, 144–48.
Swedborg, Robert, and Harriet Swedborg. *American Oak Furniture*. Radnor, PA: Wallace-Homestead, 1988.
Sweet, Frank H. "The Bridge Keeper." *The Craftsman* 10:2 (May 1906): 213–18.
Symonds, John Addington. Introduction to *The Life of Benvenuto Cellini*, by Benvenuto Cellini. New York: Scribner's, 1920: ix–liv.
——. *The Renaissance in Italy*. Vol. 3, *The Fine Arts*. New York: Scribner's, 1901.
Thackeray, William Makepeace. *Novels by Eminent Hands*. In *The Complete Works of William Makepeace Thackeray*. New York: Harper and Brothers, 1903.

"Tiffany & Co. at the St. Louis Exhibition." *The Craftsman* 7:2 (November 1904): 169–83.

Tolles, Bryant F., Jr., with Carolyn K. Tolles. *Architecture in Salem: An Illustrated Guide*. Hanover, NH: University Press of New England, 2004.

"Tools and Table for Carving." *The Craftsman* 14:5 (August 1908): 550.

Trachtenberg, Alan. "Seeing and Believing: Hawthorne's Reflections on the Daguerreotype in *The House of the Seven Gables*." *American Literary History* 9:3 (Fall 1997).

Traubel, Horace. "Keeping in the Historic Line." *The Artsman* 1:7 (April 1904).

Triggs, Oscar Lovell. *Chapters in the History of the Arts and Crafts Movement*. Chicago: Bohemia Guild of the Industrial Arts League, c. 1902.

Ulrich, Laurel Thatcher. *The Age of Homespun: Objects and Stories in the Creation of an American Myth*. New York: Vintage, 2002.

Vasari, Giorgio. *The Lives of the Artists*. Translated by Julia Conaway Bondanella and Peter Bondanella. Oxford: Oxford University Press, 1991.

——. *Le Vite de' più eccellenti pittori, scultori, e architettori*. Edited by Gaetano Milanesi. Florence, 1878.

Veblen, Thorstein. *The Instinct of Workmanship*. New York: Macmillan, 1914.

——. *The Theory of the Leisure Class*. New York: Penguin, 1994.

Vitruvius, Marcus Pollio. *De Architectura*. Leipzig: Teubner, 1867.

Voragine, Jacobus de. *The Golden Legend; or, The Lives of the Saints, as Englished by William Caxton*. Vol. 3. London: J. M. Dent, 1900.

Walker, T. L., and A. W. N. Pugin. *Examples of Gothic Architecture Selected from Various Ancient Edifices in England*. Vol. 3. London: Henry Bohn, 1838.

Wallace, Kevin V. "Todd Hoyer and Hayley Smith," *Craft Arts International* 55 (2002).

"Wallpaper Reviews." *Decorator and Furnisher*, 15 (1894).

Waugh, Evelyn. *Brideshead Revisited*. Boston: Little, Brown, 1945.

Weinstein, Cindy. *The Literature of Labor, The Labors of Literature*. Cambridge: Cambridge University Press, 1995.

Wharton, Edith. *The Age of Innocence*. New York: Collier, 1968.

Wheeler, Gervase. *Rural Homes; or, Sketches of Houses Suited to American Country Life with Original Plans, Designs, & c.* Auburn, NY: Alden, Beardsley, 1853.

Whitman, Walt. "Poem of the Daily Work of the Workmen and Workwomen of These States." In *Leaves of Grass*. Brooklyn, 1856.

Wigglesworth, Michael. *The Day of Doom*. New York, 1867.

Wilde, Oscar. "The Decay of Lying." In *Intentions*, 1–55. New York: Brentano's, 1905.

Wilentz, Sean. *Chants Democratic: New York City and the Rise of the American Working Class, 1788–1850*. Oxford: Oxford University Press, 1984.

Wineapple, Brenda. *Hawthorne: A Life*. New York: Random House, 2004.

Wulff, Eric. "An Ingrained Aesthetic." *Craft Arts International* 54 (2002).

Zandy, Janet. *Hands: Physical Labor, Class, and Cultural Work*. New Brunswick: Rutgers University Press, 2004.

INDEX

Page numbers in italics refer to illustrations.